Vauxhall Viva HC 1971-76 Autobook

By Kenneth Ball
and the Autobooks Team of Technical Writers

Vauxhall Viva, 1159cc, 1256cc, 1971-75
Vauxhall Viva SL, 1159cc, 1256cc, 1971-75
Vauxhall Firenza, SL, 1159cc, 1256cc, 1971-73
Vauxhall Viva 1300, L, SL, 1975-76

Autobooks

Autobooks Ltd. Golden Lane Brighton BN1 2QJ England

The AUTOBOOK series of Workshop Manuals is the largest in the world and covers the majority of British and Continental motor cars, as well as all major Japanese and Australian models. For a full list see the back of this manual.

46012383 ı

CONTENTS

Acknowledgement

Introduction

Chapter 1   The Engine   9

Chapter 2   The Fuel System   25

Chapter 3   The Ignition System   39

Chapter 4   The Cooling System   45

Chapter 5   The Clutch   49

Chapter 6   The Transmission   53

Chapter 7   Propeller Shaft, Rear Axle, Rear Suspension   67

Chapter 8   Front Suspension and Hubs   77

Chapter 9   The Steering Gear   87

Chapter 10   The Braking System   95

Chapter 11   The Electrical System   107

Chapter 12   The Bodywork   123

Appendix   133

ISBN 0 85147 600 7

First Edition   1972
Second Edition, fully revised   1972
Reprinted   1972
Reprinted   1972
Third Edition, fully revised   1973
Fourth Edition, fully revised   1974
Reprinted   1974
Fifth Edition, fully revised   1975
Sixth Edition, fully revised   1976

© Autobooks Ltd 1976

860

Printed and bound in Brighton England for Autobooks Ltd by G. Beard & Son Ltd

D

ACKNOWLEDGEMENT

We wish to thank Vauxhall Motors Ltd for their co-operation and also for supplying data and illustrations. Considerable assistance has also been given by owners, who have discussed their cars in detail, and we would like to express our gratitude for this invaluable advice and help.

INTRODUCTION

This do-it-yourself Workshop Manual has been specially written for the owner who wishes to maintain his car in first class condition and to carry out his own servicing and repairs. Considerable savings on garage charges can be made, and one can drive in safety and confidence knowing the work has been done properly.

Comprehensive step-by-step instructions and illustrations are given on all dismantling, overhauling and assembling operations. Certain assemblies require the use of expensive special tools, the purchase of which would be unjustified. In these cases information is included but the reader is recommended to hand the unit to the agent for attention.

Throughout the Manual hints and tips are included which will be found invaluable, and there is an easy to follow fault diagnosis at the end of each chapter.

Whilst every care has been taken to ensure correctness of information it is obviously not possible to guarantee complete freedom from errors or to accept liability arising from such errors or omissions.

Instructions may refer to the righthand or lefthand sides of the vehicle or the components. These are the same as the righthand or lefthand of an observer standing behind the car and looking forward.

CHAPTER 1

THE ENGINE

1:1 Description
1:2 Removing the engine
1:3 Lifting the head
1:4 Servicing the head
1:5 Refitting the head
1:6 Removing timing gear and camshaft
1:7 Refitting timing gear
1:8 Removal of sump and oil pump
1:9 Servicing the oil pump
1:10 Removing the clutch and flywheel

1:11 Big ends and connection rods
1:12 Pistons, rings and gudgeon pins
1:13 Removing crankshaft and main bearings
1:14 External oil filter, crankcase breather
1:15 Reassembling the stripped engine
1:16 Refitting the engine in car
1:17 1256cc engines, piston rings
1:18 Positive crankcase ventilation
1:19 Fault diagnosis

1:1 Description

The engine is a conventional four cylinder in-line unit with pushrod operated overhead valves. Up to 1971 the capacity was 1159cc (70.7 cu inch) but for 1972 this was increased to 1256cc (76.6 cu inch) by increasing the bore diameter. On the earlier models an extra-performance version was included in the range and a choice of compression ratios for the standard engine. With the larger engine the extra performance version was dropped. The servicing information given in this chapter applies equally to all engines and where any exceptions occur the appropriate engine type will be mentioned.

Two sectional views of the engine are given in **FIGS 1:1** and **1:2** which show most details of the internal construction. The crankshaft has three main bearings, with end float being controlled by the centre bearing flanges. Spring-loaded oil seals are provided at both ends of the shaft. The solid skirt pistons have offset gudgeon pins. The three bearing camshaft is driven by a chain from the crankshaft with an automatic tensioning device.

The cylinder head has the inclined valves working directly in the head with no guides being used. Pressed-steel rockers are mounted on individual hollow studs pressed into the cylinder head and operate on a hemispherical seating retained on a stud by a self-locking nut as shown in **FIG 1:3**.

The fuel supply is by means of a mechanical pump driven from an eccentric on the camshaft which feeds the single carburetter. This may be a downdraught Zenith instrument or one of a range of Zenith-Stromberg side-draught units in the 150 CD series. On late model cars the air intake is not only filtered but also temperature controlled for optimum performance.

Lubrication is provided by a gear type pump driven by skew gears from the camshaft, the upper end of the pump driving spindle having an offset slot to engage with the distributor shaft. The pump includes a spring-loaded plunger type relief valve. An external fullflow oil filter is included mounted on the lefthand side of the engine.

Cooling is by means of a conventional radiator with a belt driven fan and centrifugal water pump mounted on the front of the cylinder head. This belt also drives the electrical alternator.

1:2 Removing the engine

A number of servicing operations can be carried out with the engine still mounted in the car, but for work on the lower part including the servicing of pistons, crankshaft and bearings the engine must be removed in order to take off the sump. It is possible on these cars to remove

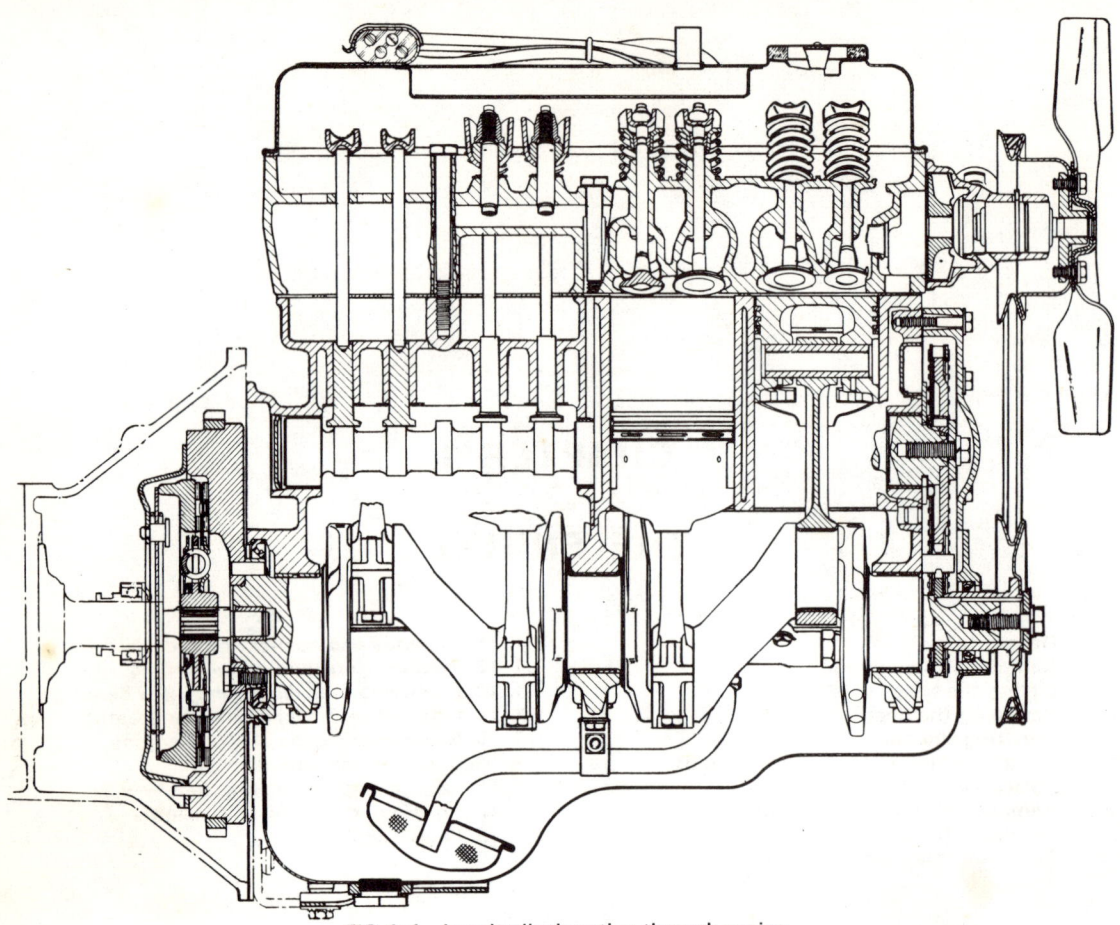

FIG 1:1 Longitudinal section through engine

the engine and leave the transmission, either synchromesh or automatic in place. The sequence of operation is as follows:

Drain the sump. Disconnect the battery. Remove the bonnet.

Drain the cooling system, remembering to retain the coolant if antifreeze has been added. Disconnect water and heater hoses and remove the radiator.

Remove the air cleaner, carburetter controls and the bracket attached to the bulkhead. Disconnect the fuel feed pipe, plugging it to prevent leakage.

Remove the exhaust pipe from the manifold. Disconnect the engine wiring harness, starter cable and earth strip.

Remove the bolts attaching the front engine mountings to the brackets on the crossmember.

On cars with manual gearbox: Support the front of the gearbox. Take the weight of the engine in a sling as shown in **FIG 1:4,** then disconnect the gearbox brace and remove the bolts securing the gearbox to the crankcase. Moving the engine slightly forwards will now disengage the gearbox first motion shaft from the hub of the clutch disc, but care must be taken to ensure that at no time does the weight of the engine hang on the shaft during the operation.

On cars with automatic transmission:

Support the transmission from underneath and take the weight of the engine in a sling. Remove the top bolts securing the converter housing and the starter to the crankcase.

Remove the engine braces and the converter housing front cover.

Remove the bolts securing the torque converter to the flexplate and the remaining bolts securing the converter housing to the crankcase. Having checked that all connections are free, lift out the engine.

1:3 Lifting the head

It should be noted that it is possible to withdraw one or more pushrods without removing the head, see operation 7. To remove the cylinder head with the engine in the car proceed as follows:

1 Disconnect the battery.
2 Drain the cooling system (**Chapter 4**). Disconnect radiator and heater hoses.
3 Disconnect the carburetter feed pipe, ignition control suction pipe and servo vacuum pipe (disc brake models).
4 Remove the carburetter.

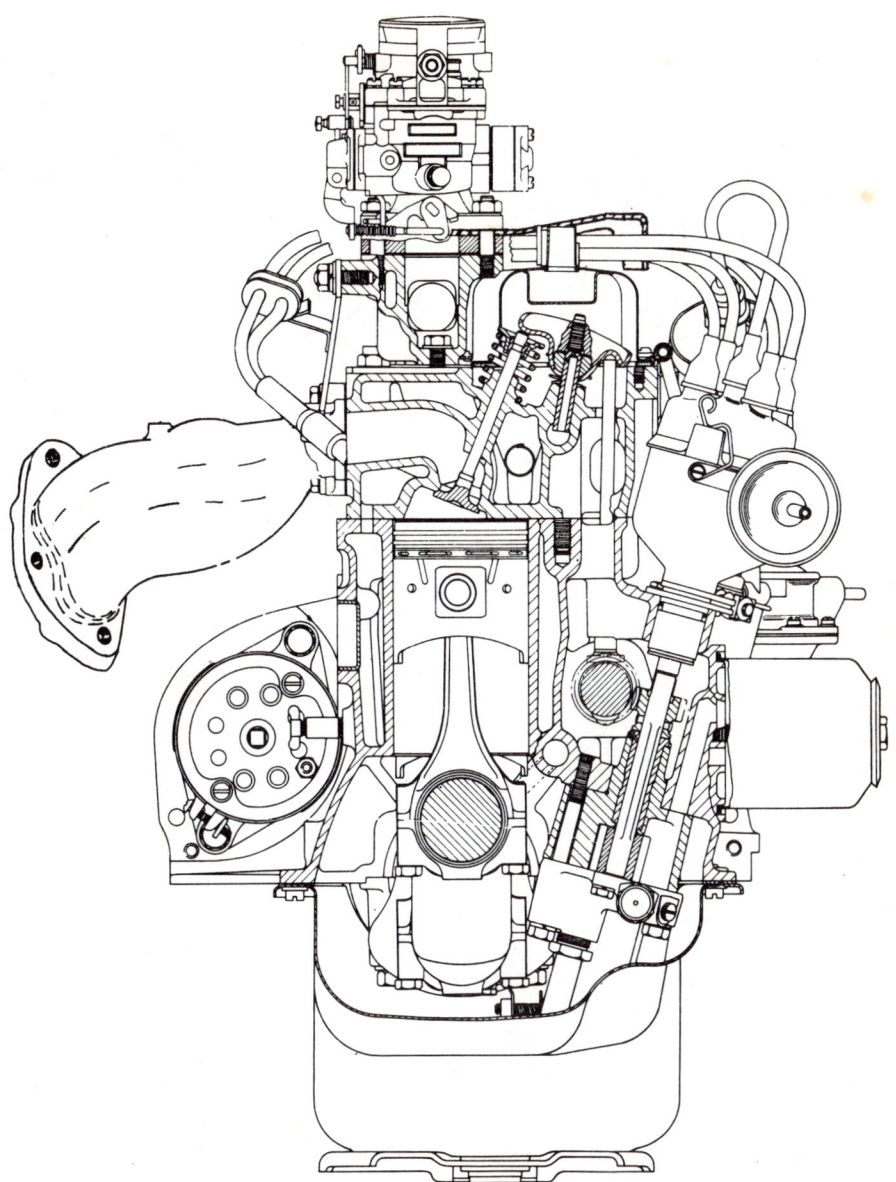

FIG 1:2 Transverse section through engine

5 Remove the inlet manifold. On standard engines one of the bolts is inside the manifold (**FIG 1:5**). Disconnect the exhaust pipe and remove the sparking plugs.

6 Slacken the generator pivot bolts and both ends of the slotted brace and remove the fan belt. Remove the ignition coil. Disconnect the wire from the temperature gauge unit if fitted.

7 Remove the rocker cover. If the head is to be completely stripped, the rockers may be removed next by undoing their centre nuts. Otherwise the nuts need only be slackened enough to allow the rockers to be swung round for the pushrods to be removed as shown in **FIG 1:6**. Ensure that each valve is closed before slackening its rocker nut and take care not to drop the pushrod back once it is disengaged from the tappet. Mark the pushrods so that they can be refitted in the same order and the same way up.

8 Remove the cylinder head bolts, slackening each bolt a little at a time in the reverse order to that shown for tightening in **FIG 1:9**. Lift off the head and gasket. If the head sticks do not try to prise it off with a screwdriver as this may damage the joint faces. Light hammer blows on a block of wood may help.

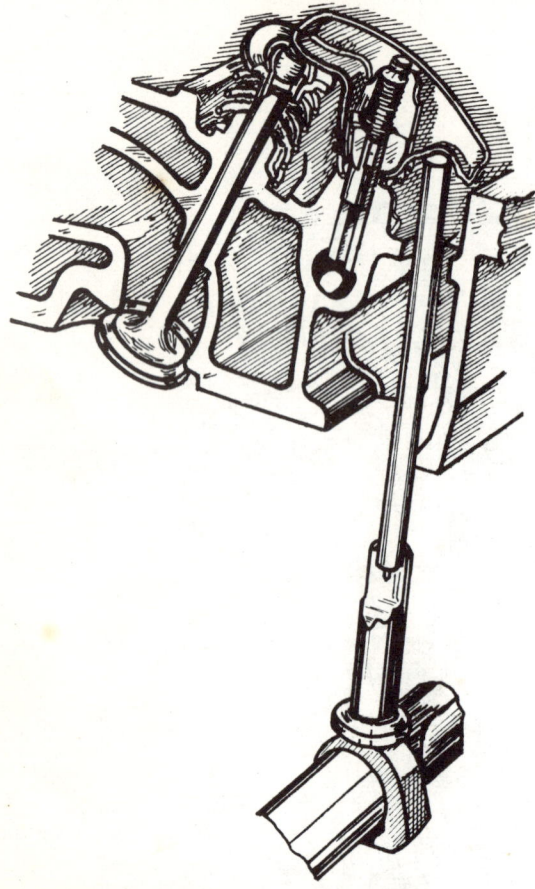

FIG 1:3   Section through rocker gear

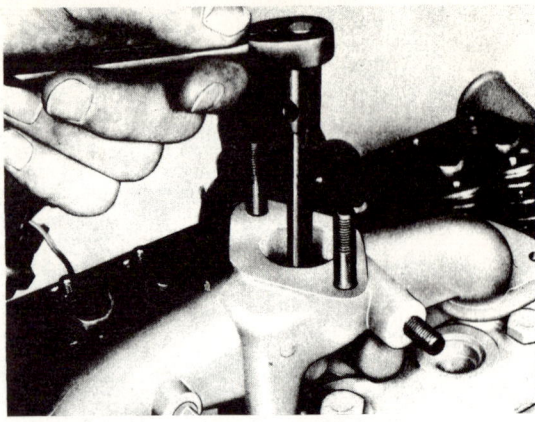

FIG 1:5   Inlet manifold centre bolt

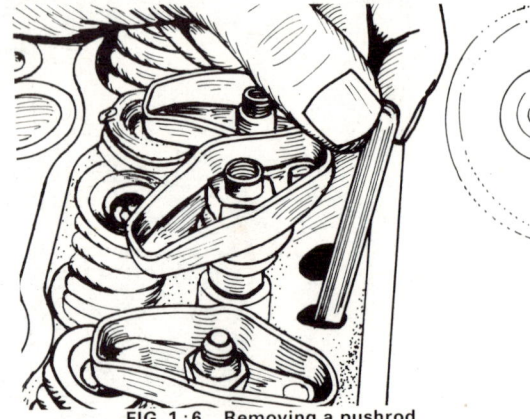

FIG 1:6   Removing a pushrod

1:4 Servicing the head, attention to valves

FIG 1:7 shows the cylinder head, valves and rocker gear. It should be noted that valve clearance is controlled by adjusting the height of the fulcrum of each individual rocker. This is achieved by means of a self-locking nut at its centre. It is essential for this nut to be sufficiently tight on its stud thread. A method of checking this point is given later.

To remove the rockers unscrew the centre nut and place each rocker and its small parts in a numbered rack or take other steps to ensure that it goes back on the same stud. Valves and their parts should be kept in sequence in the same way.

When decarbonizing, scrape most of the carbon from the head before removing the valves, to prevent damage to the valve seats. To remove the valves, compress each spring with a suitable valve tool so that the split cotters can be removed and the spring released.

Inspect the valves for burnt or cracking heads and the valve faces for pitting. Check the valve stems to see whether the clearance is within the limits shown in Technical Data. No valve guides are fitted, but valves are supplied with standard stems and four oversizes, identified by the number (in thousandths of an inch) stamped on the stem. The valve stem bore in the head must be reamered to suit.

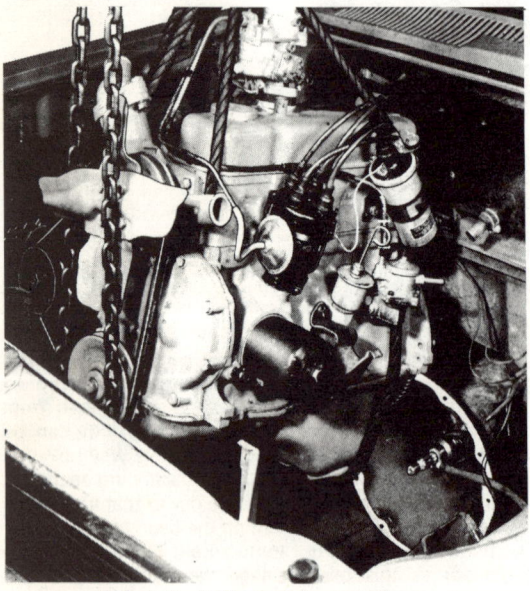

FIG 1:4   Lifting engine out of car

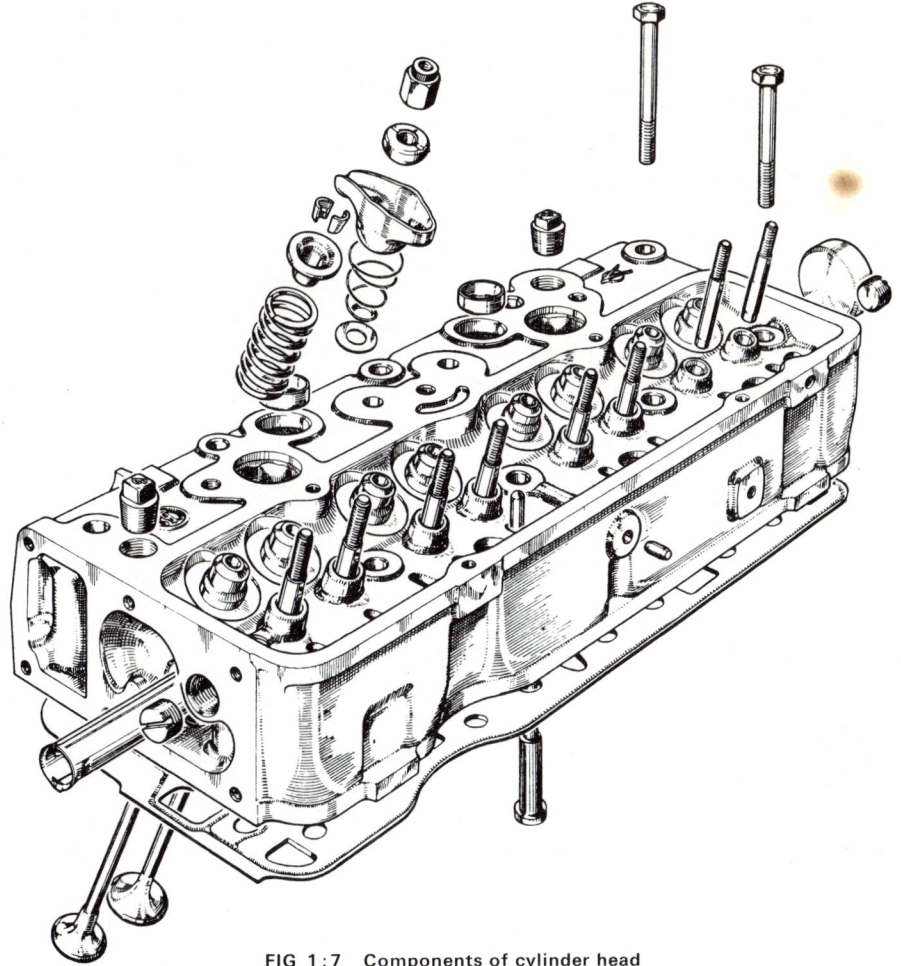

FIG 1:7 Components of cylinder head

To ensure an accurate bore at the valve port, ream from the top of the cylinder head. The valve seats are cut directly in the head and valves and seats must be faced to conform with dimensions given in Technical Data. After refacing valves and especially after reamering valve stem bores, check valve faces and seats for concentricity. A valve stem showing excessive wear on one side may indicate a bent valve. In view of the need for special reamers and cutters the owner may find it more economical to entrust the work of reamering stem bores and refacing valves and seats to a Vauxhall service agent.

Next inspect the rocker studs. They are press-fitted into the head so check that none have worked loose. Then check the fit of the nut on the stud. Lubricate the thread with hypoid gear oil and test for a minimum reading on a torque wrench of 3 lb ft when the nut is fully engaged on the thread. If a **lower** reading is obtained the nut is too slack and is liable to unscrew. If the stud appears to be in good condition the fitting of a new nut may overcome the trouble, but if this still gives a reading of less than 3 lb ft the stud must be renewed. This involves extracting the old stud, reaming the hole and

pressing in an oversize stud. This work calls for special reamers, a special cylinder head jig and the use of a power press, and is therefore better entrusted to a Vauxhall service agent. Check also that each rocker ball (**FIG 1:3**) is a free fit on its rocker stud shank.

Before refitting the valves, make sure that all traces of loose carbon have been removed from the head and ports and that the valve stems and valve stem bores are perfectly clean. Lubricate the stems and valve stem bores with a mineral oil containing colloidal graphite. It is generally advisable to fit a set of new valve springs. Weak springs can cause premature burning of valves and seats and other more serious troubles.

If new valves are fitted a new set of split cotters should also be fitted. In other cases examine the existing cotters. They have an internal projection to engage in a narrow groove in the valve stem. Any showing signs of wear at this point should be discarded. When fitting the valve springs, ensure that the tapered hole in the valve spring collar is clean. Compress the spring and after inserting the split cotters release the spring slowly, making quite sure that the cotters are fully home.

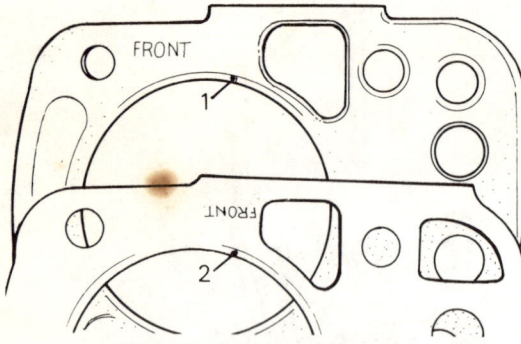

FIG 1:8   Cylinder head gaskets

Key to Fig 1:8   1 Low compression   2 High compression and extra-performance engines

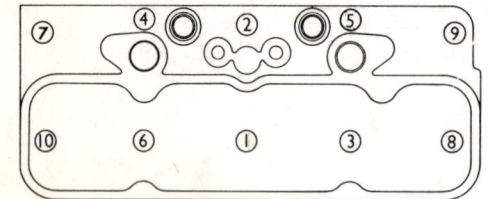

FIG 1:9   Sequence for tightening cylinder head bolts

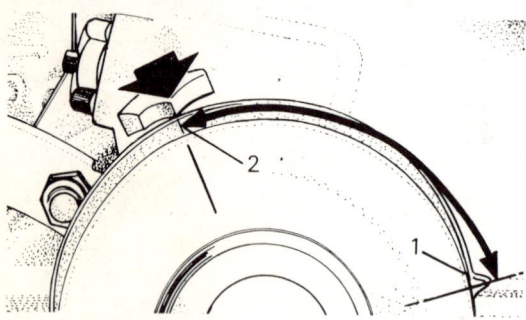

FIG 1:10   Valve timing check

Key to Fig 1:10   1 Crankshaft pulley pointer   2 Mark on pulley rim at 4.60 inches

1:5 Refitting the head

The exhaust manifold can be refitted to the cylinder head before fitting the head. Installation of the rockers is best left until later. A new cylinder head gasket should be fitted, as well as small gaskets which have been disturbed. Note that low compression engines, identified by a letter B adjacent to the engine number of the cylinder block, have a thick copper-asbestos gasket shown at 1 in FIG 1:8. The high compression and the high performance engines have a thinner asbestos-steel gasket as shown at 2 in the same illustration. Ensure that the contact faces of both cylinder block and the head are clean. Smear both sides of the gasket with Wellseal jointing compound. On later 1256 cc engines a reinforced asbestos-based material is used, identified by its dark grey colour, and must be installed dry. **Do not use jointing compound.**

The cylinder head bolts should have clean dry threads and be tightened in the sequence shown in FIG 1:9. Tighten each bolt at first little more than finger tight. Go round several times in the same order gradually tightening until the torque figure of 49 lb ft is obtained. A torque wrench is essential for accurate results.

Install the pushrods taking care not to drop them past the tappets into the crankcase. See FIG 1:6. A tight fitting rubber grommet temporarily fitted to the pushrod will prevent this trouble. Refit the rockers. Adjust the valve clearances by means of the rocker adjusting nuts to .006 inch inlet and .010 inch exhaust for standard engines and .008 inch inlet and exhaust for high performance and 1256 cc engines, with the appropriate piston on compression stroke in each case. Refit and adjust the fan belt as described in **Chapter 4,** and assemble the remaining components in the reverse order to that of dismantling, but leaving the rocker cover off. Start the engine and run it until it reaches normal working temperature. Then with the engine still running at idling speed, recheck the valve clearances to the figures quoted. Adjust the four inlet valves (Nos. 2, 3, 6 and 7 counting from the front) and then the four exhaust valves (1, 4, 5 and 8). Refit the rocker cover using a new gasket and refit the breather hose.

1:6 Removing timing gear and camshaft

To remove timing gear and camshaft it is necessary to remove the engine from the car. The valve timing can be checked however without removing or dismantling the engine.

To check the valve timing, remove the rocker cover and sparking plugs. Referring to FIG 1:10, from the centre of the pointer 1 on the crankshaft pulley, mark a point 2 on the pulley rim 4.60 inch in an anticlockwise direction. Mount a dial gauge over the inlet valve of No. 1 cylinder (the second valve from the front of the car) so that its button rests on the valve spring collar. Turn the engine in its normal (clockwise) direction until the gauge shows the valve is fully open. The mark 2 should now be in line with the TDC pointer, shown arrowed in the illustration, on the timing case.

To remove the timing gear and camshaft, remove the engine as described in **Section 1:2.** Remove the fan belt, fuel pump and distributor. If the head is not to be removed remove the pushrods **(Section 1:3)** and lay the engine on its side. If the head is to be removed, do so now and invert the engine. Proceed as follows:

1 Remove sump and oil pump **(Section 1:8).**
2 Remove the crankshaft pulley bolt and crankshaft pulley.
3 Remove the timing case.
4 Remove the bolt securing the camshaft chainwheel. Withdraw the two wheels together with the endless chain. The dowel locating the camshaft chainwheel is an interference fit in the chainwheel and should come away with it.
5 Remove the camshaft thrust plate. Ensure that the tappets are clear of their cams and withdraw the camshaft.
6 Remove the tappets, keeping them in order so that each can be refitted in the same bore. Remove the timing chain tensioner from the timing case.

1:7 Refitting timing gear and camshaft

Before reassembling, all parts should be examined for wear. Check the camshaft and see that the measurement from base to peak of each cam is within the limits given in Technical Data. Examine the skew gear. If this is badly worn or damaged both camshaft and oil pump drive gear must be renewed. Inspect the timing chain and examine both chain wheels for worn teeth. If they are badly worn, renew them as well as the chain. Renew any tappets which are worn or pitted on the bottom face.

Replacement camshaft bearings are supplied with bores finished to size, so that if renewal is necessary they do not need to be bored in line. Removal and refitting is facilitated by using special tools available from the makers.

To remove the camshaft bearings the flywheel or flexplate must be removed. Insert a plug SE.655 in the front bearing and drive it out. Drive out the other two bearings in turn using the pilot SE.667 to support and align the drift SE.8454. The expansion plug sealing the rear bearing is driven out with it.

To install the new bearings, start at the rear and work towards the front of the crankcase. Locate each bearing so that the notch is facing away from the crankshaft and towards the front (see **FIG 1:11**). This ensures that the oilways line up with those in the crankcase. The centre bearing has two oil holes, the smaller one lining up with an oil feed to the rocker gallery, as shown in **FIG 1:12**.

Make sure the front bearing does not project beyond the crankcase front face. Remove any overlapping bearing metal obstructing the oilways in the crankcase. Fit a new expansion plug behind the rear bearing, ensuring that there are no burrs or flats on the rim of the plug. Use jointing compound to ensure an oil-tight joint.

To renew the timing case oil seal, drive out the old seal taking care not to damage the front bore of the case, indicated by the arrow in **FIG 1:13**. Press in the new seal with the open side towards the rear of the case and the closed side contacting the shoulder as shown.

Lubricate and refit tappets. Ensure that each tappet is at the limit of its travel so as to clear its cam, especially when working with the engine on its side. Smear the cams and tappet faces with graphited oil and carefully insert the camshaft. Refit the camshaft thrust plate as shown in **FIG 1:15**.

Immerse the timing chain in engine oil and assemble the two wheels with the chain so that the timing marks align as shown in **FIG 1:16**. Install the timing chain and wheels on the shafts. Ensure that the dowel, which is an interference fit in the camshaft chainwheel, locates in the hole in the camshaft. When fitting the chain make sure that the tension pad, 1 in **FIG 1:14**, is held fully in the body 4 until the chain and sprocket are in position, otherwise it will have to be removed and reset before the chain can be fitted.

Excessive timing chain wear may indicate that the oil nozzle, arrowed in **FIG 1:17** is blocked or defective. The nozzle is an interference fit in the crankcase and if renewed must be fitted with the bleed hole aligned as shown.

Lubricate the timing case oil seal with engine oil. Attach a new timing case gasket to the crankcase with grease and fit the timing case, making sure the tensioner pad lines up with the chain. Before tightening the timing

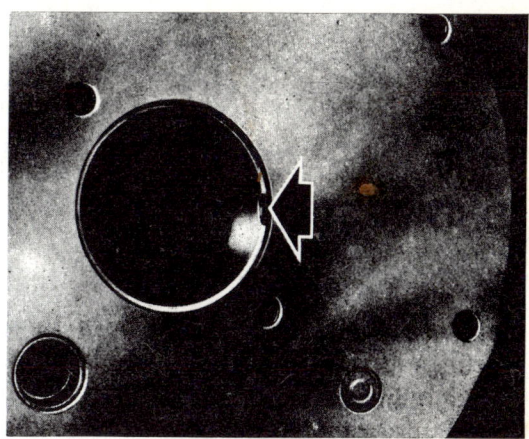

FIG 1:11 Camshaft bearings must be located with the notch towards the front of the block

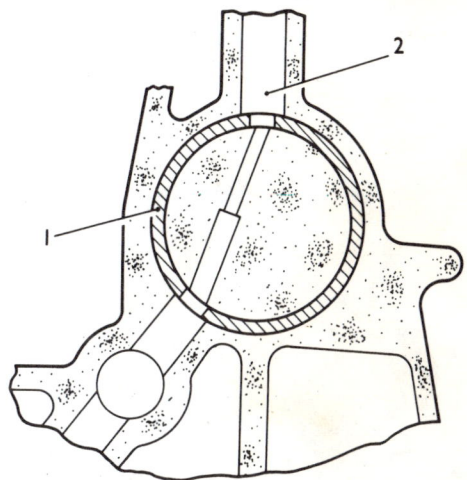

FIG 1:12 Section through camshaft centre bearing showing alignment of oilways

Key to Fig 1:12   1 Bearing   2 Oil feed to rocker gallery

case bolts the oil seal must be concentric with the crankshaft. An aligner No. Z-8556 is available for this purpose. Tighten the bolts fully.

1:8 Removal of sump and oil pump

To remove the sump the engine must be removed from the car as described in **Section 1:2**. Invert the engine, undo the sump bolts and lift off the sump. Discard the sump gasket and also the seal in the groove of the rear main bearing cap.

Using a spanner on the pulley bolt, turn the crankshaft until the pointer on the pulley is aligned with the TDC pointer on the timing case, with the distributor rotor corresponding with the No. 1 cylinder segment. Do not turn the engine after this unless it is to be fully dismantled. Remove the distributor. Referring to **FIG 1:18**, disconnect the pump suction pipe 1 from the centre main bearing cap. Remove the two bolts marked 2 from the pump cover and remove the pump and its gasket.

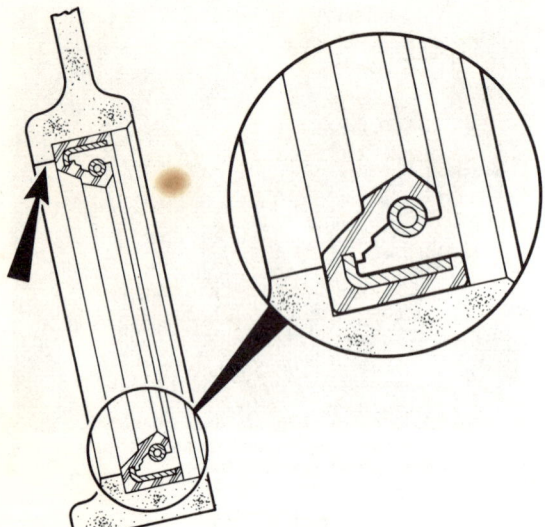

FIG 1:13 Timing case oil seal

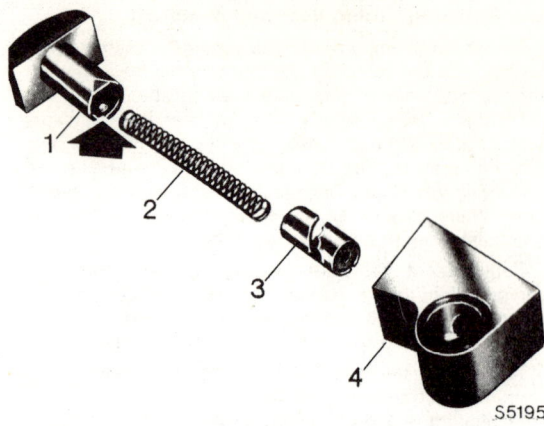

S5195

Key to Fig 1:14 Timing chain tensioner showing pip (arrowed) which engages the stepped groove in the piston

Key to Fig 1:14   1 Sleeve and pad assembly   2 Spring
3 Piston   4 Body

FIG 1:15 Camshaft thrust plate showing legs positioned for correct location of chain tensioner

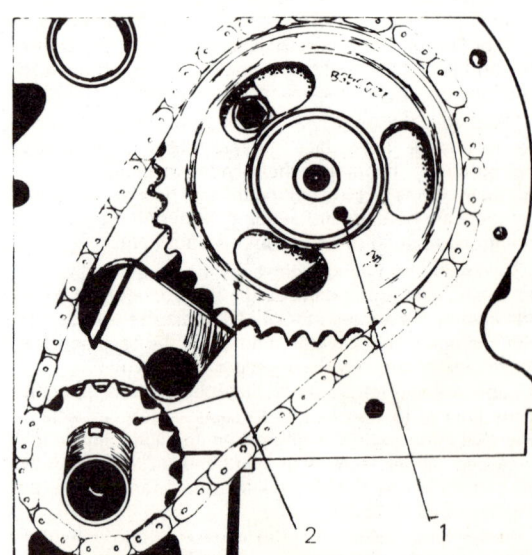

FIG 1:16 When fitting timing chain ensure that dowel 1 is in position and timing marks 2 are in line

1:9 Servicing the oil pump

The oil pump components are shown in **FIG 1:19.** The efficient action of the gear-type pump depends on precise clearances between component parts. Overhaul does not call for special tools but involves accurate measurement of the various dimensions which will be found in Technical Data. If wear is discovered it is also essential to know in which cases the renewal of mating parts is also necessary. Testing pump output requires a special rig designed for the purpose, but if the dimensional checks are carried out according to instructions this should not be necessary.

To dismantle the pump, remove the suction pipe from the pump cover. Remove the two remaining bolts in the cover and lift off the cover. Mark the meshed teeth of the two impellers so that if serviceable they can be re-assembled in the same mesh. Withdraw the driven impeller. Mark the position of the drive gear teeth in relation to the offset slot in the spindle. Unrivet the driving gear and withdraw the driving spindle and impeller assembly. Do not remove the impeller from its spindle as it is an interference fit.

Carry out the following checks, bearing in mind that if several parts need renewal it may be better to fit a replacement pump.

1 Check both impellers for end clearance, radial clearance in the body and backlash between the teeth, using feeler gauges. Note that a worn driven impeller

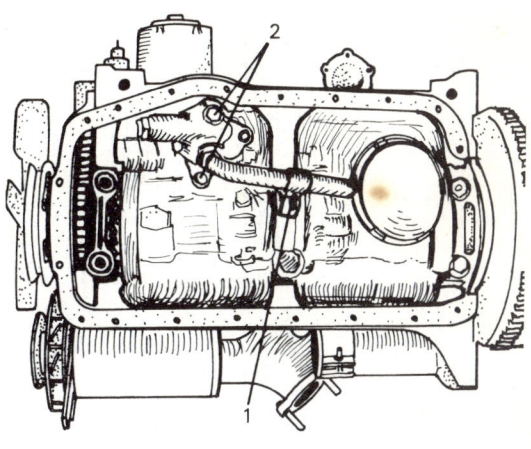

FIG 1:17   Timing chain oil nozzle

Key to Fig 1:17   1   Camshaft thrust plate   2   Oil nozzle

FIG 1:18   Oil pump removal

Key to Fig 1:18   1   Suction pipe support   2   Pump securing bolts

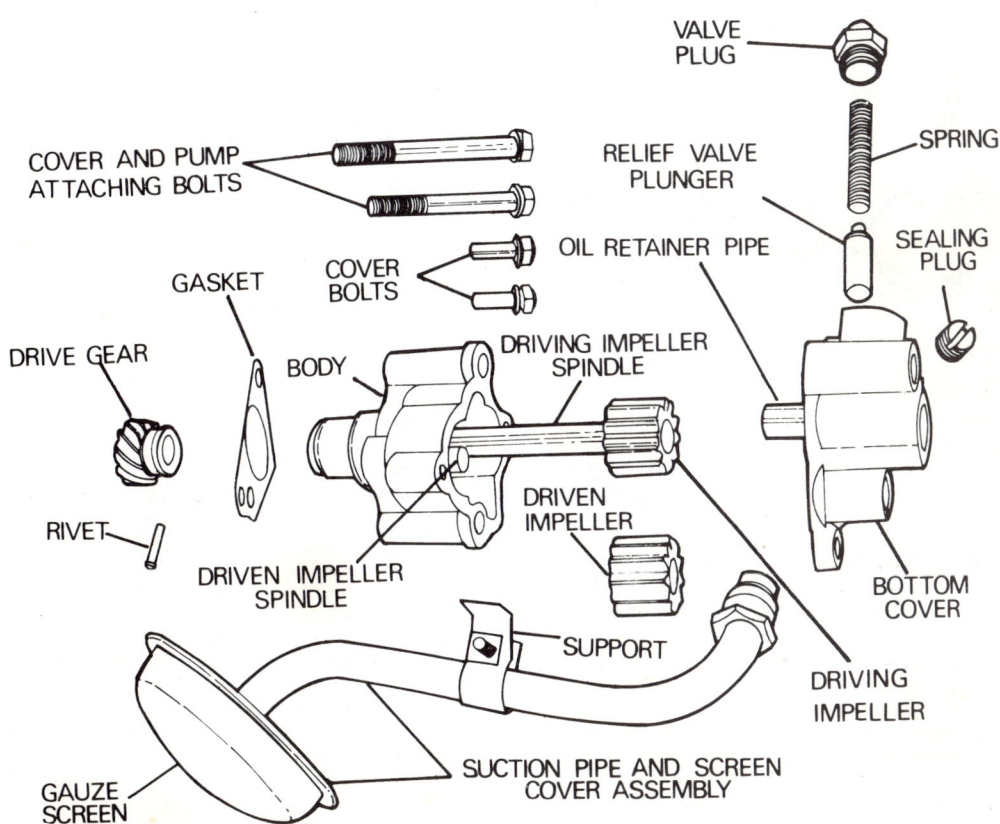

FIG 1:19   Exploded view of oil pump. To facilitate reassembly, mark the meshing teeth of the driven and driving impellers and also drive gear. Do not remove the impeller from the spindle

VIVA HC

17

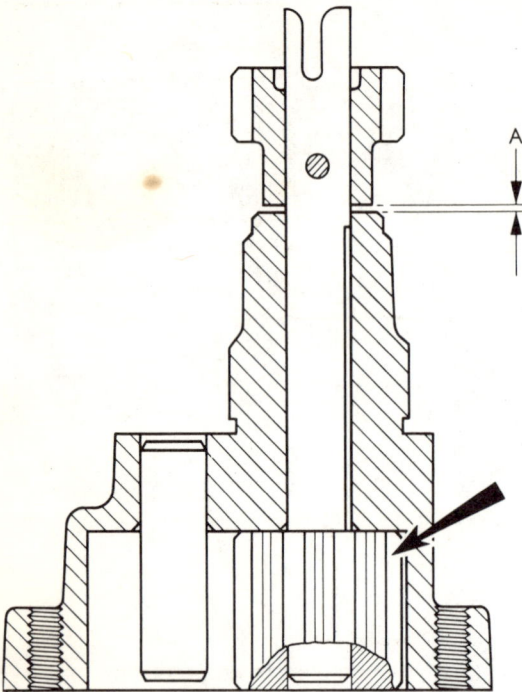

FIG 1:20 Sectional view of oil pump. Measure end float at **A**

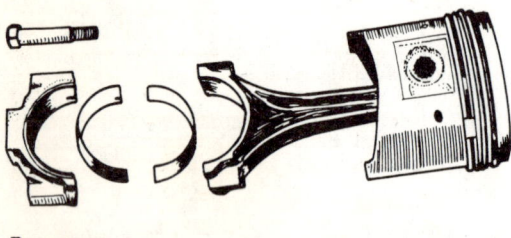

FIG 1:21 Piston and connecting rod assembly

spindle or driving impeller spindle bore call for renewal of pump body and impeller assembly. The steel bush in the body on earlier models is not renewable. If either the driven gear, driving spindle or driving impeller is worn, all three parts must be renewed.

2 Check that the driving impeller is tight on its spindle.

3 If the attaching face of the pump cover shows signs of wear it must be renewed complete with oil retainer pipe.

4 The oil pressure relief valve plunger must slide freely in the bottom cover but without slackness. Renew the spring if its condition is doubtful.

5 When assembling the pump ensure that all oilways are clear and all parts clean. After a final wash in petrol the parts must not be touched with rag, as the smallest piece of fluff could block a vital oilway.

6 Lubricate the spindles with graphited oil (not engine oil). The driving impeller must be pressed on to its spindle so that when the impeller, arrowed in

FIG 1:20, is in contact with the pump body, the end float measured at A is .007 to .010 inch.

7 Refit the relief valve and sealing plug but do not use sealing compound on the plug.

1:10 Removing clutch and flywheel

Before removing the clutch from the flywheel, mark the clutch cover to flywheel relationship. Unscrew the cover attaching bolts evenly, slackening each a turn at a time diagonally until the spring pressure is released and the clutch assembly can be removed.

To remove the flywheel unscrew the four bolts holding it to the crankshaft flange. Supporting the weight of the flywheel and keeping it square, tap it off the flange with a copper or lead hammer. If the flywheel is not kept square it will be found to have a tendency to jam on the shaft.

Check the spigot bearing for wear or slackness. For renewal of bearing and for overhaul of clutch, reference should be made to **Chapter 5.**

Examine the clutch friction face of the flywheel. If scored or cracked it should be renewed. Inspect the crankshaft key or dowel for wear or slackness and check the bolt holes for elongation due to the flywheel running loose. Examine the bolts for signs of stretching or of damaged threads. If the flywheel has been running loose, remove any embedded metal from the crankshaft flange with carborundum taking care to protect the spigot bearing and the crankshaft oil seal from abrasive.

If the starter ring or any portion of it has badly worn or broken teeth it should be renewed. It is a shrink fit on the flywheel and renewal is better entrusted to a service agent with the necessary equipment for the work. Check the condition of the starter pinion and renew this also if necessary.

1:11 Big ends and connecting rods

For removal of connecting rods and pistons the engine must be removed from the car and the cylinder head and sump removed as described in previous Sections.

FIG 1:21 shows a piston and connecting rod assembly. Before splitting the big ends, mark each piston and connecting rod assembly and its cap with the cylinder number. Do not use a file or punch as such marks can lead to fatigue failure. The numbers or symbols found on the rods and caps indicate matching pairs but not the cylinder number. The piston crown has a notch which must face the front. The small figures 1 to 8 show the graded size (see Technical Data).

Unscrew the big end bolts and remove the caps and bearing shells. Keep these to their respective rods and caps. Place the engine on its side. Remove the carbon from the top of each bore and withdraw the pistons upwards with their connecting rods. Carefully remove the piston rings. The gudgeon pins are an interference fit in the connecting rods and no attempt must be made to remove them. For replacement, the complete assembly of piston, gudgeon pin, connecting rod and cap is supplied. Bearing shells can be renewed if the dimensions of crankpin journal and connecting rod housing bore are within the limits given in Technical Data. Note that rods or caps which have been 'taken up' by filing cannot be renewed on an exchange basis.

Examine the cylinder bores for scoring or wear. The diameter should be measured at the point of maximum wear, just below the highest point of piston travel. This can only be accurately measured by means of a cylinder gauge. If the bores are scored or the wear exceeds .010 inch the cylinder block must be rebored, linered or renewed. If the bores are not scored and wear is less than .010 inch new piston rings can be fitted.

1:12 Pistons, rings and gudgeon pins

For production purposes, pistons are graded into eight sizes numbered 1 to 8 (stamped on the piston crown) representing variations of .00025 inch in an overall range of .002 inch. Replacement standard pistons are in grades 5, 6, 7 and 8. Oversize pistons are supplied in grades 5 and 8 in each of the three nominal oversizes.

Pistons must be measured in line with the top of the cut-out in the skirt and at right angles to the gudgeon pin. The vertical clearance of piston rings in their grooves should be checked. If the grooves are badly worn new piston and connecting rod assemblies will be required.

If pistons and connecting rods are still serviceable and cylinder bore wear is within the specified limits, new piston rings should be fitted. Always remove the ridge round the top of the cylinder bores when fitting new rings. Check the gaps in the new rings, placing them about $1\frac{1}{2}$ inch down the bore and squaring up with a piston. The gap must on no account be less than that specified. If the ends of the ring butt at working temperature serious damage may result.

Fit the piston rings in the following order (see **FIG 1:22**):

1 A scraper ring or special oil control ring in the bottom groove.
2 A stepped compression ring in the centre groove.
3 A compression ring in the top groove.

Markings on piston rings 'top' and 'bottom' indicate the right way up in the groove, not whether to fit in top or bottom groove.

On 1159 cc engines where slight bore wear causes increased oil consumption but is not sufficient to justify reboring, special Vauxhall Oil Control ring sets can be fitted to the bottom groove instead of the scraper ring. These are installed as follows, see inset in **FIG 1:22**:

1 Assemble the insert against the bottom land of the groove.
2 Install the spring expander.
3 Install the rails and spacer which are a unitized assembly, i.e. temporarily bonded together with an oil-soluble material, and should not be separated before installation. Gaps in the rails and spacer should be in line.

Vauxhall Oil Control rings must not be used in unworn bores.

The bottom diagram in **FIG 1:22** shows the scraper ring fitted to 1256 cc engines, the ends A and B of the expander must not overlap. When fitting position the ends of the expander, and the rails C, equally round the piston.

1:13 Removing crankshaft and main bearings

The crankshaft runs in three main bearings of the shell type. Bearing shells are machined to size and no attempt should be made to 'take up' bearings by filing the caps.

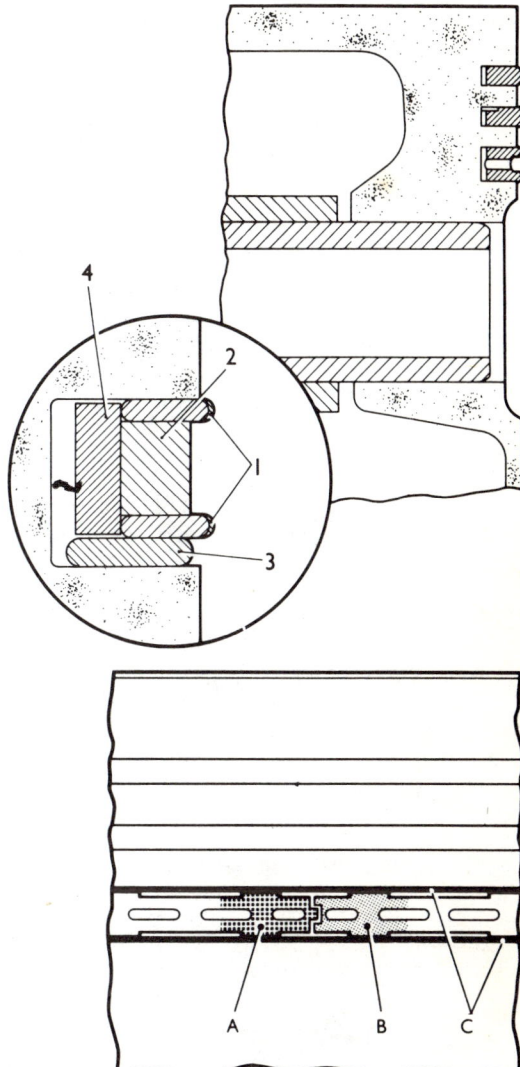

FIG 1:22 Piston ring location. Inset shows Vauxhall oil control ring components, below is scraper ring of 1256 cc engine

Key to Fig 1:22 1 Rails 2 Spacer 3 Insert 4 Expander

Crankshaft end float is controlled by the centre main bearing, on the 1159 cc engine, with synchromesh transmission the upper shell only is flanged and positively located in the crankcase.

To remove the crankshaft, the sump, flywheel and piston and connecting rod assemblies must first be removed as described in previous Sections. Mark the main bearing caps to ensure that if serviceable they are refitted in their respective positions. Remove the main bearing bolts and caps, also keeping each shell with its own cap. Check that the crankshaft end float is between .002 and .008 inch. Lift out the crankshaft. Discard the crankshaft oil seal. Remove the bearing shells from the crankcase, again noting their respective positions.

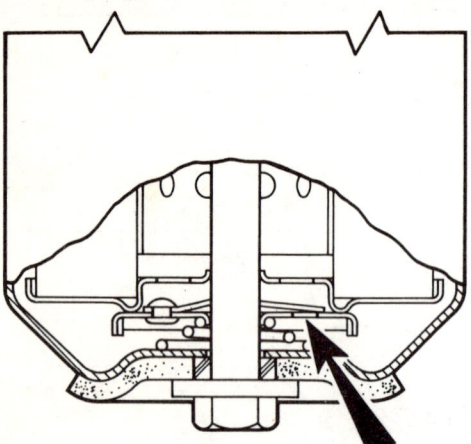

FIG 1:23   Oil filter bypass holes

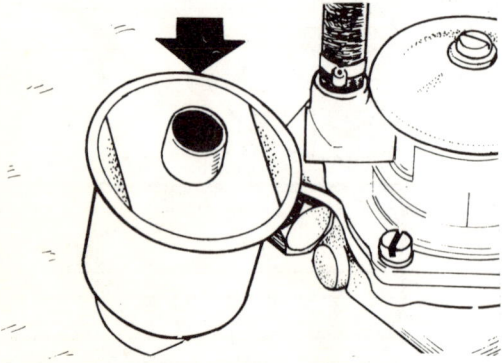

FIG 1:24   Crankcase breather

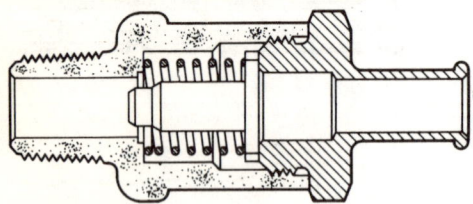

FIG 1:25   Section through breather valve

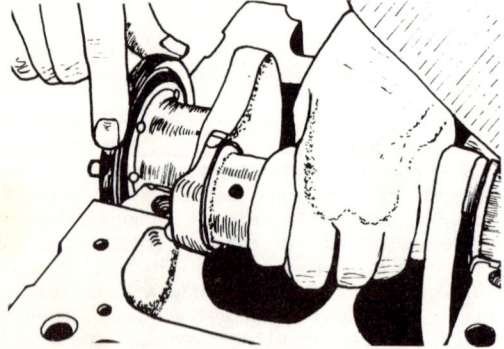

FIG 1:26   Supporting the weight of the crankshaft while inserting the seal

To check that the bearing caps have not been filed, refit the caps without the crankshaft or bearing shells and tighten the bolts to 58 lb ft. Measure the vertical diameter of each housing bore. If this is less than the minimum shown in Technical Data the cap has been filed. This trouble however can be rectified by fitting the special main bearing caps supplied for the purpose. Unlike the caps supplied with an engine or cylinder block, these are not machined as an assembly with the block but have their faces .004 to .005 inch below the axis of the housing. They are supplied with shims .002 and .003 inch thick. By using shims with a difference of .001 inch on opposite sides the diameter can be controlled to within .0005 inch and brought within the specified limits.

The crankshaft main journals and crankpins should be checked for wear and ovality. If worn below the specified limits or badly scored, the crankshaft must be reground and undersize bearing shells fitted. Crankshaft oilways should be cleared by forcing through paraffin or petrol under pressure, especially if the bearings have 'run'. The crankshaft should be checked for truth by mounting it between centres, but the average owner will not have facilities for carrying out this check.

To check bearing clearances do not use steel feeler gauges as these will damage the shells. A more satisfactory method is to use Plastigage, a material whose thickness after being compressed in a bearing can be measured by measuring its width against a scale provided. The manufacturer's instructions for its use should be carefully followed.

1:14 External oil filter, crankcase breather

The external oil filter is of the fullflow type, that is to say the whole of the oil passes through the filter on its way from the pump to the main oil gallery in the engine. The filter has a renewable element and a bypass device which allows oil to pass directly from the pump to the engine if the filter is allowed to become blocked.

The filter is on the lefthand side of the crankcase. Before removal, place an oil tray underneath as some oil will escape even if the sump has been drained. Unscrew the centre bolt and remove the casing. Discard the element. Remove the old gasket from the seating in the crankcase. In case of difficulty, spear the gasket with a sharply pointed instrument and pull it out. Do not prise it by levering against the edge of the groove. Clean out the filter casing and ensure that the bypass holes, arrowed in **FIG 1:23,** are clear.

Refit the filter casing with the new element and a new gasket. Ensure that the casing seats on the gasket and does not foul the edge of the groove, then tighten the nut to a torque of 14 lb ft. If the sump has been drained it should be refilled, otherwise top up to compensate for oil drained from filter. Run the engine to check for leaks.

For crankcase ventilation, air enters the crankcase through a wire gauze type breather. Air is extracted from the rocker cover through a hose connected to the carburetter air cleaner or to a ventilator valve in the inlet manifold. **FIG 1:24** shows the crankcase breather which incorporates the dipstick orifice. To clean the breather, unscrew it by hand, rinse in clean paraffin and blow out with compressed air. Oil the wire gauze and allow surplus oil to drain off. Check that the sealing ring is present and in good condition before installing the breather. **FIG 1:25** shows a sectional view of the ventilator valve. Where fitted, the ventilator valve should be checked to ensure that its spring is not weak or distorted and that the valve operates freely.

1:15 Reassembling the stripped engine

Before starting the work of reassembling the engine ensure that all components are scrupulously clean. If the block has been rebored pay particular attention to any corners where swarf could have collected. On a major overhaul the plugs should be unscrewed from the main oil gallery and the gallery blown out with compressed air. Waterways in the cylinder block and head should be flushed out with water. New gaskets and oil seals should be fitted throughout the engine.

To refit the crankshaft proceed as follows. Ensure that the new rear oil seal is clean and undamaged. Check the periphery of the crankshaft flange, including the chamfer, for scores, burrs or scratches, which can damage a new oil seal. Lubricate the oil seal lip and the crankshaft flange with antiscuffing paste. Assemble the seal squarely on the flange, taking care that the seal lip which faces towards the main bearing is not turned back or damaged. Ensure that all traces of old jointing compound have been removed from the oil seal groove and rear bearing cap faces on the crankcase and remove all traces of oil from these surfaces with solvent. After drying apply jointing compound sparingly to the seal groove. Install the crankcase halves of the main bearing shells. The flanged shell is for the centre bearing. Lubricate the shells with engine oil.

Carefully lower the crankshaft into place, taking the weight while guiding the oil seal into its groove in the crankcase, as shown in **FIG 1:26**. On no account must the weight of the crankshaft rest on the seal lip or the seal will be permanently damaged. Check the crankshaft end float, which should be between .002 and .008 inch.

Install the main bearing caps with their shells. The centre cap has the tapped hole for the oil suction pipe bolt on the side nearest the camshaft. If the special service caps with shims are being used, ensure that the shims are not trapped by the ends of the shells. The shims can be temporarily located with a little petroleum jelly while tightening up the cap bolts.

The rear main bearing cap needs special treatment as follows:

1 Remove all traces of jointing compound from the cap. Remove all traces of oil with solvent and dry the surfaces.
2 Apply jointing compound sparingly to the (inner) seal groove of the cap.
3 Apply Silastic 732 RTV sealant in a $\frac{1}{8}$ inch wide bead on cap register 2 (see **FIG 1:27**) far enough from the vertical face to prevent sealant being squeezed onto the face 1 during installation of the cap. The sealant air hardens so the cap must be installed within five minutes of the sealant application.

Fit the main bearing bolts with oiled threads and tighten to a torque of 58 lb ft. **It is essential for these bolts to be tightened to the specified torque as no locking device is provided.**

Fit the piston rings in the order described in **Section 1:12**. Lubricate the gudgeon pins with graphited oil and

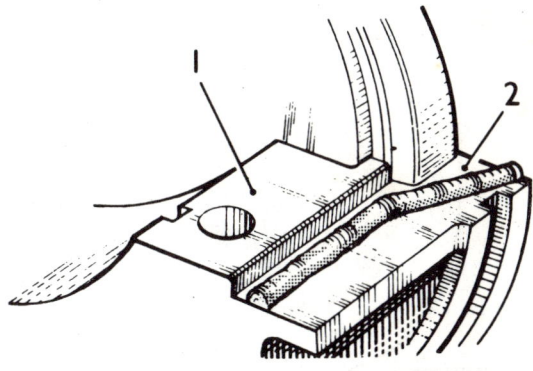

FIG 1:27 Application of sealer to register of rear main bearing cap

FIG 1:28 Position of oil pump drive spindle slot before installation. This will give correct installed location

the cylinder bores, pistons and rings with clean engine oil. Using a piston ring compressor install each piston through the top of the cylinder bore, with the notch in the piston crown facing the front. Ring gaps should be evenly spaced with the bottom one towards the camshaft. When refitting original pistons fit each in its original bore.

Make sure the bearings shells are properly fitted in the connecting rods. Assemble the big end caps and shells so that the pairing marks coincide. Install the big end bolts with oiled threads and tighten to a torque of 25 lb ft. **It is essential for this point to be observed as insufficiently tightened bolts may work loose while over-tightened bolts may stretch or shear.**

Refit the timing gear as described in **Section 1:7**. Check that the pointer on the crankshaft pulley is aligned with the TDC pointer on the timing case, with No. 1 piston on the compression stroke. Fit a new gasket to the oil pump and lubricate the pump drive gear teeth. Position the pump spindle as shown in **FIG 1:28** and install the pump. Check that, after fitting, the driving spindle slot has taken up the position shown in **FIG 1:29**, or within 12 deg. anticlockwise of that position. Fit the suction

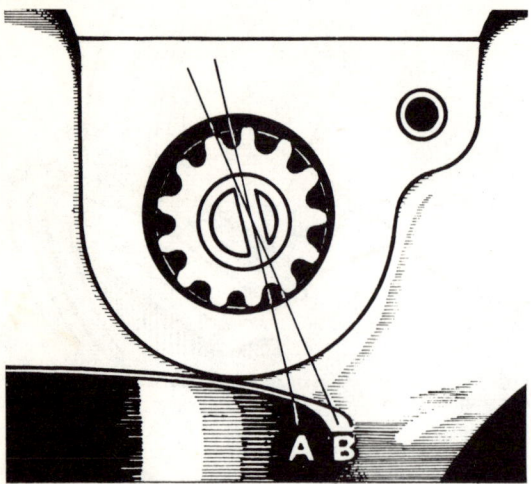

FIG 1:29 Installed position of oil pump drive spindle slot should be as shown at **A** or within the range **A-B**

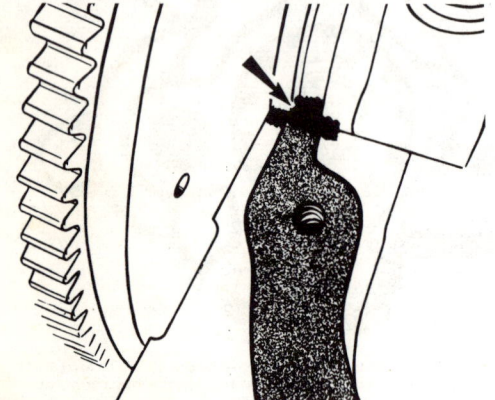

FIG 1:30 Sealer applied in corner when fitting sump gasket

pipe to the pump cover with the union finger tight. Install and tighten the pipe support and finally tighten the union. Check that the nut of the support screw is adjacent to the support attaching bolt.

In refitting the sump the following instructions must be carefully observed or leakage may result:

1 Inspect the sump contact faces for damage or distortion.
2 Clean old jointing compound from the crankcase face. Clean sealer from the rear main bearing cap groove unless this has been recently installed in which case if the sealer has not hardened it should not be removed. Dry the cleaned areas.
3 Apply jointing compound to the sump gasket area of the crankcase and timing case. Apply Silastic 732 RTV sealer to the corners formed by the rear bearing cap seal groove and the crankcase.
4 Fit the new sump gasket on to the crankcase, ensuring that the ends are fully engaged in the rear bearing cap groove then apply Silastic 732 RTV sealer as indicated by the arrow in **FIG 1:30**.

5 Warm the bearing seal and shape it to the contour of the bearing cap with the chamfered portions facing inwards. Fit the seal, arrowed in **FIG 1:31** in the cap groove ensuring that it overlaps the sump gasket equally at each side. Apply Silastic 732 RTV sealer to the junction of seal and gasket on both sides.
6 Jointing compound is not used between the gasket and the sump face and both these surfaces should be clean and dry. Install the sump within five minutes of sealant application, owing to sealant hardening, making sure that the seal remains correctly seated in its groove. Tighten the sump bolts evenly.

Check that the sump to gearbox brace is correctly assembled. In **FIG 1:32,** 1 is the brace, 2 the sump bracket. The internal and external toothed washer 3 must be assembled between brace and bracket as shown.

If the bolts securing the front engine mounting brackets to the crankcase have been disturbed, degrease the bolt threads and the internal threads in the crankcase with solvent. Refit the bolts after smearing the threads with Loctite Grade AVV to ensure an oil and watertight seal, and prevent the bolts working loose.

Install the flywheel. The faces of the crankshaft flange and the mating surfaces of the flywheel must be clean and dry and the weight of the flywheel must be supported until it is squarely home on the flange. Apply Bostik 771 to the centre portions of the bolts only and tighten evenly to a torque of 25 lb ft. The clutch must be refitted, carrying out the disc aligning operation described in **Chapter 5, Section 5:6**.

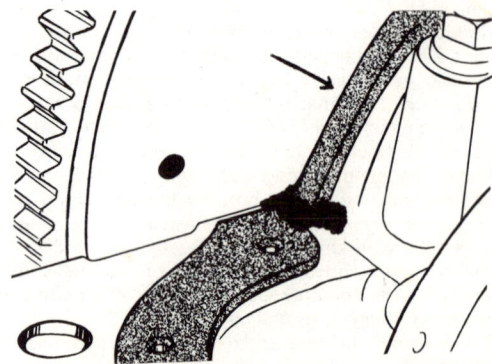

FIG 1:31 Ends of seal (arrowed) overlap gasket equally on each side. Apply sealer as shown

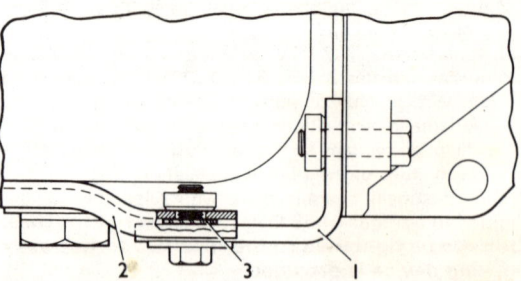

FIG 1:32 Gearbox brace 1, Sump bracket 2, Lock washer 3 correctly fitted when securing gearbox brace

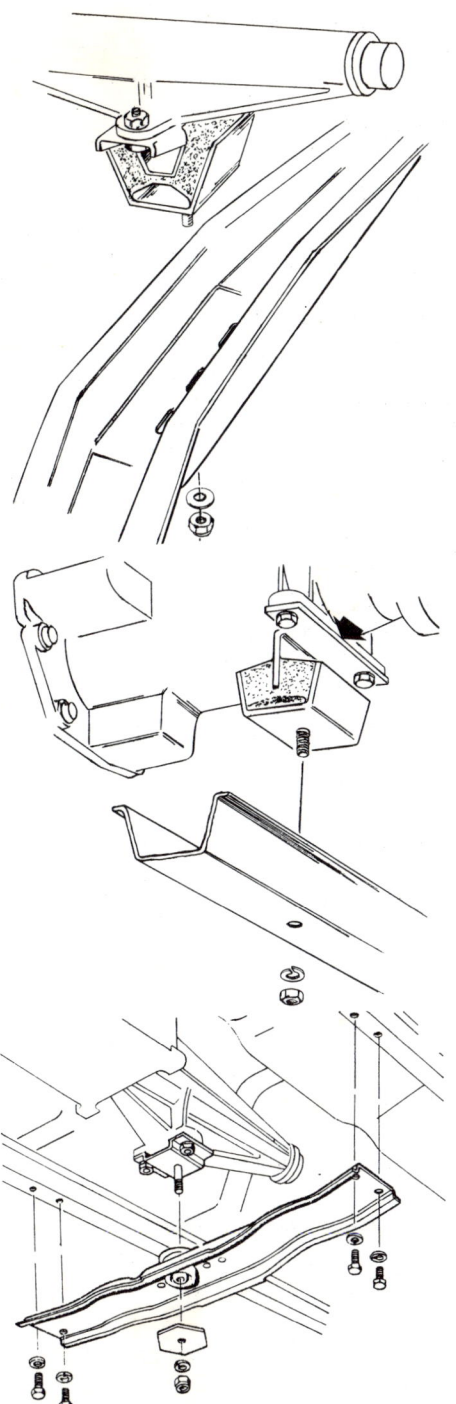

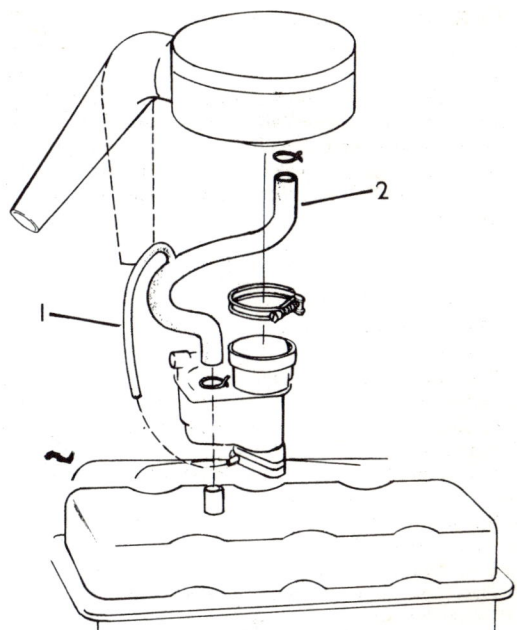

FIG 1:34 Positive crankcase ventilation 1256 cc engine

FIG 1:33 Engine rear mounting. Top, synchromesh gearbox; centre, automatic transmission; bottom, 1974 1256 cc engine. Large hexagon washer on latest type, must be positioned with two flats transversely across the car to clear crossmember on rebound

1:16 Refitting the engine in the car

Refit any other item removed from the engine after it was removed from the car. Note that when fitting the alternator mounting bracket there is a reinforcing web at the end nearest the rear of the block.

Apply a light smear of grease on the splines of the gearbox first motion shaft and then ensure that the clutch fork and release bearing are correctly positioned.

Sling the engine in the manner used for its removal (see **FIG 1:4**) and lower it into position, lining it up most carefully to allow the first motion shaft to enter the splined clutch disc hub and the crankshaft spigot bearing. It is most important to ensure that the weight of the engine at no time is allowed to hang on the shaft as considerable strain and damage will be caused.

Tighten all bolts and refit components in the reverse order to their removal. For instructions on adjustments to the controls on automatic transmission see **Chapter 6**.

Refill the sump with the recommended grade of engine oil and refill the cooling system. Start the engine and run it until normal working temperature is reached, then check the carburetter settings and examine the engine for leaks.

Check the tightness of the cylinder head bolts and the valve clearances.

1:17 1256 cc engines, piston rings

On these engines the chromium plated top ring is conventional, but the centre ring is externally stepped on its lower face. The plain face is marked TOP.

A three-piece rail-type scraper ring is used in the third position and care should be taken to see that the ends of the expander/spacer do not overlap, and also that this gap and those of the rails are spaced equally around the piston.

1:18 Positive crankcase ventilation

The system illustrated in **FIG 1:34** is used on 1256cc engines.

The main ventilation hose 2 is connected between the rocker cover and the air cleaner, while a smaller diameter hose 1 runs between the main hose and a connection on the carburetter heat insulator. There is no breather with this system, the dipstick locating in a plain hole in the crankcase.

1:19 Fault diagnosis

(a) Engine will not start

1 Defective coil
2 Faulty distributor capacitor
3 Dirty, pitted or incorrectly set contact points
4 Ignition leads loose or insulation faulty
5 Water on plug leads
6 Battery discharged or terminals corroded
7 Faulty or jammed starter
8 Sparking plug leads wrongly connected
9 Vapour lock in fuel pipes
10 Defective fuel pump
11 Overchoking, or 'pumping' accelerator pedal
12 Underchoking
13 Blocked petrol filter or carburetter jets
14 Leaking valves
15 Sticking valves
16 Valve timing incorrect
17 Ignition timing incorrect

(b) Engine stops

Check 1, 2, 3, 4, 10, 11, 12, 13, 14, 15 in (a)
1 Sparking plugs defective or gaps incorrect
2 Retarded ignition
3 Weak mixture
4 Water in fuel system
5 Petrol tank vent blocked
6 Incorrect valve clearances

(c) Engine idles badly

Check 1 and 6 in (b)
1 Air leak at manifold joints
2 Slow running jet blocked or out of adjustment
3 Air leak in carburetter
4 Over-rich mixture
5 Worn piston rings
6 Worn valve stems or stem bores
7 Weak exhaust valve springs

(d) Engine misfires

Check 1, 2, 3, 4, 5, 8, 10, 13, 14, 15, 16, 17 in (a); 1, 2, 3, 6 in (b)
1 Weak or broken valve springs

(e) Engine overheats

See **Chapter 4** (first check fan belt)

(f) Compression low

Check 14, 15 in (a); 5, 6 in (c); 1 in (d)
1 Worn piston ring grooves
2 Scored or worn cylinder bores

(g) Engine lacks power

Check 3, 10, 11, 13, 14, 15, 16, 17 in (a); 1, 2, 3, 6 in (b); 5, 6 in (c) and 1 in (d); also check (e) and (f)
1 Leaking joint washers
2 Fouled sparking plugs
3 Automatic advance not operating

(h) Burnt valves or seats

Check 14, 15 in (a); 6 in (b) and 1 in (d). Also check (e)
1 Excessive carbon around valve seat and head

(j) Sticking valves

Check 1 in (d)
1 Bent valve stems
2 Scored valve stem
3 Incorrect valve clearance

(k) Excessive cylinder wear

Check 11 in (a) and see **Chapter 4**
1 Lack of oil
2 Dirty oil
3 Piston rings gummed or broken
4 Badly fitting piston rings
5 Connecting rods bent

(l) Excessive oil consumption

Check 5, 6 in (c) and check (k)
1 Ring gaps too wide
2 Oil return holes in piston blocked
3 Scored cylinders
4 Oil level too high
5 External oil leaks

(m) Crankshaft and connecting rod bearing failure

Check 1 in (k)
1 Restricted oilways
2 Worn journals or crankpins
3 Loose bearing caps
4 Extremely low oil pressure
5 Bent connecting rod

(n) Internal water leakage (see **Chapter 4**)

(o) Poor circulation (see **Chapter 4**)

(p) Corrosion (see **Chapter 4**)

(q) High fuel consumption (see **Chapter 2**)

(r) Engine vibration

1 Loose generator bolts
2 Fan blades out of balance
3 Incorrect adjustment or worn rubbers on engine mounting
4 Exhaust pipe mountings too tight

CHAPTER 2

THE FUEL SYSTEM

2:1 Fuel pump operating principles
2:2 Routine maintenance
2:3 Dismantling pump
2:4 Reassembling pump
2:5 Pump testing
2:6 Zenith carburetter type 30 IZ
2:7 Routine maintenance. Slow running
2:8 Dismantling
2:9 Reassembly
2:10 Air cleaner
2:11 Fault diagnosis
2:12 Zenith Stromberg carburetter 150 CDS

2:13 Routine maintenance
2:14 Servicing the carburetter
2:15 Slow running adjustment
2:16 Zenith Stromberg 150 CDST
2:17 Throttle control linkage
2:18 Air cleaners
2:19 Zenith carburetter 34 IVET
2:20 Zenith Stromberg 150 CD-SETV
2:21 Zenith Stromberg 150 CD-SEV
2:22 Temperature controlled air cleaner
2:23 Fault diagnosis

2:1 Fuel pump operating principles

All models up to engine number 1400011 are fitted with the AC type YD mechanical fuel pump driven off the camshaft and supplying petrol to the carburetter from the tank mounted in the boot.

From engine number 1400011 a pump of sealed construction is fitted, the only work that can be carried out is the removal of the centre screw and cap to clean the filter. The fan pegs on the filter gauze must face upwards and the cap must seat correctly on the sealing ring before tightening the centre screw.

The earlier pump, shown in section in **FIG 2:1**, is mounted on the side of the crankcase and the pump rocker arm is operated by a cam on the engine camshaft. The heel of the rocker arm operates a link pivoting on the same spindle but not attached to the rocker arm. The link pulls the diaphragm down against its spring, drawing petrol in through the inlet valve. The spring then pushes the diaphragm upwards, closing the inlet valve and forcing petrol through the outlet valve to the feed to the carburetter.

As soon as the carburetter float chamber is full its needle valve closes and the back pressure in the pump holds the diaphragm down. A small spring keeps the rocker arm in contact with the cam and it continues to reciprocate but without operating the link, thus regulating the supply according to the needs of the carburetter. A

gauze filter screen traps any dirt before it reaches the pump inlet valve. A heat-insulating gasket is fitted between the pump and the crankcase.

2:2 Routine maintenance

The air vent in the petrol tank filler cap must be kept clear as the pump cannot function correctly unless there is atmospheric pressure on the petrol in the tank.

FIG 2:2 shows the filter cover and screen removed for periodic cleaning. The screen and the inside of the cover should be washed with paraffin and dried with compressed air. Cover the inlet valve orifice and flush out any sludge in the pump body. When refitting the screen and cover, renew the two gaskets, the large one between the screen and the cover and the small one under the head of the cover screw. Air leaks at these points can prevent the pump from working. Ensure that the nylon bush is assembled between the screen and the cover.

2:3 Dismantling pump

To remove the pump, disconnect the two hoses from the pump, plugging the inlet hose to prevent leakage. Undo the two bolts holding the pump to the crankcase and remove the pump and heat-insulating gasket. Dismantle the pump as follows:

1 Remove filter cover and screen.
2 Mark across flanges of pump cover and body. Undo the five screws and remove the cover.

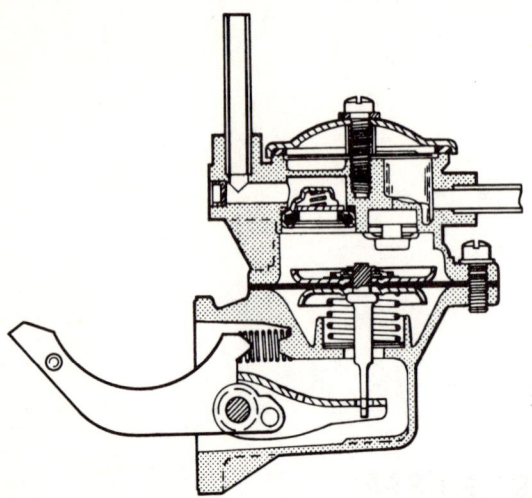

FIG 2:1   Sectional view of fuel pump

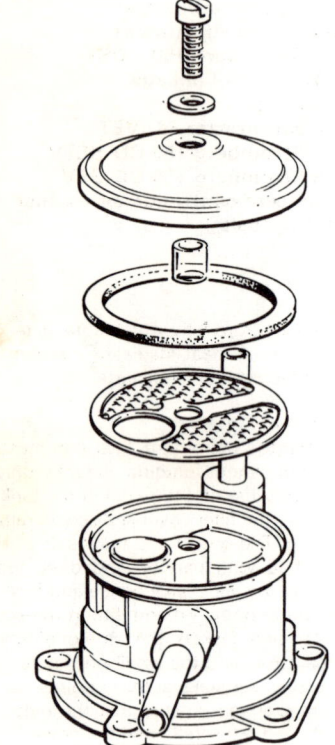

FIG 2:2   Filter cover removed for cleaning

3 Release the diaphragm assembly by depressing and turning 90 deg.

4 Carefully prise out the staked valves and remove their gaskets. Valves and seatings are supplied as an assembly.

5 Do not remove the rocker arm and link assembly unless these parts are badly worn.

If it is necessary to remove the rocker arm, grip it firmly in a vice leaving a gap between the pump body and the vice jaws. Using two flat bars, one on each side of the rocker arm, with protective packing against the body flange, lever the body away from the rocker arm. This will shear the staked metal at each end of the rocker arm pin retainers, allowing the assembly to be withdrawn. When fitting replacement rocker arm parts use the special service pin retainers, copper coloured for identification, which are shorter to allow for restaking the body.

2:4 Reassembling pump

Ensure that all parts are clean and reassemble in the following sequence:

1 Fit a new oil seal, seal retainer and diaphragm spring into the pump body. Fit the diaphragm assembly, depressing and rotating 90 deg. to engage the link and align the diaphragm tab with the lug of the body as shown in **FIG 2:3**.

2 Clean the valve recesses of the cover and remove any burrs left by previous staking. Fit new gaskets and valves as shown in **FIG 2:4**, in which (1) is the inlet valve and (2) the outlet valve. Press or tap the valves into place, using a sleeve .56 inch inside diameter and .68 inch outside.

3 Stake the cover at six positions round each valve.

4 Fit the filter screen, filter cover, nylon bush and new gaskets.

5 Push the rocker arm towards the pump body until the diaphragm is level with the body flange face. Position the pump cover so that the marks (see previous Section) align. Fit the five pump cover screws and tighten until the heads just engage the lockwashers.

6 Operate the rocker arm several times to align the diaphragm. Then, with the rocker arm released so that the diaphragm is at the top of the stroke, tighten the cover screws diagonally and evenly.

When refitting the pump to the engine ensure that the heat-insulating gasket is in position. Ensure that the hoses engage the full length of the pump connections and are not kinked.

2:5 Pump testing. Fault location

In the absence of specialized testing equipment the pump can be checked for flow while installed in the car. **Owing to the proximity of the exhaust system, this test should not be made with a hot engine.** Disconnect the feed pipe from the carburetter. If the engine is turned over a few times with the starter, petrol should gush out. If it does not, remove the other end of the pipe and test again in case the pipe itself is blocked.

If petrol is not coming from the pump, the trouble can be either in the pump or its connections or in the supply to the pump. Make sure there is adequate petrol in the tank, especially if the car is not on level ground and see that the tank cap vent is clear. Obstructions or leaks in the pipeline from the tank to the pump are possible, but the commonest trouble spots are the two gaskets of the pump filter cover. Any leakage at these points will cause air to be drawn into the pump instead of petrol. The pump filter can also be blocked.

The pump can also be tested when off the car by working the rocker arm by hand. Place a finger over the inlet port. The pump should develop an appreciable suction after a few strokes and maintain a vacuum for a few seconds. It should also hold pressure for a few seconds against a finger placed over the outlet port when the rocker arm has been pressed towards the pump and then released.

ZENITH CARBURETTER Type 30 IZ

2:6 Description

This carburetter is fitted to the early versions of the Viva HC and is a single choke downdraught instrument incorporating a diaphragm type acceleration pump operated by the throttle and an economy unit operated by the depression in the inlet manifold. An exploded view of the carburetter is given in **FIG 2:5**.

Referring to **FIG 2:5** it will be seen that there are four jets, the main jet 14, a correction jet incorporated in the emulsion tube 9, the pilot or slow-running jet 46 and the economy jet 47. The strangler flap or choke 1 is manually operated, and is designed so as to partly open as soon as the engine starts. The strangler control is also interconnected with the throttle to provide a fast idling speed until the engine reaches normal working temperature. Idling or slow running is controlled by the idling mixture volume control screw 35 and the throttle stop screw 43.

The economy unit, items 47 to 57 in **FIG 2:5** is shown in detail in **FIG 2:7**. It consists of a spring-actuated diaphragm 3, an economy jet 6 and a spring-loaded valve 9. At cruising speeds the relatively high manifold depression transmitted from a drilling below the throttle flap moves the diaphragm against a spring, allowing the economy unit chamber to fill from the float chamber and the spring-loaded valve to close. This prevents the use of fuel through the economy jet and economical cruising is obtained on the main jet only. At wide throttle openings manifold depression is reduced, allowing the diaphragm to push the valve off its seating and force petrol through the economy jet. This augments the supply from the main jet which is thus restricted in size without over-weakness at wide throttle openings.

The acceleration pump, items 10 to 12 and 24 to 31 in **FIG 2:5** is shown in detail in **FIG 2:8**. The purpose of the pump is temporarily to enrich the mixture which would otherwise be too weak when the throttle is suddenly opened but when the engine speed is low and manifold depression would not draw sufficient petrol through the main jet. The pump lever 3 is connected to the throttle and when the throttle is opened quickly the diaphragm 5 creates sufficient pressure in the pump chamber to force petrol through a metered bleed jet (not illustrated) past the ball valve 12 into the injector 10 in **FIG 2:5**. A non-return valve is also provided to prevent petrol draining back from the pump chamber into the float chamber. If on the other hand the throttle is opened slowly, there is not enough pressure to open the ball valve 12 and petrol passes through the bleed jet back into the float chamber.

2:7 Routine maintenance. Slow running

Routine maintenance is confined to a periodic removal of the carburetter for cleaning which will be described in **Section 2:8**. With the exception of the pilot jet the jets cannot be readily removed without dismantling, and

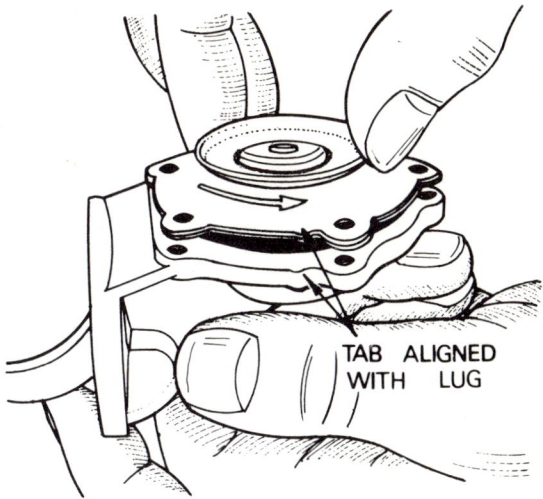

FIG 2:3 Refitting the diaphragm

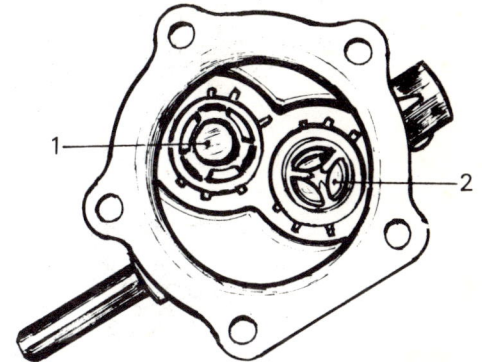

FIG 2:4 Correct installation of inlet valve 1 and outlet valve 2

this is more easily carried out with the carburetter on the bench. If however the acceleration pump injector is removed with the carburetter still on the engine, do not operate the throttle or the pump as this may dislodge the spring and ball valve, which will drop into the engine. Before setting the idling adjustment, it should be noted that conditions such as air leaks at manifold joints, incorrect petrol level, partly closed strangler, fouled sparking plugs and incorrect ignition timing will make satisfactory slow running impossible.

When adjusting idling on cars fitted with Automatic Transmission, first ensure that the handbrake is fully applied and that the selector lever is in the P or N position, otherwise the car may move with an increase in engine speed. After adjusting the idling speed, move the selector lever to the D position and check that the adjustment obtained gives smooth idling consistent with a minimum of creep.

On all models set the idling as follows: Run the engine until warmed up to normal working temperature. Referring to **FIG 2:5** the adjustment is carried out by means of the idling mixture volume control screw 35 and the throttle stop screw 43. Adjust the throttle stop screw

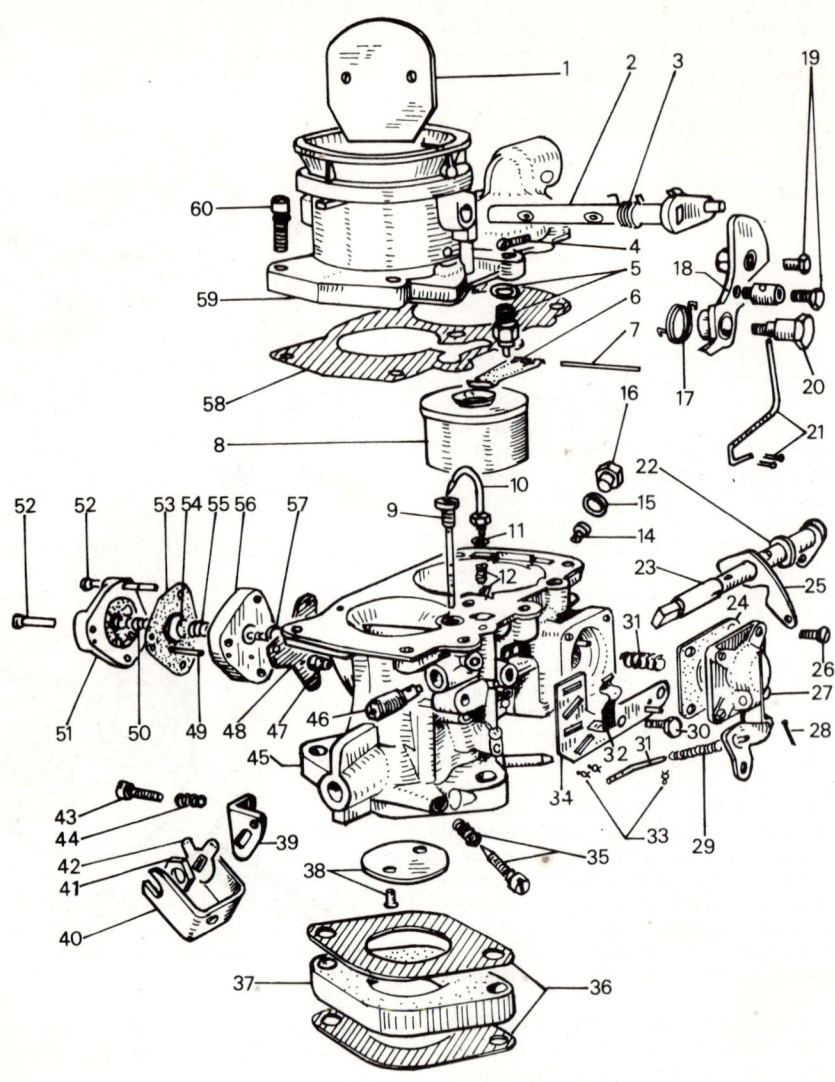

FIG 2:5   Exploded view of Zenith carburetter 30 IZ

Key to Fig 2:5   1 Strangler flap   2 Flap spindle   3 Return spring   4 Flap screw   5 Needle valve and washer
6 Float arm   7 Arm spindle   8 Float   9 Emulsion tube and correction jet   10 Pump injector   11 Sealing ring
12 Pump ball and retaining spring   14 Main jet   15 Washer   16 Sealing plug   17 Cam return spring   18 Strangler cam assembly
19 Swivel screws   20 Cam pivot   21 Rod—strangler to throttle, and split pins   22 Distance washer
23 Throttle spindle and pump rod lever assembly   24 Pump diaphragm   25 Throttle floating lever   26 Pump cover screw
27 Pump cover assembly   28 Split pin   29 Pump rod spring   30 Strangler bracket bolt   31 Pump rod   32 Cable clip
33 Rod circlips   34 Strangler bracket   35 Idling mixture volume control screw and spring   36 Gaskets   37 Heat insulator
38 Throttle flap and screw   39 Throttle abutment plate   40 Throttle lever   41 Nut   42 Lockwasher   43 Throttle stop screw
44 Spring   45 Body   46 Pilot jet   47 Economy jet   48 Gasket   49 Vacuum tube   50 Diaphragm spring
51 Economy unit cover   52 Economy unit attachment screws (3 long)   52A Economy unit cover screws (2 short)   53 Diaphragm
54 Valve washer   55 Valve spring   56 Economy unit body   57 Valve   58 Gasket   59 Float chamber cover   60 Cover screw

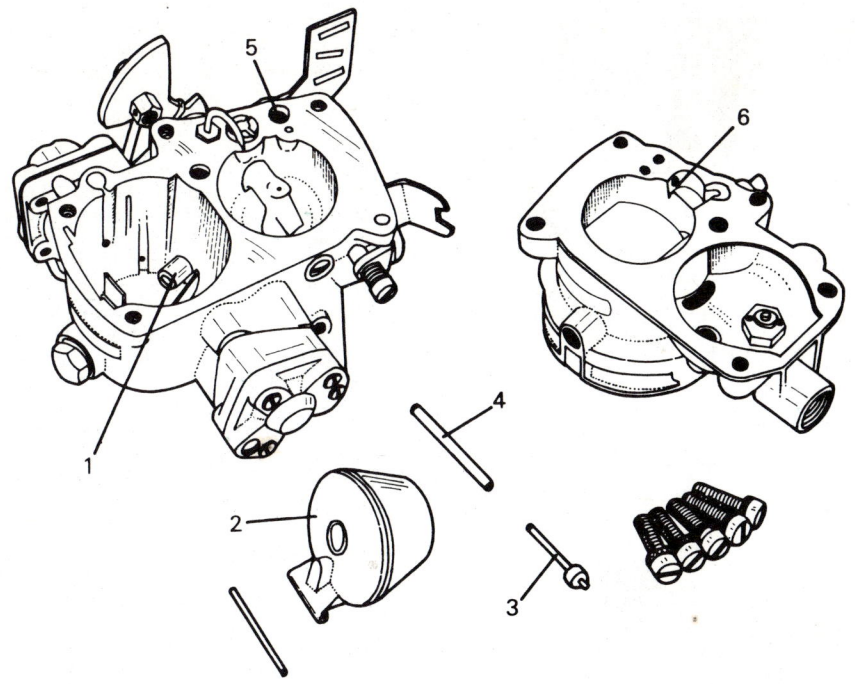

FIG 2:6   Zenith 30 IZ with float chamber cover removed

Key to Fig 2:6   1 Main jet   2 Float assembly   3 Pilot jet   4 Filter   5 Hole for pilot jet   6 Air bleed

until the engine is running at a fairly fast idling speed. Unscrew the volume control screw until the engine begins to 'hunt' (or run in a 'lumpy' manner), then screw it in again until the engine runs evenly. By this time the engine will probably be running too fast, so unscrew the throttle stop screw until a suitable idling speed is obtained. This adjustment will possibly richen the mixture enough for the engine to start to 'hunt' again, calling for a further adjustment of the mixture screw. Both adjustments should be carried out slowly. Do not screw the mixture screw fully home and do not attempt to get an exceptionally slow idling speed, or the engine may develop a tendency to stall.

Note that where European Exhaust Emission Control (Code 636) is specified, a 30 IZE unit is fitted. This carburetter has a calibrating screw sealed during manufacture and adjustment is not permissible in service.

2:8 Dismantling

Remove the carburetter from the engine as follows:
1 Remove the air cleaner.
2 Disconnect petrol and vacuum pipes and strangler control from the carburetter.
3 Disconnect the throttle control rod from the throttle lever after removing the circlip and spring.
4 Remove the nuts from the two carburetter flange studs and remove the carburetter with heat-insulator and two gaskets.

To dismantle the carburetter proceed as follows, referring to the detailed item numbers in **FIG 2:5** and the more general pictorial view in **FIG 2:6**:

1 Remove float chamber cover 59 and gasket 58.
2 Lift out float 8 and spindle 7.
3 Lift off pump injector 10 and sealing ring 11. Remove ball and spring 12.
4 Remove emulsion tube and correction jet 9, pilot jet 46 and after removing plug 16 and washer 15 take out the main jet 14. On some carburetters the petrol feed is taken to an extended pilot jet shrouded in a filter and installed in a vertical drilling in the body.

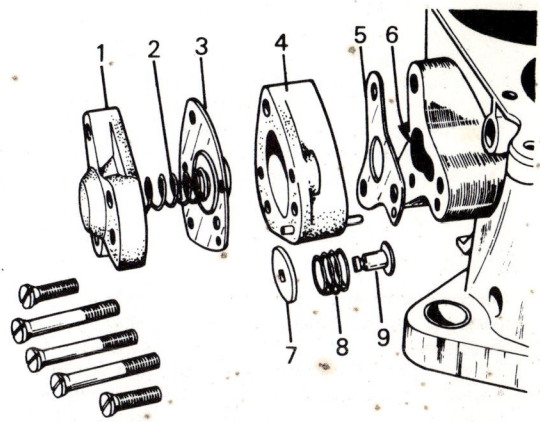

FIG 2:7   The economy unit

Key to Fig 2:7   1 Cover   2 Spring   3 Diaphragm   4 Valve body   5 Gasket   6 Jet recess   7 Valve washer   8 Valve spring   9 Valve

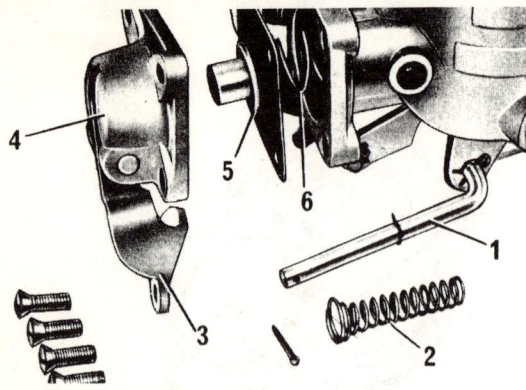

FIG 2:8 The acceleration pump

Key to Fig 2:8   1 Control rod   2 Control rod spring
3 Lever   4 Cover   5 Diaphragm   6 Return spring

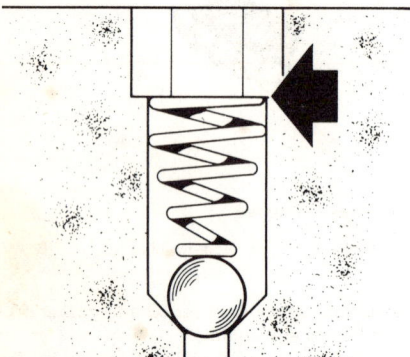

FIG 2:9 Position of injector spring

5 Referring to **FIG 2:8,** dismantle the acceleration pump, disconnecting the pump rod 1 from the pump lever 3 and detaching the rod spring 2. Remove the pump cover 4 the diaphragm 5 and the diaphragm spring 6.

6 Referring to **FIG 2:7,** dismantle the economy unit. The cover 1 has five screws. Undo the top screw and the two furthest from it to remove the unit as an assembly. Then remove the two remaining screws to separate the cover from the spring 2, diaphragm 3 and body 4. The valve 9 is removed by turning the washer 7 a quarter of a turn to release the spring 8. Unscrew the economy jet from the recess 6 in the carburetter body.

2:9 Reassembly

Reassembly of the carburetter is a reversal of the procedure given for dismantling, but the following points should be noted:

1 Blow out jets with compressed air or a foot-pump. Do not use wire prickers as this will enlarge the jets. Check the jet sizes with those given in Technical Data. Renew all gaskets, also the diaphragms of both economy and pump units if their condition is doubtful.

2 Before fitting the economy unit, ensure that the economy jet 6 in **FIG 2:7** is in place.

3 After installing the acceleration pump, connect the pump rod 1 in **FIG 2:8,** ensuring that the larger end of the spring 2 contacts the pump lever 3 and the rod is placed in the appropriate hole in the lever, namely the upper hole for winter setting or the lower hole for summer setting.

4 Install the jets in the carburetter body and fit the pump injector, items 10, 11 and 12 in **FIG 2:5.** Note that the wide end of the spring 12 is uppermost and is a tight fit in the bore. Push the spring down until it is flush with the bottom of the hexagon recess as shown in **FIG 2:9,** but do not push down further as this will apply excessive pressure to the ball. Referring to **FIG 2:5,** ensure that a sealing ring 11 is fitted to the injector 10. Position the injector radially as shown in **FIG 2:6.**

5 Adjust the strangler to throttle setting as follows:

(a) Unscrew the throttle stop screw 43 in **FIG 2:5** until the throttle is fully closed.

(b) Wedge the throttle slightly open by inserting a No. 61 or 1 mm drill between the throttle flap and the carburetter bore.

(c) Hold the strangler cam 18 against the stop pin to allow the strangler flap to be fully closed by its spring.

(d) Slacken the screw locking the rod 21 to the cam 18 and move the rod through the hole in the swivel until the throttle floating lever 25 contacts the pump rod lever 23. The latter is fixed to the spindle while the former is free to move on the same spindle.

(e) Retighten the swivel screw.

Check that the strangler flap remains closed when the engine is cranked by means of the starter. The return spring 3 should engage in the end notch of the spindle lever.

2:10 Air cleaner

The air cleaner has a detachable element. Remove the air cleaner from the carburetter before cleaning the element. Two types of element are fitted. The wire gauze type should be rinsed in clean paraffin, dried with compressed air and dipped in clean engine oil, the surplus being allowed to drain off before refitting. Wipe out the inside of the cleaner casing and ensure that the two gaskets are sound. Check the condition of the flexible hose from the rocker cover.

Paper element-type cleaners should not be cleaned but serviced by renewal of the element. Details of the engine crankcase ventilator valve which is fitted in conjunction with this type of element will be found in **Section 1:14.**

Note that different jet sizes are used with the two different types of air cleaner.

2:11 Fault diagnosis

(a) Leakage or insufficient fuel delivered

1 Air vent in tank restricted
2 Petrol pipes blocked
3 Air leaks at pipe connections
4 Pump or carburetter filters blocked
5 Pump gaskets faulty
6 Pump diaphragm defective
7 Pump valves sticking or seating badly
8 Vapour lock in pipe lines due to heat

(b) Excessive fuel consumption

1 Carburetter needs adjusting
2 Fuel leakage
3 Sticking strangler (choke) control
4 Dirty air cleaner
5 Excessive engine temperature
6 Brakes binding
7 Tyres under-inflated
8 Idling speed too high
9 Incorrect pump linkage setting

(c) Idling speed too high

1 Rich mixture
2 Carburetter controls sticking
3 Slow running screws incorrectly adjusted
4 Worn carburetter throttle flap (butterfly valve)
5 Ignition timing too far advanced

(d) Noisy fuel pump

1 Loose mountings
2 Air leaks on suction side and at diaphragm
3 Obstruction in fuel pipe
4 Clogged pump filter

(e) No fuel delivery

1 Float needle stuck
2 Tank vent blocked
3 Pipe line obstructed
4 Pump diaphragm stiff or damaged
5 Inlet valve in pump stuck open
6 Bad air leaks on suction side of pump

ZENITH STROMBERG CARBURETTER

2:12 Operating principles

The extra performance engine fitted to the early HC is equipped with a Zenith/Stromberg 150 CDS carburetter with synchromesh transmission or type 150 CDST with automatic transmission. This is of the side draught pattern and operates on the constant vacuum principle with a variable jet controlled by a piston type air valve and metering needle. A separate starter assembly is fitted to provide the rich mixture required for cold starting. Part sectional views of this carburetter are given in **FIGS 2:10** and **2:11** of which the latter shows very clearly the construction of the starter assembly of which a short description will be given to assist in understanding the operation.

The cold start device has as its main fixture a disc, 37 rotated by the choke control, in which are drilled a number of metering holes 41 through which the fuel passes from the float chamber to the throttle bore, via the passage ways 40 and 39. At the same time the fast idle cam 34 rotates and opens the throttle to its fast idle position and so provides the necessary rich mixture for cold starting and idling.

In order to cope with varying climatic conditions the two-position stop 33 is included, by means of which the position of the fast idle cam in the cold start position is determined and also the number of metering holes uncovered in the valve disc. The inset to **FIG 2:11** shows the normal position of this stop, while for conditions of extreme cold it is turned through a quarter of a turn to the position shown in the main drawing.

As the engine warms up and the choke is pushed back the number of metering holes in use is reduced and so the mixture is gradually weakened down to the normal running mixture. From this point the carburetter functions in the normal manner.

2:13 Maintenance

The bore of the air valve piston 9 in which the damper 1 fits should be kept filled with clean 10W-30 engine oil up to $\frac{1}{4}$ inch of its upper edge. Failure to do this will result in flat spots and poor acceleration.

The diaphragm should be examined and renewed if it is showing signs of deterioration or damage. This may be done by removing the screws securing the depression chamber cover 32 and lifting out the air valve when the screws holding the diaphragm retaining rings 29 may be withdrawn. When fitting the new diaphragm make sure that its locating tabs fit in the recesses in the carburetter body and the upper end of the piston (see **FIG 2:12**). Care also is needed when refitting the retaining ring on to the air valve piston.

When cleaning the carburetter parts, only petrol or paraffin should be used as any other cleaning compounds may adversely affect the diaphragm or sealing rings. Wire or other hard tools should never be used for cleaning jets or calibrated passage ways, but they should be washed in petrol and blown out with compressed air.

2:14 Servicing the carburetter

No difficulty will be experienced in dismantling the carburetter for cleaning and inspection, but before rebuilding it is recommended that new gaskets and O-rings should be obtained. Instruction for fitting the diaphragm have been given earlier.

Float level:

This must be correctly set when reassembling or checked if flooding or excessive consumption occurs and can only be done with the carburetter removed from the engine.

Hold the carburetter upside down then, with the needle valve on its seating, the two highest points of the floats should be between 15.5 and 16.5 mm above the face of the main body as shown in **FIG 2:13**.

If the float level needs correction, the float arm that contacts the float needle should be carefully bent as required.

Centralizing the jet:

Efficient operation of the carburetter depends upon the free movement of the air valve piston and the needle in the jet orifice. This may be checked by removing the hydraulic damper, lifting the air valve either by means of the lifting pin or a thin screwdriver and observing its fall on to the carburetter body. This should be quite free and result in a firm click as the underside of the valve hits the bridge of the bore. Failure to do this indicates the need to centralize the jet in its holder as follows:

Check that the needle is perfectly straight and that its shoulder is flush with the underside of the piston.

Slacken the jet bush retaining screw 18 by half a turn. Turn the jet adjuster until the jet is below the bridge. Slowly screw the jet adjuster clockwise, while at the

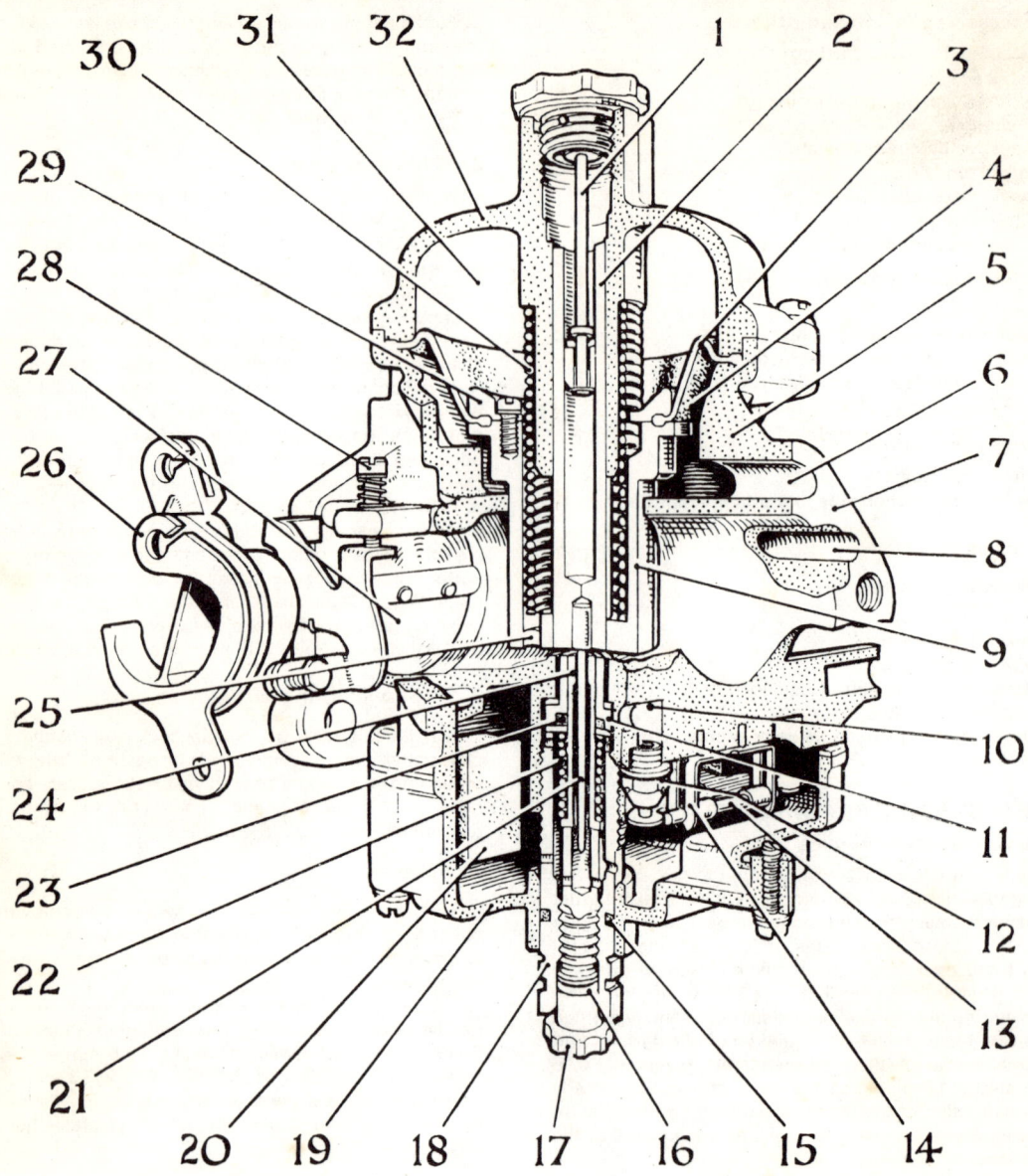

FIG 2:10 Part sectional view of Zenith Stromberg carburetter 150 CDS

Key to Fig 2:10   1 Air valve hydraulic damper   2 Guide spindle for air valve   3 Diaphragm   4 Air chamber below diaphragm   5 Carburetter body   6 Air feed to air chamber below diaphragm   7 Air cleaner mounting flange   8 Air vent hole to float chamber   9 Air valve piston   10 Fuel inlet channel   11 Centralizing bush   12 Float needle valve assembly   13 Float fulcrum spindle   14 Float fulcrum   15 O-ring   16 O-ring   17 Jet adjustment   18 Jet bush retaining screw   19 Float chamber   20 Float   21 Metering needle   22 Jet spring   23 O-ring   24 Jet   25 Depression transfer hole (1 shown)   26 Throttle spindle lever   27 Throttle valve   28 Slow running speed adjustment screw   29 Retaining ring for diaphragm   30 Air valve piston return spring   31 Depression chamber above diaphragm   32 Depression chamber cover

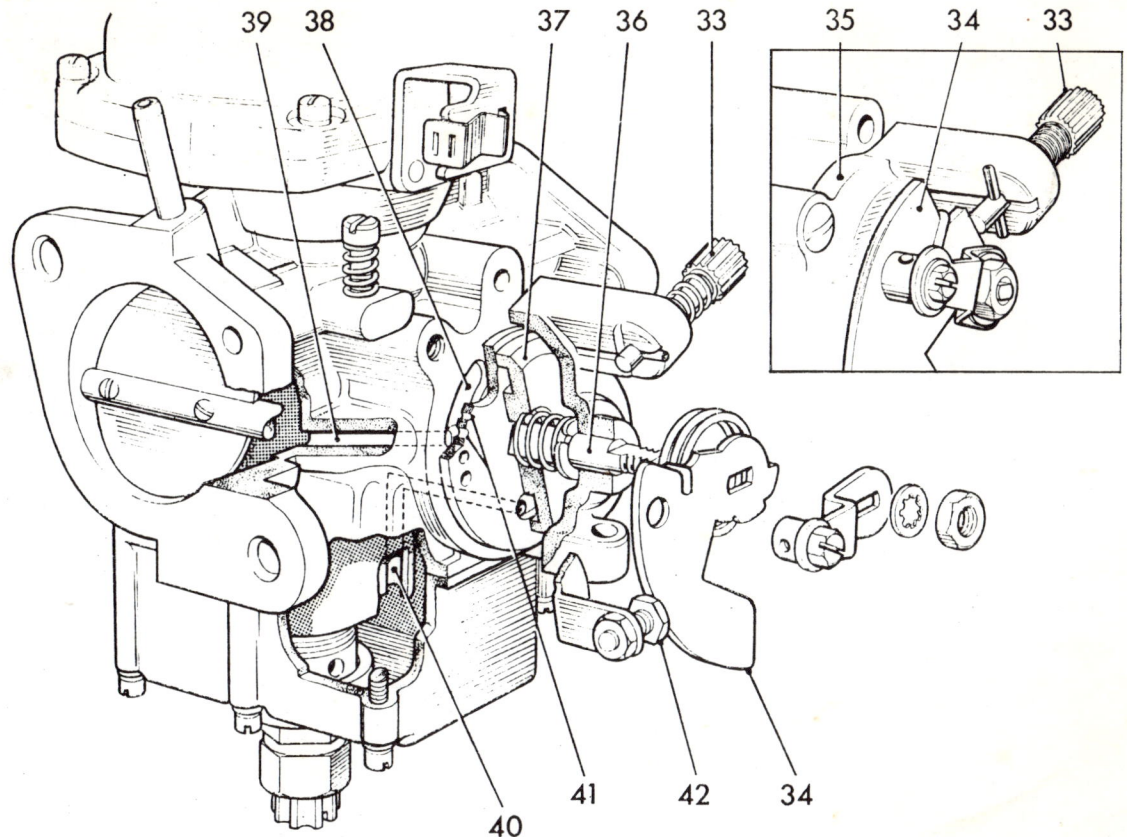

FIG 2:11 Starter assembly details. Inset shows normal position of stop

Key to Fig 2:11   33 Starter assembly two position stop   34 Fast idle cam   35 Starter assembly outer housing
36 Disc valve spindle   37 Starter assembly disc valve   38 Port feed by metering holes in disc valve   39 Fuel feed from port 38
to throttle bore   40 Fuel feed drilling to starter assembly   41 Metering holes in disc valve   42 Cold fast idle speed adjustment

same time raising and releasing the air valve, and noting
the sound made when the air valve contacts the bridge.
The sound will change when the jet comes in contact
with the air valve. Turn the jet down a quarter turn to align
the jet and bridge.

Give a sharp tap on the side of the screw 18. This will
normally centralize the jet and its bush around the
needle and allow it to pass freely in the jet orifice. In
some stubborn cases it may be necessary to give the
valve a slight push from above.

Tighten the retaining screw 18 and recheck.

Choke control:

The choke control securing screw on the cam 34
should be tightened when the choke control is $\frac{1}{8}$ inch
from its fully back position in order to ensure that the
cam rests against its stop when the control is pushed
fully back.

To ensure the correct fast idle, push the cam 34
against its stop while adjusting the screw 42 until a
.8 mm drill can be inserted between the throttle flap and
the carburetter bore.

2:15 Slow running adjustment

Although this adjustment is made at idling speed it
does in fact control the whole operating range of the
carburetter.

Start the engine and run until normal operating temperature is reached, then adjust the idle screw 28 to
obtain the specified idling speed of 800 to 850 rev/min.
Now turn the jet adjuster 17 as required to give the
smoothest running. If this results in an increase in engine
speed, the idle screw 28 may be reset to give the correct
idling speed and the process repeated.

The setting may be checked by lifting the air valve
piston with its lifting pin and observing the engine speed.
If it increases the mixture is too rich, while if it immediately
tends to stall it is too weak. Ideally it should rise for a
moment and then fade away. Note that clockwise
rotation of the jet adjusting screw weakens the mixture
and anticlockwise rotation richens it.

2:16 Zenith/Stromberg 150 CDST

This type of carburetter which is fitted on cars with
automatic transmission differs from the previous model
in that it has a water-heated automatic cold-start device

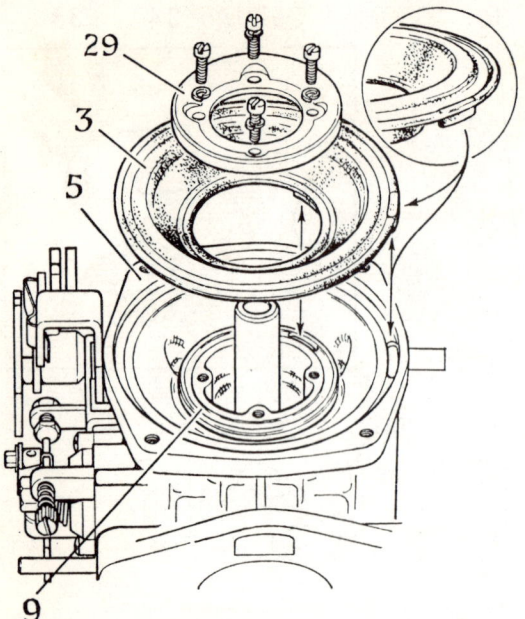

FIG 2:12 Showing correct location of diaphragm

Key to Fig 2:12   3 Diaphragm   5 Body   9 Air valve
29 Retaining ring

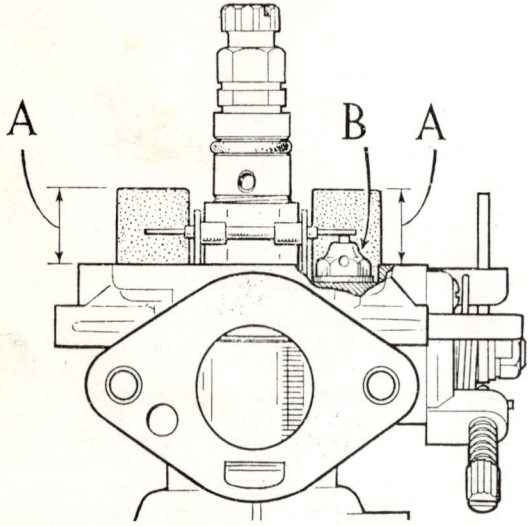

FIG 2:13 Adjusting float level. **A**=15.5 to 16.5 mm

1974 1256 16/17MM (Basket removed)

in place of the manually controlled unit. This is illustrated in **FIG 2:14**.

The tapered needle 4 admits the fuel into the carburetter bore and is operated by the thermostat lever 3 which is moved under certain conditions of manifold vacuum by the vacuum kick-rod 2 and piston 1. The kick-rod is cut away to allow some degree of independent movement by the thermostat lever.

The thermostat lever and fast idle cam 5 are mounted on a common shaft and are interconnected by a spring which controls the movement of the fast idle cam in relation to the thermostat lever. The position of the thermostat lever is controlled by a bi-metal spring thermostat 6 which is heated by water passing through the casing.

When starting from cold the accelerator pedal should be depressed once and released to allow the thermostat lever and fast idle cam to take up a rich position. The needle is thus lifted off its seat and fuel passes into the mixing chamber.

When the engine fires, the inlet manifold vacuum draws on the piston and kick-rod and so operates the thermostat lever into a position where the needle rides in a lower position and provides a weaker mixture.

As soon as operating temperature is reached, the thermostat causes the lever to seat the needle and closes off any further supply of fuel. The fast idle cam takes up its normal running position and it should be noted that the fast idle screw is sealed and should not normally be disturbed.

The correct setting of the thermostat is indicated by a dot on the rim of the housing. This must be in line with the lines on the choke body and insulator.

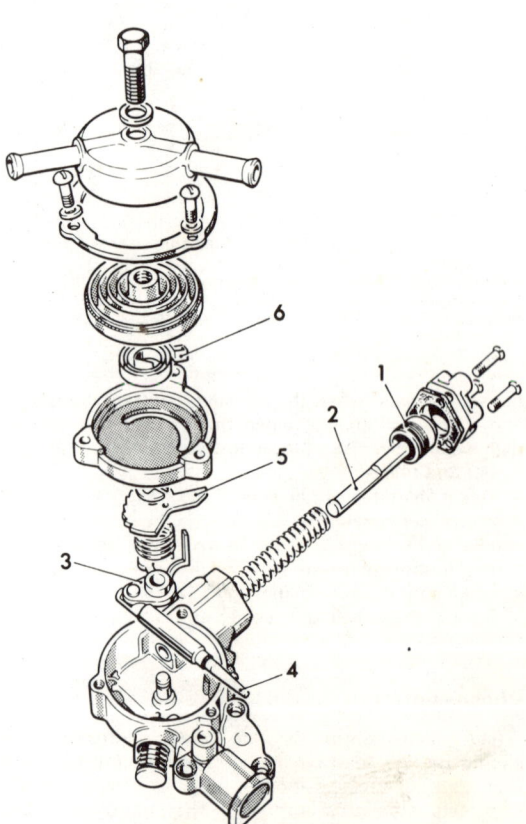

FIG 2:14 Cold start device 150 CDST

Key to Fig 2:14   1 Piston   2 Vacuum kick rod
3 Thermostat lever   4 Needle   5 Fast idle cam
6 Thermostat

2:17 Throttle control linkage

A cable-operated throttle control is used with all engines. This is illustrated in **FIGS 2:15** and **2:16** from which it will be seen that the throttle cable is operated by an organ-type pedal through a link and bellcrank mounted in a housing screwed to the floor of the car.

To renew a cable it is necessary to detach the housing from the floor panel. After assembly check the dimension A in **FIG 2:16** and, if necessary, adjust it to 2 inches. Lubricate all moving parts with grease.

Adjustment of the cable is provided at the carburetter end by means of a threaded sleeve and two nuts on the outer cable. The setting here should provide a small amount of slackness when the bellcrank of the accelerator pedal is in contact with the housing and the throttle lever is fully closed.

FIG 2:17 Resetting fast idle cam 150 CDST ensure end of rod is flat, to prevent jamming

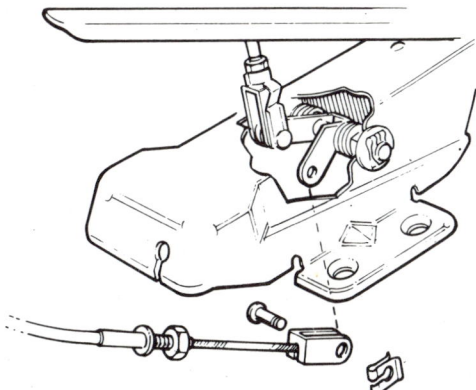

FIG 2:15 Accelerator pedal assembly

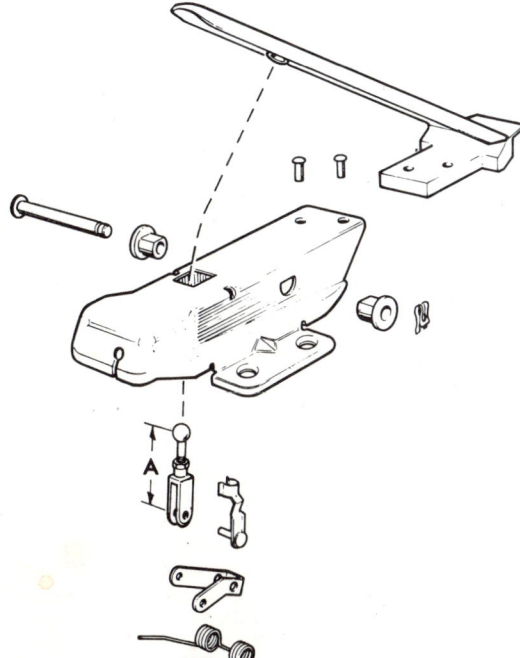

FIG 2:16 Adjusting pedal linkage. **A**=2 inches

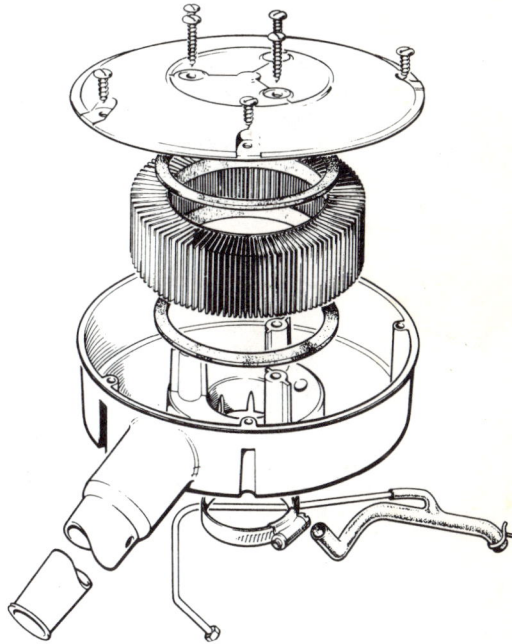

FIG 2:18 Air cleaner. Paper element

On engines with an automatic choke or cold start device the fast idle cam must be in the normal running position before adjusting the throttle cable.

With the Zenith carburetter, remove the air cleaner, hold the choke flap open and operate the throttle linkage to allow the fast idle cam to return to its normal running position. On the Zenith/Stromberg carburetter this is done by removing a brass plug with a screwdriver and inserting a $\frac{3}{16}$ inch diameter rod in the hole as shown in **FIG 2:17** and pushing the thermostat lever and fast idle cam fully anticlockwise.

2:18 Air cleaners

Two types of air cleaners are to be found on the Stromberg carburetters covered by this manual, either the paper element type shown in **FIG 2:18** or the wire mesh and oil bath type illustrated in **FIG 2:19**.

FIG 2:19 Air cleaner. Oil bath type

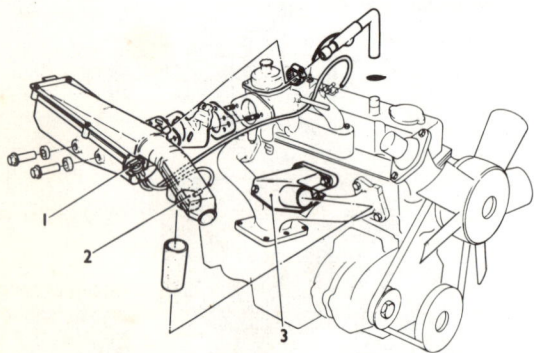

FIG 2:20 The temperature controlled air intake system

Key to Fig 2:20 1 Temperature sensing unit 2 Vacuum motor 3 Hot air shroud

The paper element should be renewed at the intervals recommended in the Owners handbook and is done simply by lifting off the snap fitting top cover and then releasing the securing screws. When fitting the new element, make sure that the sealing rings are correctly located.

It will be seen that the air intake tube is adjustable and is directed towards the exhaust manifold in winter to eliminate carburetter icing while in summer it is pivoted through 45 deg. towards the side of the engine compartment.

The oil bath type of cleaner is mounted on a bracket attached to the cylinder head and contains a wire mesh element as part of the cover which can be withdrawn after removing the cover retaining bolt.

The element and the oil bath should be washed in paraffin and allowed to dry before being refilled with SAE.50 engine oil up to the level indicated.

2:19 Zenith carburetter 34 IVET

This is fitted to 1256 cc engines and is in most respects similar to the type described earlier in **Section 2:6**. Detailed specifications will be found in **Technical Data**.

On these carburetters built to Code 636 requirements the calibrating screw is sealed and it should be noted that

the accelerator pump link pin must **always** be fitted in the upper hole of the pump spindle lever. The part throttle air bleed passage is threaded but no screw is fitted.

2:20 Zenith Stromberg 150 CD-SETV

This carburetter is fitted to 1159 cc extra-performance engines with Code 636 (European exhaust emission control) equipment.

It is similar to the 150 CDST carburetter with the exception of the following:

1 The metering needle is spring loaded to one side of the jet and centralization is not required.

2 A temperature compensator is fitted which is pre-set and must not be altered.

3 An idle trimming screw is fitted above the temperature compensator, it must not be moved.

The jet and metering needle is set at the factory and is locked by a seal and clip. An exhaust gas analyser is required for correct setting.

2:21 Zenith Stromberg 150 CD-SEV

This carburetter was introduced at engine number 1400011 on the 1256 cc model. It is similar in most respects to the 150 CD-SETV except for the following:

1 A nylon plug seals the revised jet adjuster, and must not be removed.

2 The float chamber must be removed before the jet adjuster can be withdrawn.

3 The needle valve incorporates a non-detachable filter.

The nylon washer on the needle stem is positioned between the needle flange and the plain washer.

Screw the jet adjuster fully into the body to prevent a foul when installing the float chamber.

The initial setting of the jet adjuster is two turns down from the fully in position. Run engine till hot and set idle speed with the throttle stop screw. Turn jet adjuster until engine runs smoothly.

2:22 Temperature controlled air cleaner

During 1975 a new type of air cleaner was introduced which uses a flat rectangular filter element housed in a body which also includes a temperature sensor and a vacuum motor. See **FIG 2:20**.

The paper element is removed for renewal at regular servicing intervals by undoing the six retaining screws and lifting off the top cover of the cleaner unit. The other main components also have to be renewed in the event of malfunctioning as no adjustments or repairs are possible. A fault in these will usually close the hot air entry and hold the cold air entry open. Such a fault may go un-noticed in hot weather, but may result in symptoms of weak mixture when the ambient temperature is low.

As will be seen from the illustration, air can be admitted to the cleaner housing either through the front orifice at engine compartment temperature (cold air) or by way of the hose connected to the shroud covering the exhaust manifold. The control damper is simply a device for opening and closing the hot and cold air inlets and so adjust the temperature of the air being delivered to the carburetter.

The control damper is actuated by the vacuum motor whose vacuum supply is regulated by the sensor unit which is a bi-metal temperature sensing spring responsive to the air temperature in the housing. The sensor is connected in a vacuum line from the inlet manifold to the motor and at low temperature values allows a greater depression to reach the vacuum motor which in turn closes the cold air intake. As the temperature inside the cleaner housing rises, so the sensor reduces the vacuum supply and the cold air intake is progressively opened, mixing cold with hot air as necessary to maintain an air cleaner temperature of 40°C ± 7°C.

When maximum engine power is required, as for acceleration, the vacuum level in the inlet manifold is lowered and this causes the vacuum motor to open the cold air intake fully to allow maximum air flow.

Testing:

In the event of symptoms suggesting faulty operation of the air cleaner mechanism, first check the condition of all the hoses and renew any faulty item.

Observe the position of the damper through the air cleaner intake, using a small mirror if necessary, and check the linkage for binding.

If a vacuum pump is available, the action of the damper can be observed when a vacuum is applied to the motor diaphragm. If this does not operate correctly, the vacuum motor and intake tube assembly must be renewed.

The temperature sensor can be checked as follows: With the engine cold, note the position of the damper. The cold air port should be open and the hot port closed.

Start the engine and allow it to idle. The cold air port should be closed at once and the hot air port opened. As the engine warms up the damper should move, partially opening the cold port and the air cleaner body becomes warm to the touch.

A further test, starting from cold (below 35°C) is to remove the cleaner cover and stick a thermometer with the bulb adjacent to the sensor unit. Cover the cleaner and start the engine when the cold air port should close. As the engine warms up and the cold port is opened, remove the cover and note the temperature; it should be between 33°C and 47°C. If this operation is not obtained, the sensor is defective and must be renewed.

The sensor is clipped into the cleaner housing and can be levered off after removing the vacuum pipes.

2:23 Fault diagnosis

Carburation and fuel supply faults which are common to all types of instrument have been described in **Section 2:11**. The Zenith Stromberg CD carburetter, given reasonable maintenance will not give more trouble than the more conventional types; in fact, owing to its simple jet system fuel blockages are virtually impossible. There are, however, a few possible troubles which may present difficulty to those unfamiliar with the Zenith Stromberg:

(a) Difficult starting and uneven running
1 Choke control or air valve operation faulty
2 Float level incorrect
3 Flooding due to float needle not seating, or assembly loose in body

(b) Poor idling and loss of power
1 Diaphragm split
2 Metering needle sticking
3 Metering needle incorrect size
4 Throttle spindle worn

(c) Slow response to throttle (30 to 40 mile/hr in top gear)
1 Oil level in dashpot low
2 Sluggish movement of damper caused by grit or burrs
3 Air valve movement sluggish. If caused by grit or carbon clean with paraffin (not petrol or solvent)
4 Metering needle bent or not centralized
5 Air valve spring incorrect. Correct spring identified by blue paint

(d) Fuel leaks from bottom of float chamber
1 Jet assembly not concentric with bore of float chamber boss
2 Sealing ring faulty

(e) 'Flat spot' on acceleration
1 Oil level in dashpot low

NOTES

CHAPTER 3

THE IGNITION SYSTEM

3:1 Distributor. Automatic timing controls
3:2 Distributor maintenance, contact point adjustment
3:3 Distributor removal
3:4 Dismantling
3:5 Reassembly

3:6 Refitting
3:7 Re-timing
3:8 Low tension circuit tests
3:9 HT cables. Sparking plugs
3:10 Fault diagnosis

Polarity of electrical circuits

All cars in the Viva HC series have an electrical system with negative earth. It is essential that replacement units should be of the same polarity as the system on the car. This affects the polarity of the generator and the connections on the battery and ignition coil, as well as certain accessories.

3:1 Distributor. Automatic timing controls

FIG 3:1 is a part-sectioned view of the distributor showing the automatic timing controls. The distributor components are also shown in exploded form in **FIG 3:2**. A special type distributor is fitted to 1159 cc engines which have been prepared to Code 636, that is European Exhaust Emission Control, and must not be interchanged with other types. The distributor mainshaft is driven at half crankshaft speed by the oil pump spindle, but the four-lobed cam at its upper end can be turned in relation to the mainshaft by the centrifugal control system. The upper contact breaker plate can be turned in relation to the distributor housing by the vacuum control system.

These two systems of automatic timing control are supplementary and both must be kept in good order to ensure the full range of ignition advance necessary.

1 In the centrifugal control any increase in engine speed throws the weights outwards against the pull of their springs, turning the cam anticlockwise in relation to the distributor mainshaft, thus advancing the ignition.

2 In the case of the vacuum control, not fitted to Code 636 engines (European exhaust emission control), any increase in manifold depression moves the diaphragm so that the rod turns the moveable contact breaker plate clockwise, thus also advancing the ignition.

It will be seen that each system has the effect of advancing the ignition under certain conditions. While the centrifugal control is governed entirely by engine speed, the vacuum control only advances the ignition when the engine is under light load. If the engine is pulling hard or accelerating, manifold depression will be less and the ignition will automatically be retarded.

The functioning of the centrifugal control can only be checked accurately by means of special equipment. As a rough check however, remove the distributor cap and turn the rotor anticlockwise with the fingers. When released it should return to the fully retarded position. Failure to do so indicates weak springs in the mechanism.

To check the operation of the vacuum control, start the engine and gradually increase speed from idling, while

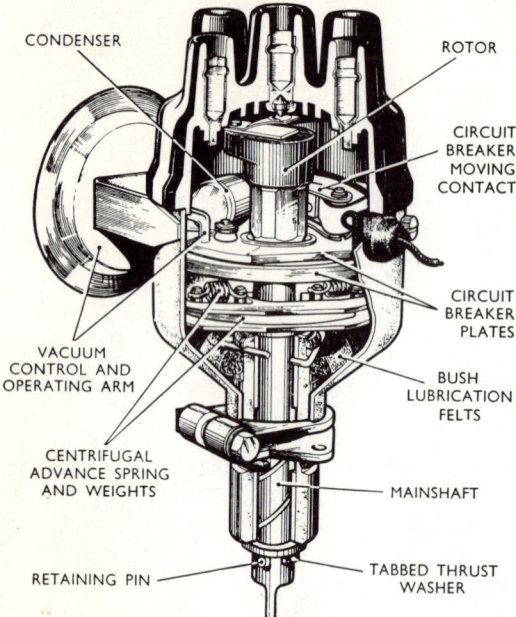

FIG 3:1 Sectional view of distributor

CONDENSER

ROTOR

CIRCUIT BREAKER MOVING CONTACT

CIRCUIT BREAKER PLATES

VACUUM CONTROL AND OPERATING ARM

BUSH LUBRICATION FELTS

CENTRIFUGAL ADVANCE SPRING AND WEIGHTS

MAINSHAFT

RETAINING PIN

TABBED THRUST WASHER

observing the control operating arm. The flange, seen in **FIG 3:3** should move until it contacts the control unit. Failure to operate indicates either a blocked or leaking vacuum pipe, contact breaker upper plate not moving freely, or a faulty vacuum unit.

3:2 Distributor maintenance, contact point adjustment

To lubricate the distributor, remove the cap by easing away the two retaining clips. Lift out the rotor arm. It should lift out easily. If any force is needed, care must be taken not to crack the insulating material of which it is composed. Before refitting, find the cause of the trouble, usually burrs on the end of the shaft. Check the rotor for cracks.

Referring to **FIG 3:3** apply a few drops of engine oil through the hole 4, to the felt pad 6 and contact pivot 3. Lightly smear the cam face 5 with petroleum jelly. On later cars a plastic foam pad impregnated with grease, not oil, is fitted to lubricate the cam.

The contact points should be clean and free from pitting. They should be cleaned with a fine grade of oil stone but their faces must be kept flat and parallel. Badly pitted points should be renewed as described below. To adjust the points, turn the engine until a cam is centralized on the moving contact rubbing block. Do not turn the engine by the fan, but remove the sparking plugs and use a spanner on the crankshaft pulley nut.

Referring to **FIG 3:3**, slacken the fixed contact screw 2, insert a screwdriver in the slot 1 and turn the plate until the required gap is obtained. Tighten the screw 2 and re-check the gap. This should be .019 to .021 inch except where new contacts have been fitted, when .021 to .023 inch should be given to allow for bedding down of the new rubbing block. After adjusting the contacts always check the ignition timing as described in **Section 3:7**.

The contact points can be renewed without removal of the distributor as follows:
1 Remove distributor cap and rotor.
2 Disconnect the LT lead at the coil.
3 Remove the capacitor mounting bracket screw and the contact breaker locking screw and withdraw contacts, capacitor and LT lead as an assembly.
4 Remove the contact stud nut from the inside of the insulating pad, withdraw the stud with the capacitor lead and LT lead attached and remove the moving contact.

The fixed and moving contacts are supplied as an assembly, generally referred to as a 'contact set'. Assemble as follows:
1 Locate the moving contact spring on the contact stud (which has the capacitor and LT lead attached). Insert the stud in the insulating pad and loosely assemble the nut.

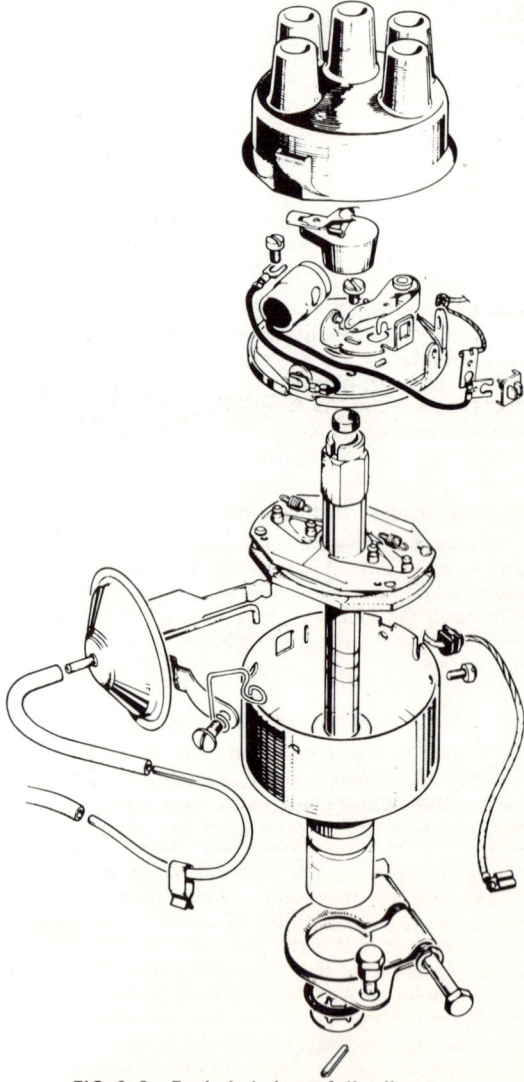

FIG 3:2 Exploded view of distributor

2 Apply a spot of oil to the moving contact pivot on the contact breaker plate and place the contact set and capacitor in position. Install the capacitor with the holes in the bracket locating on the pips in the plate.

3 Loosely install the fixed contact locking screw then tighten the contact stud nut securely.

4 Reconnect the LT lead to the coil.

5 Set the contact points to a gap of .021 to .023 inch.

6 Check the ignition timing.

When refitting the rotor, do not bear down on the contact spring. Dimension A in **FIG 3:4** should be .30 to .34 inch. To check the insulation of the rotor, remove the centre HT lead from the distributor cap and hold it about .60 inch from the edge of the rotor contact spring. Hold the insulation using a dry rag or rubber glove. Flick open the contact points. If a spark jumps the gap the rotor is faulty and must be renewed.

Before refitting the distributor cap wipe it inside and out with a clean dry cloth. Examine the carbon button for wear and the segments for burning. Examine the cap for cracks or 'tracking', indicated by thin black lines caused by electrical leakage between the segments. An electrical check for tracking can be carried out as follows:

1 Detach a sparking plug HT lead from the cap.

2 Insert the coil HT lead in its place.

3 Flick open the contact points.

4 Repeat with the coil HT lead in the opposite plug HT socket in the cap.

Tracking between any two segments will be indicated by sparking inside the cap.

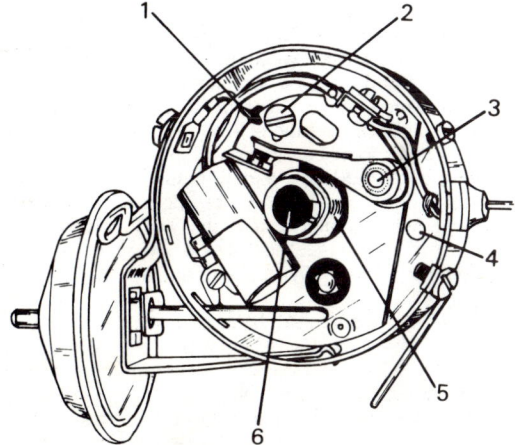

FIG 3:3 Distributor with cap and rotor removed

Key to Fig 3:3   1 Adjustment slot   2 Fixed contact screw 3 Moving contact pivot   4 Oil hole   5 Cam   6 Felt pad

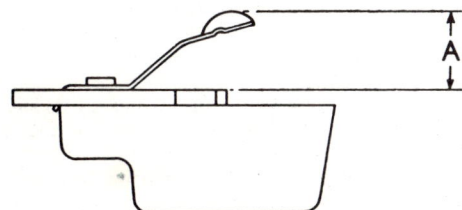

FIG 3:4   Rotor contact spring adjustment
A=.30 to .34 inch

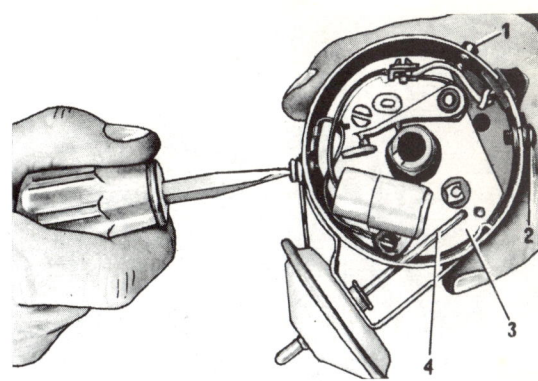

FIG 3:5   **Dismantling the distributor**

Key to Fig 3:5   1 and 2 Screws securing plate assembly 3 Contact breaker upper plate   4 Vacuum control arm

FIG 3:6   **Setting timing mark for LC and extra performance engines**

3:3 Distributor removal

To remove the complete distributor proceed as follows:

1 Disconnect the battery.

2 Disconnect the LT lead (white/black) at the coil. Mark the HT leads and remove them from the distributor cap.

3 Disconnect the suction pipe from the vacuum control unit.

4 To avoid disturbing the timing, do not slacken the horizontal bolt and nut in the distributor clamp, but remove the vertical setpin securing it to the crankcase. The distributor is then withdrawn in the form shown in **FIG 3:1**. Do not turn the engine afterwards.

3:4 Dismantling

FIG 3:2 shows the component parts of the distributor. To dismantle the distributor after it has been removed from the engine as described in the previous Section proceed as follows:

1 Remove cap and rotor.

2 Referring to **FIG 3:5,** remove the vacuum control by undoing the screw indicated and unhooking the arm 4 from the contact breaker upper plate 3.

FIG 3:7 Setting timing mark for HC engines

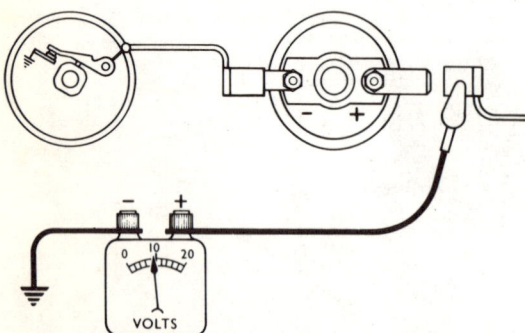

FIG 3:8 Circuit connections for checking the coil starting supply

3 Remove screws 1 and 2 and lift out the contact breaker plate assembly. Do not dismantle the plate assembly as this is serviced as a complete unit.

4 To remove the distributor mainshaft drive out the retaining pin at the bottom of the shaft and remove the tabbed thrust washer.

5 Remove any burrs from the drive end of the shaft and withdraw it from the distributor housing together with the upper thrust washer.

6 Remove the oil seal ring from the housing but do not slacken the clamp bolt if the timing is not to be disturbed.

7 Remove and discard the advance weight springs. The mainshaft with cam and weights is normally serviced as an assembly, but if the upper and lower parts of the shaft are to be separated, first note the relative positions of the rotor slot and the drive end of the shaft, to prevent a possible timing error of 180 deg.

3:5 Reassembly

Reassembly is a reversal of dismantling procedure, but the following points should be checked:

1 Check that the mainshaft is of the correct type, identified by the number 30.5 stamped on the underside of the plate. Check the fit of the mainshaft in the housing bushes and check the thrust washers for wear.

2 Clean or renew contact points (see **Section 3:2**).

3 Ensure that the hole in the oil seal groove in the housing is clear.

4 Test the rotor and distributor cap (see **Section 3:2**). Install the mainshaft as follows:

1 Ensure that there are no burrs on the end of the shaft to damage the bushes.

2 Fit new springs to the centrifugal advance weights.

3 Lubricate the shaft and the felts in the housing with engine oil.

4 With the upper thrust washer in position insert the shaft in the housing and secure the tabbed thrust washer with the securing pin.

5 Check that the end float does not exceed .010 inch.

3:6 Refitting

If the distributor housing clamp bolt has not been slackened and the engine has not been turned since the distributor was removed, line up the distributor shaft tongue with the offset in the oil pump spindle and insert the distributor. Secure the clamp plate to the crankcase by means of the setpin. Adjust the contact points, fit the rotor and cap. Connect up the HT and LT leads and reconnect the battery.

The above method ensures that the distributor shaft has been replaced in the same position in relation to the engine crankcase, but the fitting of new parts and the adjustment of contact points can affect the timing to some extent so that checking is advisable. This is described in the following Section.

3:7 Re-timing

Set the initial timing as follows:

1 Rotate the engine until No. 1 piston is at the top of the compression stroke. This will be indicated by both valves being closed when the timing pointers (see **FIGS 3:6** and **3:7**) are approximately in line. On low compression engines, identified by a letter B after the engine number, the pointer 1 on the crankshaft pulley in **FIG 3:6** should be aligned with the pointer 2 on the timing case, indicating 9 deg. before TDC. On high compression engines, set the pointer 1 midway between the pointer 2 and the TDC pointer 3 as shown in **FIG 3:7**. This gives a timing of $4\frac{1}{2}$ deg. before TDC. On all 1974 1256 cc engines the timing is 9 deg. BTDC.

2 Slacken the distributor clamp bolt and turn the distributor shaft clockwise until the points are just breaking with the rotor arm pointing towards the segment leading to No. 1 plug.

3 Tighten the clamp nut and recheck the timing.

The most accurate method of checking the ignition timing is by means of a stroboscopic timing light. This produces a flash at the precise moment at which the spark occurs at the plug, showing the exact position of the timing marks at that instant. It is used as follows:

1 Check the contact point gap (see **Section 3:2**).

2 Connect the timing light to No. 1 sparking plug.

3 Run the engine at idling speed and direct the light on the timing pointers, which should have the appearance of being stationary at the positions indicated in **FIG 3:6** for low compression engines and **FIG 3:7** for high compression engines.

4 To correct the setting, loosen the clamp bolt and turn the distributor housing slowly clockwise to advance or anticlockwise to retard the ignition. Tighten the clamp bolt and recheck the timing.

It should be noted that the ignition timing point for the extra performance engine is the same as for the standard low compression unit, i.e. 9 deg. BTDC.

Note also that the normal idling speed on 1256cc engines should be reduced to 600 rev/min to avoid faulty results due to the operation of the centrifugal advance mechanism.

3:8 Low tension circuit tests

The ignition coil is fed through a length of resistance wire incorporated in the wiring loom between the starter switch and the coil feed wire. This resistance is by-passed when starting by a feed direct from the starter solenoid to give increased voltage at this time and so facilitate starting, particularly when cold.

Ensure first that the battery is fully charged and then carry out the following tests if the engine fails to start.

Coil starting supply:

Refer to **FIG 3:8**. Disconnect the white wire from the coil and connect a 0-20 voltmeter between the wire and earth. Operate the starter switch and turn the engine. At least 8 volts should be registered. A zero or low reading could be due to a faulty solenoid or defective wiring.

Coil running supply:

Reconnect the white wire and leave the voltmeter connected as shown in **FIG 3:9**. Switch on the ignition.

With the distributor contacts closed, the voltmeter should show approximately 5 volts. Failure to do so indicates a defective resistance wire, this is not supplied separately from the wiring harness assembly.

Coil primary winding check:

Connect the voltmeter positive terminal to the black/white wire terminal, as shown in **FIG 3:10**, and the negative terminal to earth.

Open the distributor contact breaker points and switch on the ignition.

The voltmeter should read 11.5 to 12 volts. A zero reading indicates a break in the primary winding or a short circuit in either the contact breaker connections or the capacitor.

Contact breaker check:

Close the contact breaker points and switch on the ignition. The voltmeter should read between 0 and .2 volt. If it is more than .2 volt either the contacts are dirty, the contact breaker base plate and/or the distributor body to earth connection is faulty or there is a break in the black/white wire.

3:9 HT cables. Sparking plugs

HT cables should be examined for cracked and defective insulation. Cars are supplied for UK with suppressor type leads with a non-metallic graphited core having a resistance of 4000 to 8000 ohms per foot of cable. To test for continuity an ohmmeter is necessary.

Sparking plugs should be of the recommended type, details of which are given in Technical Data. The gaps

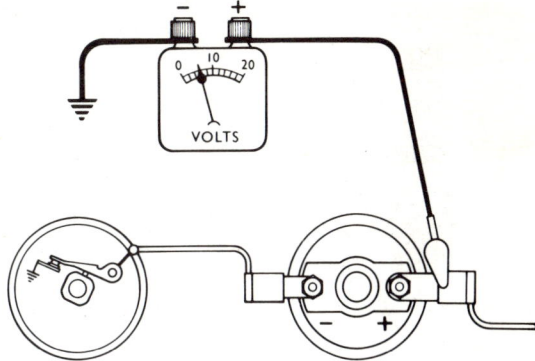

FIG 3:9 Circuit connections for checking the coil running supply

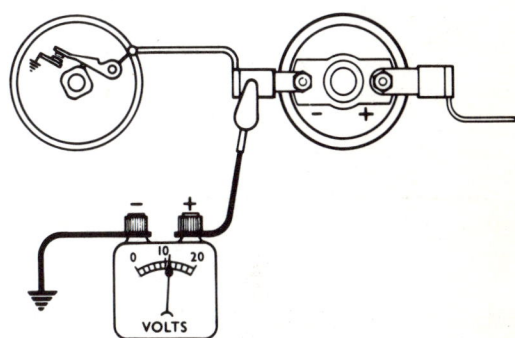

FIG 3:10 Circuit connections for checking the coil primary winding and contact breaker points

should be set to the correct dimension by bending the outer electrode only. Plugs can be cleaned and tested under working pressure on a machine used by most service stations. Those which fail the test should be renewed.

Tighten to a torque of 25 lb ft.

3:10 Fault diagnosis

(a) Engine will not fire

1 Battery discharged
2 Distributor points dirty, pitted or out of adjustment
3 Distributor cap dirty, cracked or 'tracking'
4 Rotor contact spring not touching carbon stud in cap.
5 Faulty cable or loose connection in low tension circuit
6 Distributor rotor arm cracked
7 Faulty coil
8 Broken contact breaker spring
9 Contact points stuck open

(b) Engine misfires

1 Check 2, 3, 5, 7 in (a)
2 Weak contact spring
3 HT plug and coil leads defective
4 Loose sparking plug
5 Sparking plug insulation cracked
6 Sparking plug gap incorrect
7 Ignition timing too far advanced

NOTES

CHAPTER 4

THE COOLING SYSTEM

4:1 Principles of system
4:2 Maintenance, flushing, belt tension, antifreeze, heater pipes
4:3 Water pump removal
4:4 Dismantling water pump
4:5 Reassembly
4:6 Thermostat removal and testing
4:7 Fault diagnosis

4:1 Principles of system

The cooling system is pressurized and incorporates a water pump, fan, thermostat and tube type radiator. The water pump, shown in exploded form in **FIG 4:1,** is of the centrifugal type with a self-adjusting seal. It is driven from the crankshaft by an endless belt which also drives the generator. The pump body is bolted to the cylinder head. Water which has been cooled by the radiator is pumped from the rotor chamber into a water distributor tube leading to the areas of the exhaust valve seats and sparking plug bosses. The body houses a shaft and bearing assembly secured by a locking ring. The bearing is packed with lubricant on assembly and periodic lubrication is unnecessary. Ventilation holes in the body communicate with the front face of the seal.

A rotor pressed on to the rear of the shaft contacts the seal. Contact is maintained by the seal spring which also compensates for normal wear. A flange pressed on to the front of the shaft carries a four- or eight-bladed fan. Later cars are fitted with a viscous coupling to the five-bladed fan which allows slip to take place at over approximately 1000 rev/min. The coupling and fan are a balanced unit and their relationship to one another must be maintained. In case of oil leakage the unit must be renewed as it is not repairable. The centre bolt has a left-hand thread and should be tightened to a torque of 14 lb ft.

A thermostat is fitted to facilitate rapid warming up to normal running temperature. The thermostat housing is integral with the pump body and during the warming up period the thermostat valve is closed, preventing warm water from leaving the cylinder head. Pressure is relieved by a bypass drilling between the pump rotor chamber and the thermostat housing. As soon as the thermostat reaches working temperature its valve opens and water is allowed to flow from the cylinder head through the water outlet and back to the radiator.

A pressure vent type radiator filler cap shown in section in **FIG 4:2** creates a pressurized cooling system which raises the boiling point of the coolant. The pressure valve allows steam and water to escape through the overflow pipe when the pressure exceeds the specified limit.

Where automatic transmission is fitted an oil cooler is included in the bottom radiator tank.

4:2 Maintenance, flushing, belt tension, antifreeze, heater pipes

Before draining the cooling system, the radiator filler cap must be removed and the heat control lever set to HOT to prevent air locks. **When removing the radiator filler cap on a hot engine, hold the cap with a large piece of rag. Turn the cap anticlockwise and wait a few moments for the pressure to be released before lifting off the cap.**

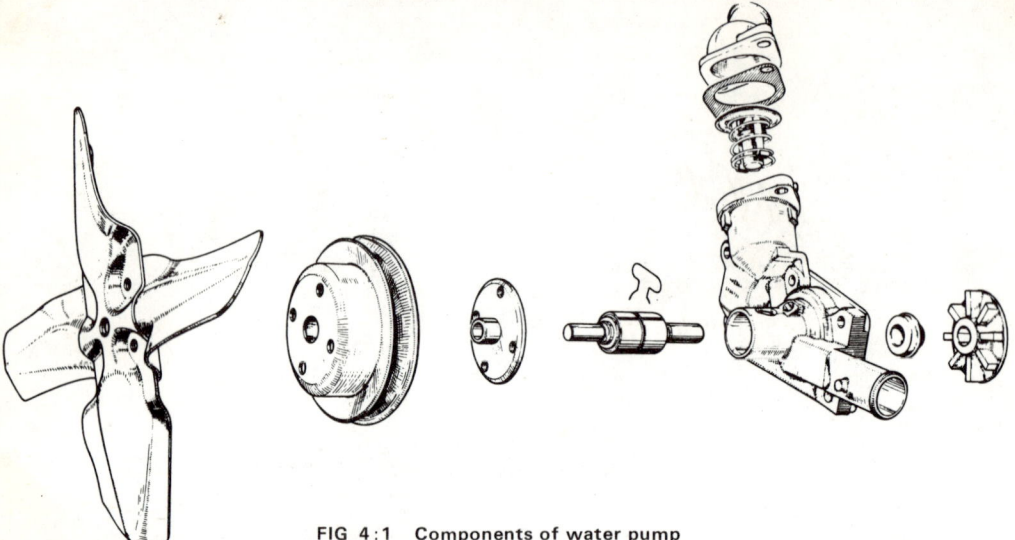

FIG 4:1   Components of water pump

There are two drain taps as shown in **FIG 4:3** on early models, one in the radiator bottom tank, the other in the cylinder block, on later models drain plugs are fitted. To drain the system, open both taps and ensure they are clear. A tap can become blocked by sludge after a certain amount of water has run out. The vehicle must be on level ground. When refitting drain plugs apply Hylomar SQ32/M or similar to the threads.

The radiator and engine water passages should be flushed from time to time to clear away clogging sediment. A service agent or radiator repair specialist will carry out this work by means of a special flushing gun. This introduces water and compressed air into the system, and by 'reverse flushing', that is flushing in the opposite direction to the normal flow, more effectively removes deposits. The owner not possessing special equipment can devise methods of running water in a reverse direction through the system without pressure, but this will not be as effective as pressure flushing.

The repair of a damaged or leaking radiator should be entrusted to a specialist repairer. The latter will have facilities for flow testing, flushing and testing under pressure and will be able to advise whether the fitting of a replacement radiator will be more satisfactory than repair.

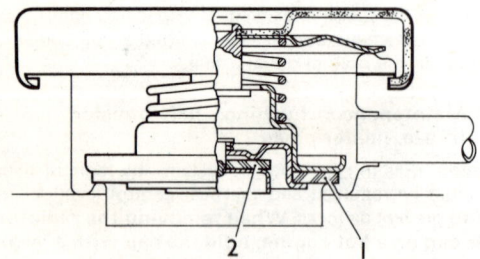

FIG 4:2   Radiator cap in section

Key to Fig 4:2   1 Pressure valve   2 Vacuum valve

When refilling the cooling system add $\frac{1}{8}$ pint of Vauxhall corrosion preventative. Note that if antifreeze is used it must be of a type specially treated to mix with the corrosion preventative. Water level should be one inch below the bottom of the radiator filler neck.

To remove the radiator:

1 Drain the cooling system.

2 Disconnect the hoses from the radiator.

3 Remove the screws attaching the radiator to the support panel and lift away the radiator.

If for any reason, as for instance when carrying out engine overhauls, the radiator has to be left unused for any length of time, it should not be allowed to dry out. It should be reverse flushed, the inlet and outlet pipes plugged and the radiator filled with water. Neglect of this precaution may cause sediment to harden and block the radiator.

Radiator hoses and heater hoses should be renewed if they show any signs of cracking or interior fouling. It is generally advisable to fit a complete new set of hoses when filling with antifreeze.

In addition to the cooling fan the belt also drives the water pump and the electric alternator and it is important to ensure that it is kept at the right tension with $\frac{1}{2}$ inch movement in the centre of the longest run. Adjustment is carried out by slackening the mounting bolts and pivoting the instrument away from the engine. If it is necessary to use a lever for this, it must be applied to the drive end bracket only (see **FIG 4:4**).

It will be seen that the alternator has a split sliding bush in the slip ring end shield lug to allow it to be mounted without imposing side loading on the lugs. It is important that the drive end shield bolt 1 should be tightened before the slip ring shield bolt 2.

In winter and in cold climates the use of a suitable antifreeze mixture is preferable to draining the cooling system. Complete draining is difficult to ensure and when a heater is fitted this does not drain with the system. Note that if a corrosion preventative is used, the antifreeze must be of a type specially treated to mix with this. The degree of

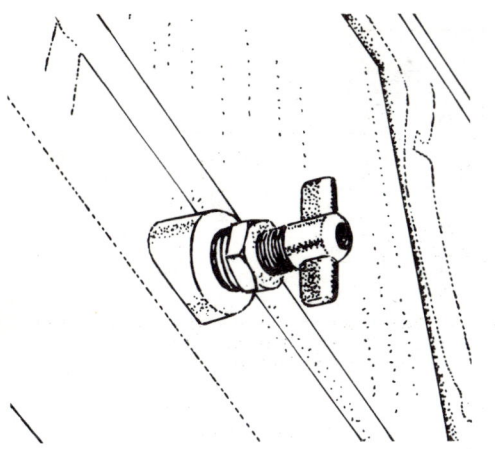
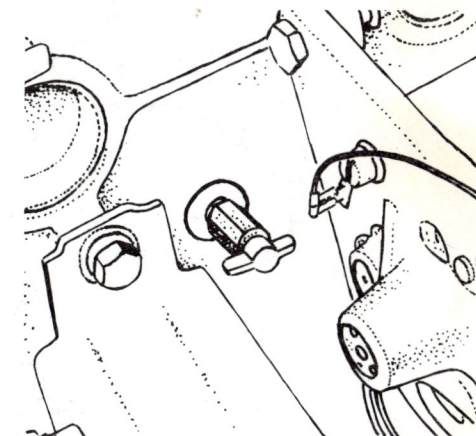

FIG 4:3   Radiator and cylinder block drain taps

protection afforded by antifreeze varies with the proportions used, and the instructions of the makers of the antifreeze should be carefully followed. Before filling with antifreeze the radiator should be flushed and radiator and heater hoses renewed.

4:3 Water pump removal

1 Drain the cooling system.
2 Disconnect the radiator hoses from the pump.
3 Remove the fan belt.
4 Remove the six bolts securing the pump and lift away the pump.

4:4 Dismantling water pump

The component parts of the water pump and fan assembly are shown in **FIG 4:1**. Proceed as follows:

1 Remove fan and pulley, water outlet and thermostat.
2 Withdraw the rotor, using a two-legged puller as shown in **FIG 4:5**. The puller should preferably have split claws or claws specially machined to straddle the rotor, as shown in the inset to **FIG 4:5**.
3 Withdraw and discard seal.
4 Inspect the condition of the shaft and bearing. If renewal is necessary, (a) withdraw the bearing

locking ring and (b) heat the pump body in water to 82°C (180°F) and remove the shaft.

5 Clean all parts and ensure that the bypass drilling is clear.

Later 1159 cc water pumps have a ceramic counter face between the rotor and the seal. This is installed in the rotor recess with the ceramic face towards the seal.

4:5 Reassembly

If several parts of the pump need renewal, the fitting of a replacement pump may be more satisfactory. The water pump is available on an exchange basis. If the existing pump is to be reassembled, proceed as follows:

1 Reheat the body and install the shaft and bearing, noting that the shorter end of the shaft is the front end.
2 Ensure that the groove in the shaft coincides with the groove in the body before installing the locking ring (see **FIG 4:1**).
3 Press on a new pulley flange plain side first, so that the dimension A in **FIG 4:6** is 3.46 inch.
4 Smear 'rubber grease' (castor-based grease harmless to rubber) on the seal front face and around the body bore and install the seal. Do not put grease on the carbon face.

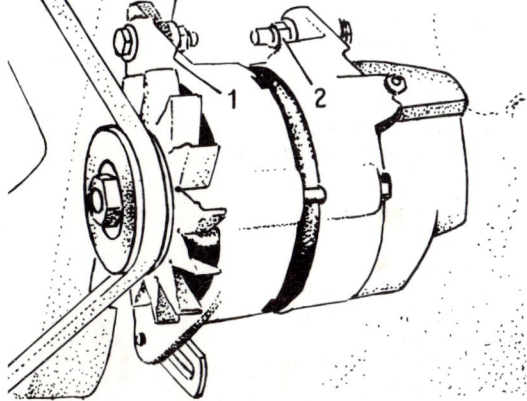

FIG 4:4   Fan belt adjustment

Key to Fig 4:4   1 Drive end bolt   2 Slip ring end bolt

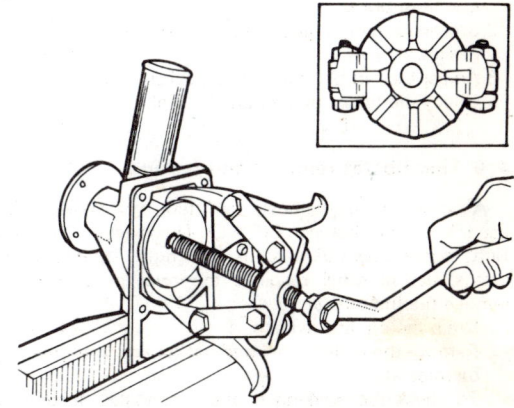

FIG 4:5   Withdrawing water pump rotor. Inset shows split claw of puller straddling rotor vanes.

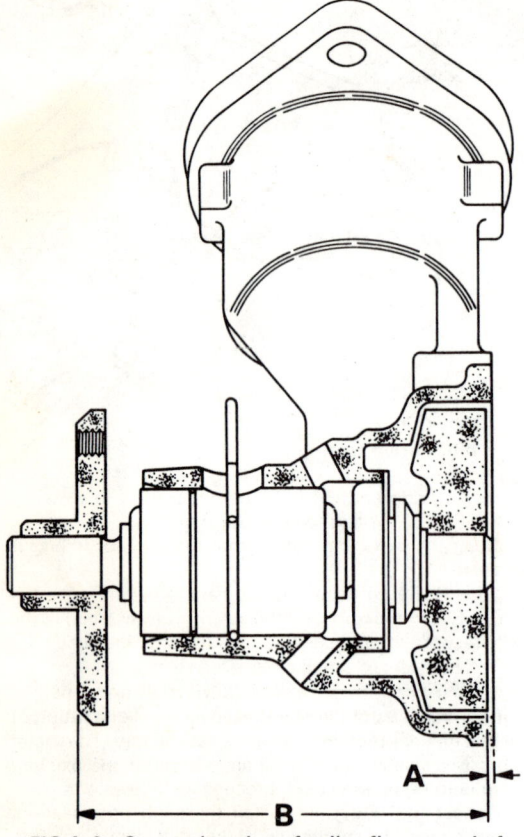

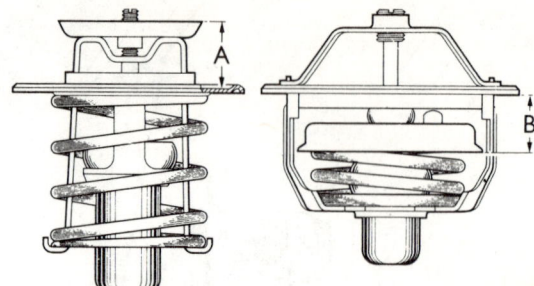

FIG 4:7 Two types of thermostat shown in section
Left—Western Thomson   Right—AC
A and B show fully open positions

temperature. Do not let either thermometer or thermostat touch the container or a false reading will be obtained. Note the temperature at which the thermostat starts to open and the temperature at which it is fully open, also the amount of valve opening as shown at A and B respectively in **FIG 4:7**. Specified temperatures and valve openings are given in Technical Data. If the thermostat is found to be defective it must be renewed. When refitting, ensure the thermostat housing and bypass drilling are clear. Refit the water outlet using a new gasket and after refilling the system check for leaks.

4:7 Fault diagnosis

(a) Internal water leakage

1 Cracked cylinder wall
2 Loose cylinder head nuts
3 Cracked cylinder head
4 Faulty head gasket
5 Cracked tappet chest wall

(b) Poor circulation

1 Radiator core blocked
2 Engine water passages restricted
3 Low water level
4 Loose fan belt
5 Defective thermostat
6 Perished or collapsed radiator hoses

(c) Corrosion

1 Impurities in the water
2 Infrequent draining and flushing

(d) Overheating

1 Check (b)
2 Sludge in crankcase
3 Faulty ignition timing
4 Low oil level in sump
5 Tight engine
6 Choked exhaust system
7 Binding brakes
8 Slipping clutch
9 Incorrect valve timing
10 Weak mixture

FIG 4:6   Correct location of pulley flange on shaft
A=.044 to .046 inch   **B**=3.46 inch

5 Press on the rotor until the shaft projects a distance of .044 to .046 inch beyond the face of the rotor.
6 Install the thermostat and water outlet. Reassemble the fan and pulley.

When installing the pump on the engine, note the following:

1 Ensure that the pump attaching faces are clean and free from burrs.
2 Smear jointing compound on each side of a new gasket.
3 Adjust the fan belt tension (**Section 4:2**).
4 Check the hose connections for leaks.

4:6 Thermostat removal and testing

A capsule type thermostat is fitted, two makes being used. These are shown in **FIG 4:7**. The Western Thomson (left) opens upwards and the AC (right) opens downwards, but in other respects the two are similar. To remove the thermostat:

1 Drain the cooling system.
2 Remove the water outlet and gasket and withdraw the thermostat.

To check the working of the thermostat, suspend it with a thermometer in water, gradually heating the water and stirring to bring water and thermostat to the same

CHAPTER 5

THE CLUTCH

5:1 Construction and operation

5:2 Routine maintenance

5:3 Clutch removal and dismantling

5:4 Clutch inspection and reconditioning

5:5 Main drive spigot bearing

5:6 Reassembling, refitting, plate alignment

5:7 Clutch pedal and cable

5:8 Fault diagnosis

5:1 Construction and operation

The clutch is of the diaphragm spring type and is enclosed in a housing integral with the gearbox. The lower front half of the housing has a detachable cover.

FIG 5:1 shows the principal components of the clutch, namely the flywheel with starter ring, the disc or driven plate, the pressure plate and cover assembly, the release bearing and clutch fork.

The disc, also shown in FIG 5:2, has riveted friction linings and drives the gearbox main drive pinion (first motion shaft) through a spring-loaded hub with internal splines. The disc is sandwiched between the rear surface of the flywheel and the pressure plate.

The pressure plate is lug-driven by the cover which in turn is bolted to the flywheel. The diaphragm spring is dished, and being located by the fulcrum rings attached to the cover, exerts pressure at its outer edge on the pressure plate, thus taking up the drive to the driven plate.

FIG 5:3 shows the clutch fork and release bearing. The inner end of the fork pivots on a ball stud pressed into the clutch housing and is held in position by a spring retainer. The fork jaw pins engage in the sleeve of the release beaing. The outer end of the fork projects through an aperture in the housing as shown in FIG 5:4 and is operated by cable from the clutch pedal.

When the pedal is depressed the clutch fork moves forward and the release bearing exerts pressure on the centre of the diaphragm spring. The diaphragm spring is prevented from moving forward by the fulcrum ring so that its outer edge moves in the opposite direction. This releases the pressure on the pressure plate and at the same time, by means of three retractor clips, moves the pressure plate away from the clutch disc, thus completing the disengagement.

Since September 1972 some of the 1256 cc variants have a larger clutch but the operating principle remains the same. However, take care when obtaining spares and quote the numbers on the vehicle's service parts identification plate attached to the righthand front wheel valance, in front of the battery.

5:2 Routine maintenance

With the cable type control, the clutch pedal does not give a reliable indication of the amount of play at the clutch fork. This play is necessary to compensate for wear in the clutch friction linings. Insufficient play can cause clutch slip and a burnt out clutch. Excessive play will prevent the clutch disengaging properly, but this fault will make itself evident by difficulty in engaging the gears.

To adjust the cable, slacken the locknut shown in FIG 5:4 and turn the adjusting nut until there is .26 inch free travel at the point A. Tighten the locknut, operate the clutch pedal two or three times and recheck adjustment. The clutch inner cable is enclosed in a nylon outer casing which is graphited on initial assembly and must not be lubricated, but a little grease should be applied to the ball end of the adjusting nut.

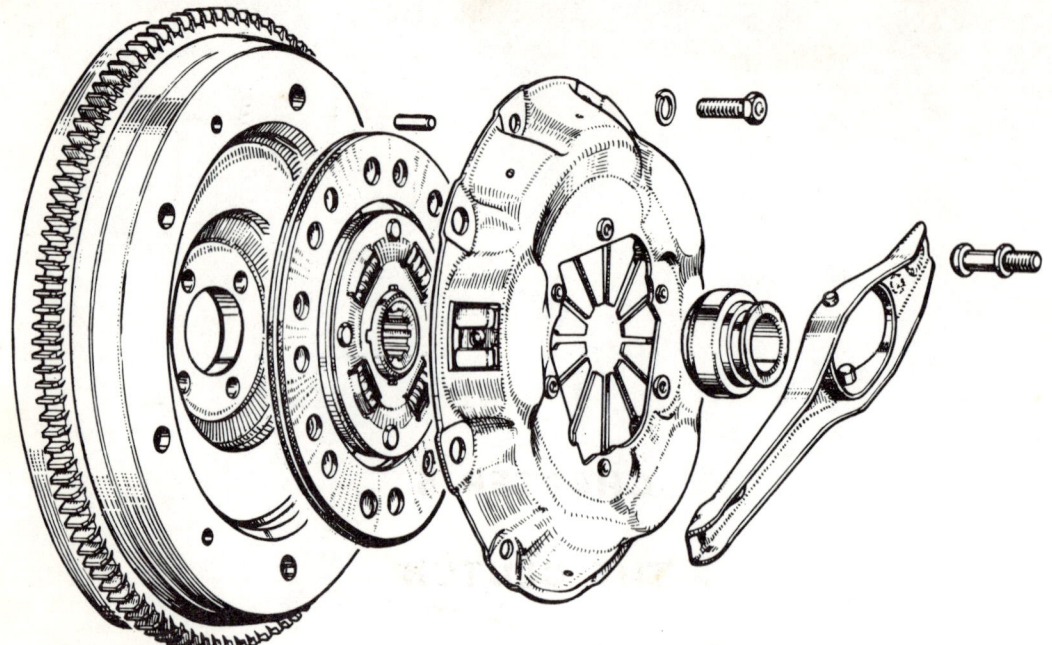

FIG 5:1   Components of clutch and flywheel

5:3 Clutch removal and dismantling

To remove the clutch, the engine should be removed from the car as described in **Section 1:2**. The clutch fork and release bearing remain in the clutch housing on the gearbox as can be seen in **FIGS 1:4** and **5:5**.

Alternatively, the gearbox can be removed, leaving the engine and clutch in position (see **Section 6:3**).

In each case before proceeding to dismantle the clutch, mark the clutch cover to flywheel relationship. Unscrew the clutch cover attaching bolts evenly, slackening each a turn at a time until the spring pressure has been released and the clutch assembly can be removed.

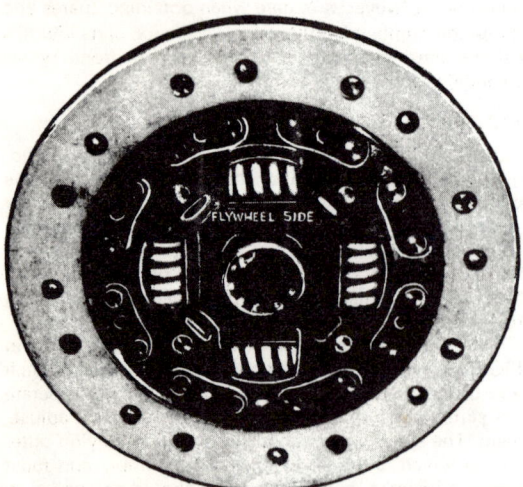

FIG 5:2   Clutch disc

If the engine is not being dismantled the flywheel need not be removed, but the starter ring should be examined and the flywheel checked for security of fixture on the crankshaft flange. The rear surface of the flywheel acts as a friction surface for the clutch, so that it should be examined for scoring or pitting. For flywheel removal reference should be made to **Section 1:10**.

5:4 Clutch inspection and reconditioning

Examine the friction face of the flywheel as described in the previous Section. Inspect the clutch disc, shown in **FIG 5:2**. Check for worn hub splines and broken or weak damper springs. Examine the friction linings for excessive wear, loose rivets, cracks or discolouration. The polished glaze is normal and does not affect the ability to transmit power, but the linings should be light in colour with the grain of the material clearly visible through the glaze. Evidence of oil on the linings is seen in a much darker colour which obliterates the grain. This condition can cause both clutch slip and clutch drag. No attempt should be made to reline the disc as it is serviced as a complete assembly.

Next examine the pressure plate and cover assembly. There must be no scoring or pitting on the friction surface of the pressure plate. Excessive wear or scoring of the centre portion of the diaphragm spring indicates a defective release bearing. The pressure plate and diaphragm are also serviced as an assembly and should not be dismantled.

Examine the fork and release bearing, which remain in the housing attached to the gearbox as shown in **FIG 5:5**. To remove, pull the clutch fork 1 to release it from the ball pin 2 and remove the fork and release bearing. **Do not wash or degrease the bearing.**

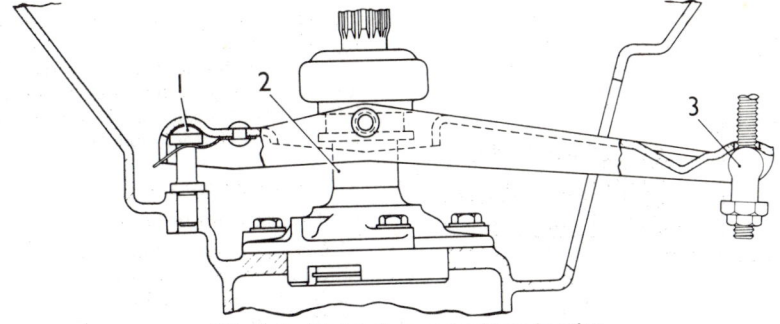

FIG 5:3　Clutch fork and release bearing

Key to Fig 5:3　　　1 Ball pin　　　2 Gearbox front cover sleeve　　　3 Cable adjusting nut

Remove the fork ball if it is worn by tapping the ball shank out of the housing. When installing a new ball, use a soft hammer to avoid damaging the ball end. Lubricate the ball with a recommended grease.

5:5 Main drive spigot bearing

Check the main drive spigot bearing (clutch pilot bush) in the crankshaft flange for wear or slackness. If it is necessary to renew the bush, the worn bush is withdrawn by means of a special drawer tool No. Z.8527. The new bush is saturated with engine oil using finger pressure on the ends after filling it with oil. It is then assembled on the installer tool No. Z.8566 as shown in **FIG 5:6** so that the pilot end projects slightly through the bush 1 with the nut in contact with the sleeve. The pilot is used for correct sizing of the bush bore so it must be free from burrs. Drive the bush squarely into the crankshaft until the installer sleeve contacts the shaft 2. Withdraw the pilot by screwing down the nut.

5:6 Reassembling, refitting, plate alignment

When installing the clutch, note the following:
1 Refit the clutch driven plate with the marked face towards the flywheel as shown in **FIG 5:2**, on early Laycock unmarked discs install the disc with spring segments on damper spring housing towards the flywheel. Later Laycock discs are marked 'FW side'.
2 Before tightening the clutch cover attaching bolts in the flywheel, the clutch disc must be aligned so that the main drive pinion (first motion shaft) will enter the clutch disc hub and the crankshaft spigot bearing when the engine and gearbox are fitted together. For this purpose a spare main drive pinion is first inserted in the clutch disc hub.
3 Next tighten the clutch cover bolts evenly a turn at a time diagonally, finally tightening to a torque of 14 lb ft.
4 Refit the clutch fork and release bearing if these have been removed from the clutch housing on the gearbox. Lubricate the release bearing sleeve (but not the bearing itself) and the main drive pinion splines sparingly with grease before assembly.
5 The engine is refitted as described in **Section 1:16** or the gearbox fitted to the engine as described in **Section 6:6**. In each case it is important that the weight of the engine or gearbox must not be allowed to bear on the clutch disc until the main drive pinion is fully home in the spigot bearing.

5:7 Clutch pedal and cable

The pendant type clutch pedal is mounted on a common shaft with the brake pedal. Both pedals are nylon bushed and the shaft is carried in nylon bushes in the pedal support bracket bolted to the dash panel. A spring pin at each end of the shaft retains the pedals and shaft. The clutch cable clevis pin is also nylon bushed.

FIG 5:7 shows the complete pedal and support assembly and it will be noted that although the pedals may be removed while leaving the support in position, the clutch pedal cannot be removed without also withdrawing the brake pedal.

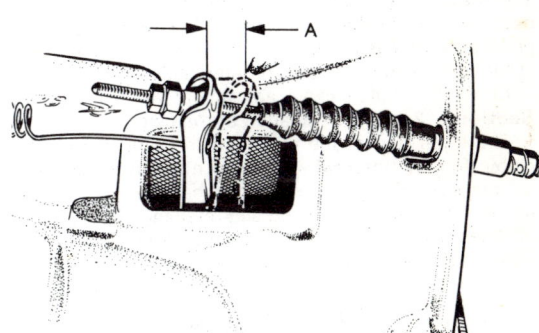

FIG 5:4　Clutch cable adjustment
A=.26 inch

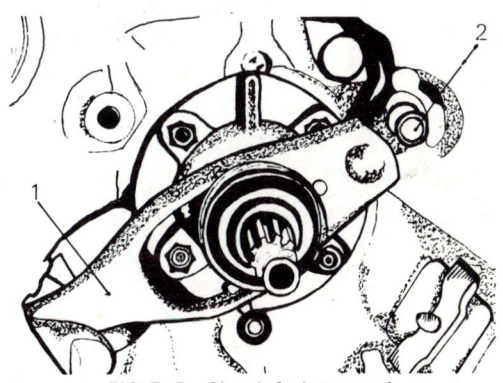

FIG 5:5　Clutch fork removal
Key to Fig 5:5　　　1 Clutch fork　　　2 Ball pin

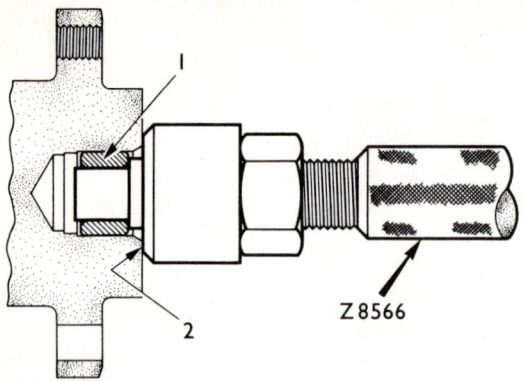

FIG 5:6 Installing main drive spigot bearing bush using Tool Z.8566

Key to Fig 5:6   1 Bearing bush   2 Crankshaft

To remove a pedal, first remove the parcel shelf and the dash insulator panel, then extract the spring pin retaining the pedal shaft at the clutch end and pull out the shaft from the mounting bracket as shown. This will release the pedal and the cable is detached from the pedal by sliding off the spring clip and withdrawing the clevis pin as shown.

When refitting the pedal, lubricate the pedal shaft and clevis with a recommended grease and ensure that the straight shank portion of the spring pin 3 at the brake pedal end of the shaft is located in the swageing in the pedal support. Ensure also that the gasket 2 is assembled at the upper end of the clutch outer cable.

Check the clutch cable adjustment as described in **Section 5:2** and the operation of the clutch.

The lower end of the clutch cable is freed from the clutch fork by unscrewing the ball nut and locking nut off the shaft. The cable may then be disengaged from its hole in the clutch housing and retaining clip.

When refitting, do not omit the rubber insulator in the clutch housing in which the lower end of the cable

locates and the circular washer between the insulator and the cable abutment.

Lubricate the adjusting nut with the recommended grease and adjust the cable as described in **Section 5:2**. The cable itself is packed with graphite on assembly and needs no further lubrication.

5:8 Fault diagnosis

(a) Clutch drag or spin

1 Excessive play in clutch cable
2 Oil or grease on linings
3 Flywheel face not running true
4 Misalignment between engine and gearbox
5 Clutch disc binding on splines
6 Main drive pinion (first motion shaft) binding in spigot bearing
7 Clutch disc distorted
8 Cover or pressure plate distorted
9 Disc linings broken
10 Dirt or foreign matter in clutch

(b) Clutch fierce or judders

Check 2, 3, 4, 7 in (a)
1 Worn clutch linings
2 Pressure plate not parallel with flywheel face
3 Contact area of linings not evenly distributed
4 Bent main drive pinion (first motion shaft)
5 Faulty engine or gearbox mountings
6 Worn rear suspension arm bushes
7 Backlash in transmission

(c) Clutch slip

1 Check 2, 3, 4 in (a)

(d) Rattles and knocks

1 Broken damper springs in clutch disc hub
2 Badly worn splines in disc hub
3 Release bearing loose on fork
4 Worn or loose fork ball
5 Play in main drive spigot bearing
6 Loose flywheel

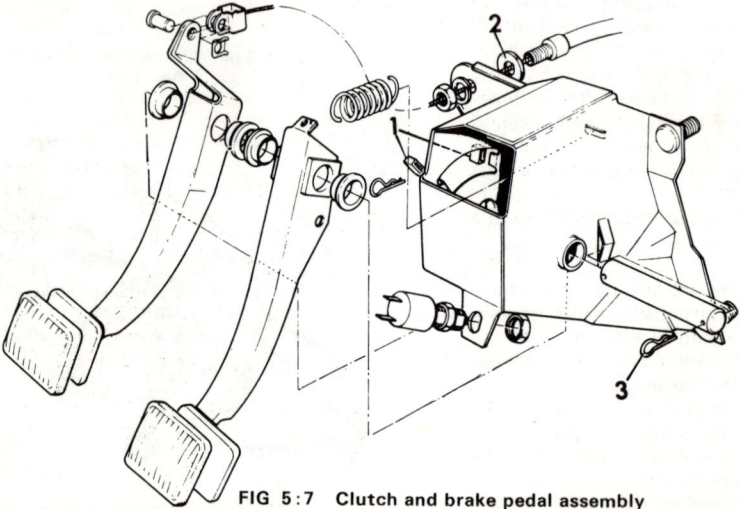

FIG 5:7 Clutch and brake pedal assembly
Key to Fig 5:7   1 Rubber stops   2 Washer   3 Spring pin

He'll face 30ft. waves, blizzards, force 9 gales and sub-zero temperatures.

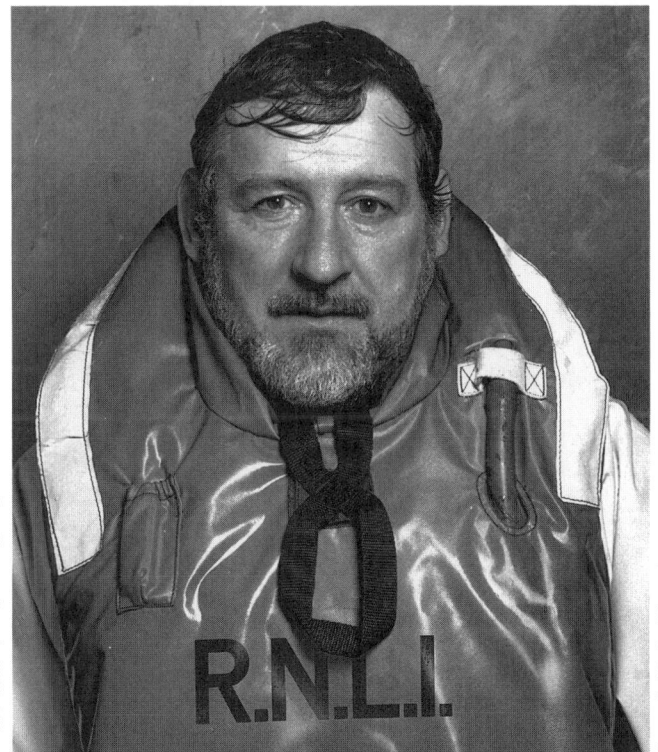

Peter Thomson: Coxswain, Whitby Lifeboat.

Photography John Londei.

R.N.L.I.

All we ask of you is £9.

How your Membership helps the Lifeboat Crews.

For over 160 years Britain's lifeboat crews have been putting to sea to save lives.

And today, as in 1824, we still rely entirely on voluntary contributions.

Which is why your membership is so vital to us.

Without your help, and that of thousands like you, there wouldn't be a lifeboat service.

Consider also that almost a third of rescues take place in darkness and you'll begin to understand the qualities of Britain's lifeboatmen and women.

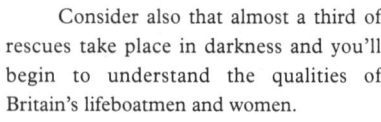

Counting the cost.

It costs a staggering £130,000 per day to run Britain's lifeboats.

To keep a single lifeboat running at full speed takes £1 for 1½ minutes.

(And remember that, on average, a lifeboat is called out every 2 hours, every day of the year.)

Our aim is to progress our 3 year plan to replace older and slower boats with modern ones at an overall cost of £24 million.

Looked at another way, we need over thirty new members to kit out just one lifeboatman in protective gear, because it costs more than £300 per man.

And with 210 lifeboat stations around Great Britain, The Channel Islands and the Republic of Ireland, the task is, quite simply, immense.

The people who never count the cost to themselves.

Selfless devotion to the service and undeniable bravery, have marked out lifeboat crews throughout our history.

Their skills and courage, given voluntarily, have resulted in over 123,000 lives saved since 1824.

They are prepared to put to sea in terrifying conditions and are on call 24 hours a day, 365 days of the year.

What you'll receive as a member.

Joining us means you'll receive our quarterly magazine 'Lifeboat'. In it you'll find facts about the service, stories of recent rescues and profiles of the people involved. It also keeps you abreast of fundraising activities and the many social events organised nationwide.

You'll also receive details of the RNLI insignia (badges, flags, ties, etc) which you can buy.

Young people have the opportunity to join our Storm Force scheme. They'll receive a special magazine with various posters, badges and stickers to collect.

Most importantly, you'll also know that your membership has actively helped to support this vital service. And for this you'll receive our thanks. Join us today.

Royal National Lifeboat Institution, West Quay Road, Poole, Dorset BH15 1HZ.
Tel: Poole (0202) 671133.

Royal National Lifeboat Institution

Reg. Charity No. 209603.

CHAPTER 6

THE TRANSMISSION

MANUAL (SYNCHROMESH) GEARBOX

6:1 Construction and operation
6:2 Maintenance
6:3 Gearbox removal
6:4 Dismantling
6:5 Reassembly
6:6 Refitting gearbox
6:7 Speedometer drive. Reverse light switch
6:8 Fault diagnosis

AUTOMATIC TRANSMISSION

6:9 Construction and operation
6:10 Maintenance
6:11 Adjustments
6:12 Testing
6:13 Transmission removal
6:14 Fault diagnosis

MANUAL (SYNCHROMESH) GEARBOX

6:1 Construction and operation

The four-speed manually-operated gearbox has synchromesh on all forward speeds, with a centrally mounted remote control gearlever. The 1256 cc models have a slightly more robust transmission fitted to cope with the extra torque but the working principle is exactly the same. However, take care when ordering spares. The gearbox is shown in section in **FIG 6:1** while its components are shown in exploded form in **FIG 6:2**. The gearbox casing is integral with the clutch housing (or bell housing) and is provided with a top cover. All gears are of helical tooth formation except those in the reverse train which are straight-toothed spur gears.

The rear end of the main drive pinion (or first motion shaft) runs in a ballbearing in the front cover, while its front end engages in the spigot bearing in the rear of the engine crankshaft (see **Section 5:5**).

The mainshaft is supported at the front end by needle rollers in the main drive pinion, and by a ballbearing in the rear cover. The mainshaft gears run directly on the shaft journals which are copper-plated.

The synchromesh mechanism incorporates two clutch and clutch hub assemblies (see **FIG 6:2**) one at the front

end of the mainshaft between the main drive pinion and the third speed gear, the other at the rear between the first and second speed gears. The clutch hubs are a press fit on splines on the mainshaft. The clutches have internal splines sliding on external splines on the hubs.

Three equally spaced slots in the hub periphery house sliding keys which are pressed outwards by two circular springs in the clutch hub bore. A pip formed on the outer face of each key engages a detent groove in the clutch bore. Two synchronizing rings with taper bores threaded to form a friction surface are located one at each end of the clutch and hub assembly, and engage the synchronizing cone on the adjacent mainshaft gear. Both rings are slotted to engage the sliding keys and have external teeth to engage the clutch splines. The first and second speed clutch has external teeth to engage the reverse pinion.

The layshaft gear assembly is supported at each end by needle rollers on a stationary layshaft. Steel spacers are provided at each end of the rollers. A thrust washer is installed at each end of the layshaft gear and has a pip on its thrust face engaging in a slot in the casing to prevent it from turning.

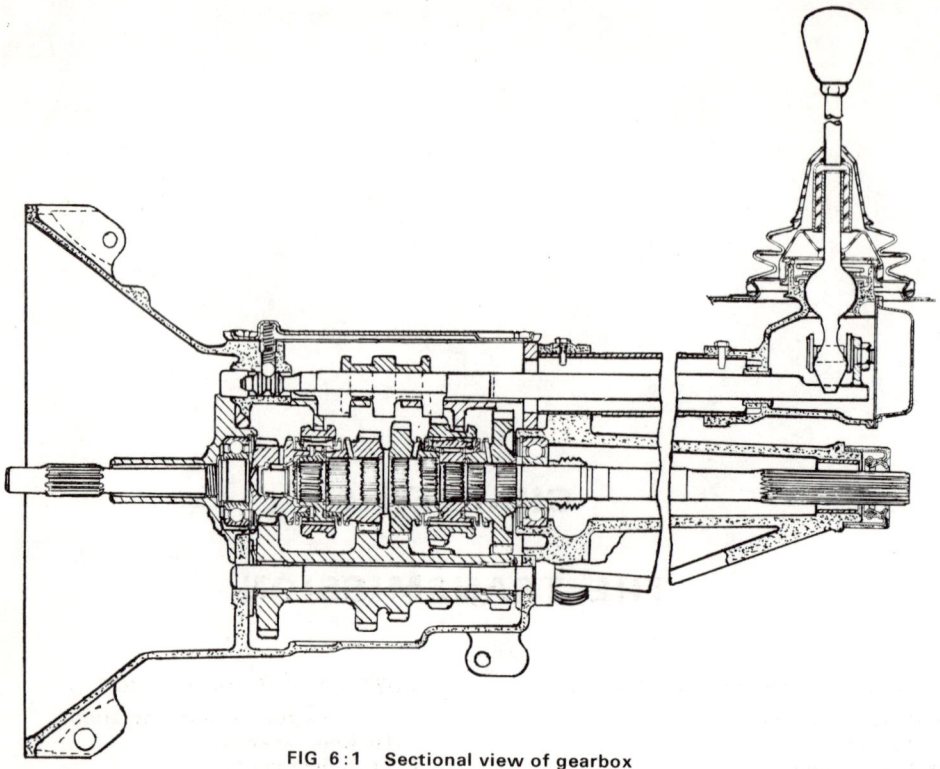

FIG 6:1 Sectional view of gearbox

The reverse pinion incorporates two bushes and runs on a fixed shaft. It can also slide on the shaft and has a groove taking the reverse striking lever.

The speedometer driving gear is a press fit on the mainshaft and is located immediately behind the mainshaft bearing by a circlip. The driven gear shaft runs directly in the rear cover and has an oil seal to prevent oil leaking into the speedometer cable.

Referring again to **FIGS 6:1** and **6:2**, the gearlever is carried in a housing on a tubular extension secured to the gearbox rear cover. Movement of the gearlever is transmitted to a selector shaft, the front end of which is slotted to engage the selector forks and reverse striking lever, shown diagrammatically in **FIG 6:3**. A spring-loaded detent ball engages in grooves at the front end of the shaft as shown in **FIG 6:1**.

Two selector forks carried on a common rail in the top of the gearbox casing, and a reverse striking lever pivoting on a fulcrum pin in the side of the casing as shown in **FIG 6:4**, engage with one or the other of the slots in the selector shaft. The forks and striking lever also engage in grooves in an interlock collar assembled to the selector shaft (see **FIGS 6:2** and **6:3**). This collar is slotted through its length and rotates with the shaft, but is prevented from moving endwise by a pin in the gearbox casing.

FIG 6:3 shows the operation of the selector mechanism. When the gearlever is moved to the left from neutral to select first or second gear, the selector shaft is rotated in the opposite direction to bring the first and second selector fork into engagement with the rear slot in the selector shaft. At the same time the interlock collar is rotated so that its longitudinal slot coincides with the first and second selector fork and allows longitudinal movement to engage first or second gear. The third and fourth selector fork is prevented from moving by the front groove in the interlock collar. The reverse striking lever is prevented from moving by the rear groove in the interlock collar.

When the gearlever is moved to the right to select third or fourth gear, the front slot in the selector shaft engages with the third and fourth selector fork jaw. The first and second selector fork and the reverse striking lever are prevented from moving by the rear groove in the interlock collar.

When moving the gearlever to the left for first or second gear its travel is limited by the lower end of the lever coming into contact with the selector shaft. To select reverse gear the lever must be lifted so that its lower end rides over the flat on the selector shaft, allowing further rotation of the shaft beyond the first or second gear position. The rear slot in the selector shaft can then engage the reverse striking lever, shown in **FIG 6:4**. At the same time both forward gear selector forks are locked by the grooves in the interlock collar.

The synchromesh on the four forward gears operates as follows. Forward or rearward movement of the gearlever is transmitted by the appropriate selector fork to the synchronizer clutch. The clutch together with the three sliding keys (see **FIG 6:2**) is moved along the hub until the keys contact the bottom of the slots in the synchronizing ring, which is then moved into contact with the

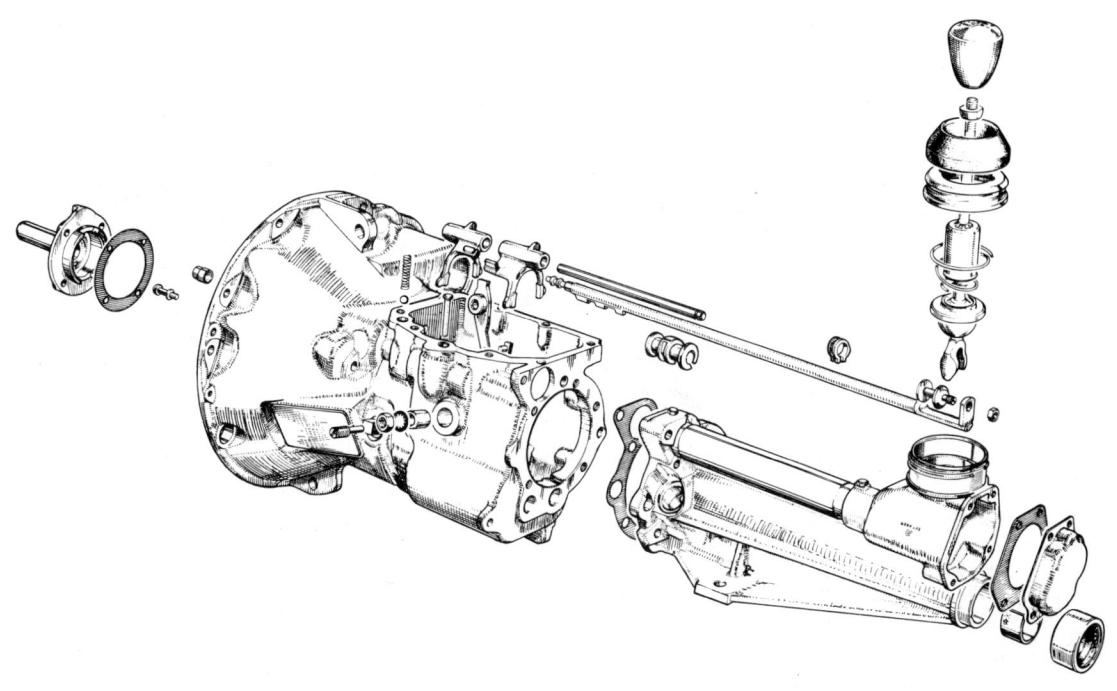

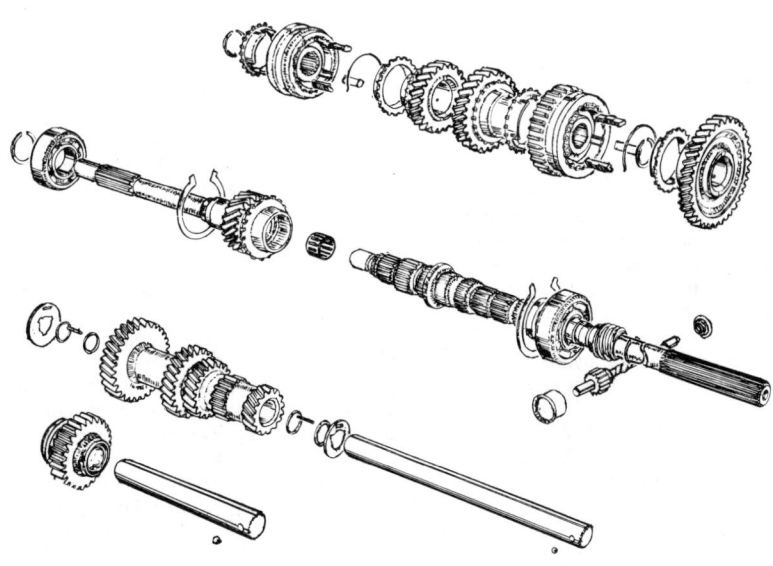

FIG 6:2   Components of gearbox

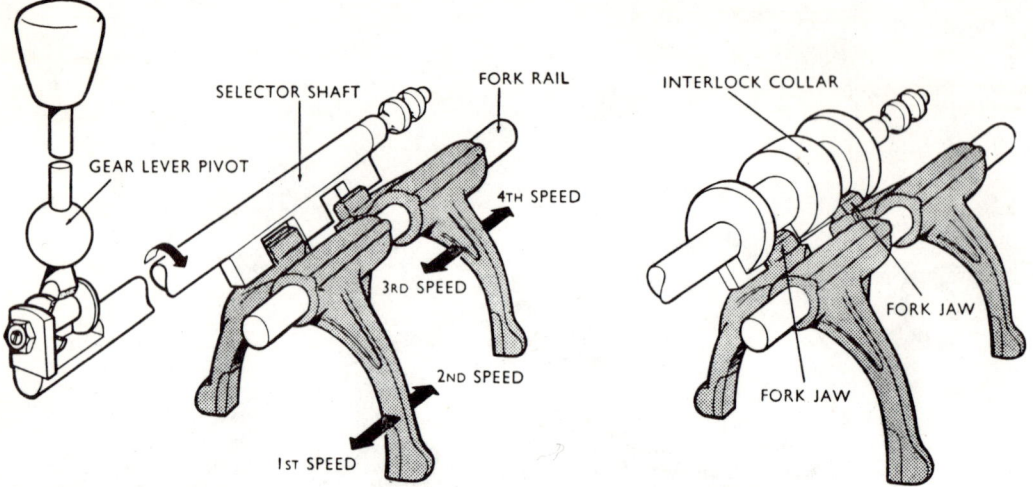

FIG 6:3 Diagrammatic view of gear change mechanism (left) with interlock collar removed and (right) with collar in place

synchronizing cone on the appropriate gear. This commences pre-synchronization and the friction between ring and cone causes the ring to rotate in relation to the hub, but only to the extent that the slots in the ring are wider than the keys.

At this point gear engagement is prevented as long as there is a difference in speed between the mating cones. As the speeds between the appropriate gear and clutch are synchronized, the ring teeth line up with the internal splines of the clutch, allowing the clutch to ride past the ring and silently engage the teeth of the appropriate mainshaft gear.

Forward movement of the gearlever when in the reverse position is transmitted via the selector shaft to the reverse striking lever (see **FIG 6:4**) thus moving the reverse pinion into mesh with the first and second speed clutch gear and the layshaft gear.

6:2 Maintenance

The combined oil level and filler plug is on the left-hand side of the gearbox casing and is accessible from underneath the car. Periodic draining and refilling are not necessary and no drain plug is provided. When checking the oil level clean away all dirt from around the plug before removing it. The oil should be level with the bottom of the plug hole, with the car standing on level ground.

If oil leakage takes place from the rear gearbox cover oil seal (see **FIG 6:2**), the seal can be renewed without removing the gearbox as follows:

1 Remove the propeller shaft (see **Chapter 7**).
2 Drive off the oil seal using a sharp drift alternately on each side of the seal outer casing as shown in **FIG 6:5**.
3 Soak the new seal in oil and drive it home on the rear end of the cover using the installer Z.8426 as shown in **FIG 6:6** or Z.8426.
4 Refit the propeller shaft.
5 Run the engine for a few minutes to circulate oil from the gearbox into the rear cover. Stop the engine and top up the gearbox with the correct grade of oil.

6:3 Gearbox removal

On all HC models with manual gearbox the gearbox is removed as a separate unit from the engine:

1 Unscrew the gearlever retaining cap and remove the lever.
2 To allow the engine to tilt, disconnect the throttle linkage from the carburetter. On cars with HB.23 engine, remove also the exhaust system support bolts.
3 Disconnect the clutch cable from the clutch fork and remove the clutch housing front cover. Disconnect the speedometer cable from the gearbox.
4 Have ready a spare sliding sleeve (arrowed in **FIG 6:7**) to prevent oil loss when the propeller shaft is withdrawn from the gearbox rear cover.
5 Remove the propeller shaft (see **Chapter 7**) and insert the spare sleeve.
6 Remove the gearbox support crossmember.
7 Remove the bolts securing the gearbox to the engine and withdraw the gearbox as shown in **FIG 6:7**, taking care not to allow its weight to rest on the main drive pinion and hence on the clutch disc during withdrawal.

6:4 Dismantling

Complete dismantling of the gearbox entails the use of a hydraulic press for the removal of the gears from the mainshaft, so that this part of the work at least must be carried out by a Vauxhall service agent. If extensive repairs are needed, it may be better to fit a replacement gearbox, obtainable on an exchange basis. The components, however, can be removed from the gearbox for inspection as follows:

1 Remove the top cover and withdraw the selector shaft detent spring (see **FIG 6:2**).
2 Invert the gearbox to drain the oil, and collect the detent ball which will drop out of the casing (see **FIG 6:8**). The interlock collar retaining pin (see 2 in **FIG 6:9**) may also drop out.
3 Mount the gearbox in a fixture which will hold it firmly but without distortion. The Vauxhall fixture D.1157 is shown in use in **FIG 6:10**.

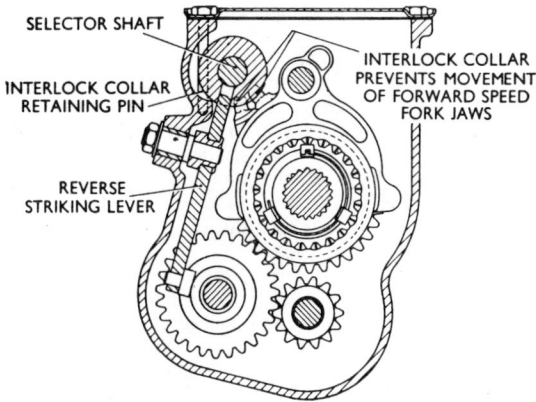

FIG 6:4 Diagram showing reverse gear operation

Labels on figure:
SELECTOR SHAFT
INTERLOCK COLLAR
INTERLOCK COLLAR RETAINING PIN
INTERLOCK COLLAR PREVENTS MOVEMENT OF FORWARD SPEED FORK JAWS
REVERSE STRIKING LEVER

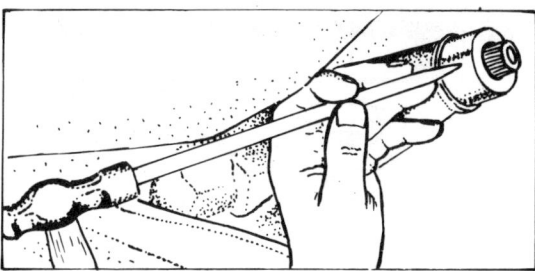

FIG 6:5 Removing rear oil seal

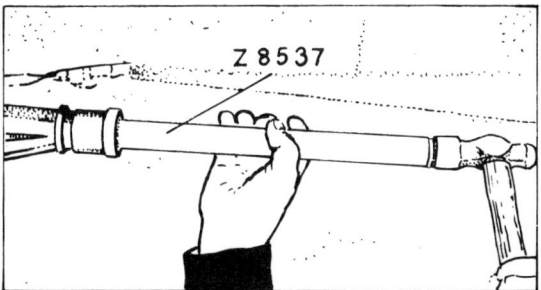

Z 8537

FIG 6:6 Fitting rear oil seal

FIG 6:7 Removing gearbox

4 Unhook the return spring and detach the clutch fork from the fork ball. Remove the fork and the release bearing. (See **FIG 5:5** in the Clutch chapter).

5 Remove the gearlever housing cover (**FIG 6:2**).

6 Referring to **FIG 6:9**, lift out the retaining pin 2 and rotate the selector shaft 3 so that the key is clear of the selector forks 4 and reverse striking lever and withdraw the shaft. Remove the interlock collar 1.

7 Remove the rear cover bolts and rotate the cover to expose the rear end of the selector fork rail. Drive out the rail from the front and lift out the forks.

8 Remove the front cover bolts and withdraw the cover and main drive pinion (first motion shaft) **FIG 6:11**.

9 Engage top gear and withdraw the mainshaft until its spigot is clear of the main drive pinion counterbore. The mainshaft can now be raised at the front end sufficiently to allow the third and top gear clutch to clear the layshaft third speed gear and to be withdrawn from the casing as shown in **FIG 6:10**. Detach the top gear synchronizing ring and spigot bearing spacer.

10 Drive out the layshaft from the front end and retain the locking ball at the rear of the shaft. Allow the layshaft gear to rest at the bottom of the casing.

11 Withdraw the reverse pinion shaft, using the remover Z.8547 or a similar tool as shown in **FIG 6:12**.

12 Lift out the reverse pinion and remove the striking lever from the fulcrum pin.

13 Remove the nut and washer and withdraw the fulcrum pin.

Any further dismantling of the gearbox components involves the use of a hydraulic press. Reassembly of the mainshaft gears involves the use of the press and also the selective fitting of circlips. These operations should be carried out by a Vauxhall service agent.

6:5 Reassembly

Before reassembling ensure that all parts are clean and that oil drillings are free from obstruction. Checks of wear on splines and similar mating parts are best carried out by comparison with new parts. The main drive pinion should be checked for backlash by inserting it in the splined clutch hub disc.

If the reverse pinion bushes are worn, a new pinion assembly must be fitted. If the gear selector shaft pin is removed or renewed, install it so that the punch mark indicating the high side of the eccentric is uppermost.

The rear cover oil seal can be renewed as described in **Section 6:2**. Renewal of the bush however involves the use of a press and a special tool Z.8551. The bush is pressed in so that its outer end is flush with the bottom of the chamfer on the cover.

Commence reassembly of the gearbox in the following sequence:

1 Install the reverse striking lever fulcrum pin with the centre punch mark indicating the high side of the eccentric uppermost as shown in **FIG 6:13**.

2 Install the striking lever on the fulcrum pin with the long boss towards the gearbox casing and assemble the pad to the lower end of the lever.

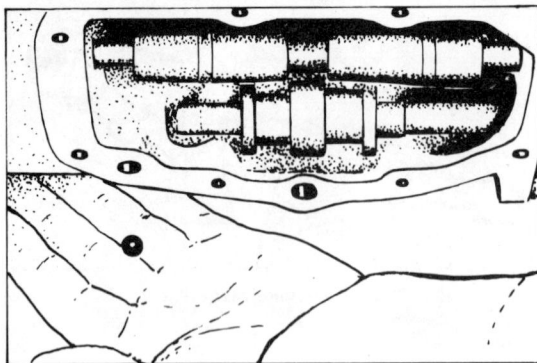

FIG 6:8 Detent ball

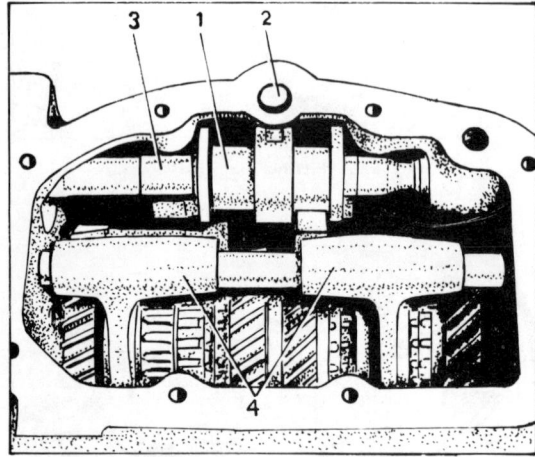

FIG 6:9 Gearbox with top cover removed

Key to Fig 6:9   1 Interlock collar   2 Retaining pin
3 Selector shaft   4 Selector forks

FIG 6:10 Removal or installation of mainshaft and rear cover assembly

3 Assemble the locking ball with a spot of grease in the drilling in the reverse pinion shaft. Engage the groove in the reverse pinion with the striking lever pad. Insert the shaft, lining up the ball with the recess in the casing and drive the shaft home with a brass drift.

4 Temporarily assemble the rear cover to the casing and locate in position with one of the cover bolts.

5 Install the selector shaft and interlock collar with the retaining pin (**FIG 6:9**).

6 Rotate the selector shaft and interlock collar away from the reverse position.

7 Adjust the reverse striking lever by means of the eccentric fulcrum pin to give a clearance of .002 to .012 inch between the rear face of the reverse pinion and the casing. Tighten the nut on the fulcrum pin.

8 Remove the selector shaft and rear cover.

9 If the main drive pinion and bearing have been removed, press them into the front cover.

10 Insert the mainshaft roller bearing in the counterbore of the main drive pinion.

11 Place a needle roller spacer in each layshaft bearing counterbore, smear the counterbore with petroleum jelly and install 25 needle rollers followed by the second spacer.

Note that on 1256 cc models the layshaft gear is supported by a double row of needle rollers at each end. Six roller spacers are used and the layshaft has a longer ground bearing track at each end.

12 Smear the layshaft thrust washers with petroleum jelly and place them on the thrust faces of the gear assembly. The larger washer goes on the front face of the gear.

Proceed with the final assembly as follows:

1 Place the layshaft gear in the bottom of the gearbox casing, at the same time locating the pips on the thrust washers in the grooves in the casing.

2 Lightly smear the front cover face with grease, place a new gasket in position and install the cover and the main drive pinion. Do not install the bolts at this stage.

3 Assemble the layshaft locking ball with a spot of grease in the drilling in the shaft. Align the layshaft gear bore with the layshaft bore in the casing. Using a brass drift, drive the shaft home, after lining up the ball with the recess in the casing face.

4 Assemble the fourth speed synchronizing ring to the third and fourth speed clutch hub on the mainshaft, ensuring that the slots of the ring engage in the clutch sliding keys. Locate the clutch well forward of the clutch hub as shown in **FIG 6:14** so that the clutch will clear the third-speed layshaft gear when installing the mainshaft assembly. Withdraw the main drive pinion as far forward as possible.

5 Lightly smear the rear cover face with grease, place a new gasket in position and install the mainshaft and rear cover. Raise the front end of the mainshaft as shown in **FIG 6:10** sufficiently for the third- and fourth-speed clutch to clear the layshaft third-speed gear and rotate the shaft to engage the layshaft gears. Do not install the rear cover bolts at this stage.

6 Assemble the selector forks on the clutches. The third and fourth selector fork can be identified by the smaller boss on the fork. Locate the rear cover radially to permit installation of the selector fork rail

as shown in **FIG 6:15**. Drive the rail home with a brass drift until it is flush with the casing rear face. Rotate the rear cover to align the bolt holes and install the bolts.

7 Using new copper washers, install and tighten the front cover bolts.

8 With the two clutches and the reverse pinion in the neutral position, locate the interlock collar over the selector forks and reverse striking lever. Insert the selector shaft through the rear cover and interlcok collar, lining up the keys on the shaft with the slot in the collar. Rotate the shaft anticlockwise until the keys are clear of the forks and locate the front end of the shaft in the casing bore.

9 Rotate the shaft clockwise and insert the interlock collar retaining pin (see **FIG 6:9**) and the detent ball and spring.

10 Temporarily install the gearlever with the long leg of the lever to the left and engage first gear. Check the clearance between the selector shaft and the reverse stop on the lever (see **FIG 6:16**) and if necessary adjust the eccentric pin on the shaft to give a clearance of .002 to .012 inch. Select neutral and remove the gearlever.

11 Install the gearlever housing cover, using a new gasket.

12 Install the top cover using a new gasket.

13 Smear the front cover sleeve and clutch fork ball with a recommended grease and install the clutch fork, release bearing and return spring.

6:6 Refitting gearbox

Refitting the gearbox involves reversal of the sequence of operations for removal given in **Section 6:3**. The following points however should be noted:

1 Prior to installing the gearbox, inject $\frac{1}{8}$ pint of gear oil through the end of the rear cover to provide initial lubrication of the speedometer gears and the rear cover bush. In addition the oil seal and felt in the rear cover must be smeared with gear oil. Insert a spare sliding sleeve into the end of the rear cover to prevent oil loss during installation.

2 Check that the starter pinion rubber boot is serviceable and correctly installed in the gearbox casing.

3 Check that the mating faces of the gearbox and crankcase are clean and free from burrs.

4 Lightly smear the main drive pinion (first-motion shaft) splines with grease.

5 Locate the seal and seal support over the gearlever housing, but do not fit the gearlever at this stage.

6 When installing the gearbox, take care not to allow the weight of the gearbox to rest on the main drive pinion and clutch disc hub until the spigot is fully home in the crankshaft bearing.

7 Ensure that the gearbox casing locates on the two dowels in the crankcase. Tighten the bolts evenly.

8 After installing the gearbox in the car, pack the recess in the gearlever housing and smear the lever ball and forked end with a recommended grease. Fit the lever so that the longer leg of the fork is towards the left.

9 After installing the propeller shaft, refill the gearbox with the recommended grade of oil. Run the engine for a few minutes and recheck oil level.

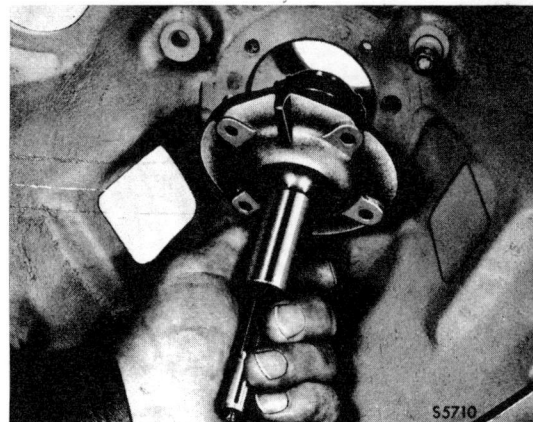

FIG 6:11 Removing first motion shaft and front cover

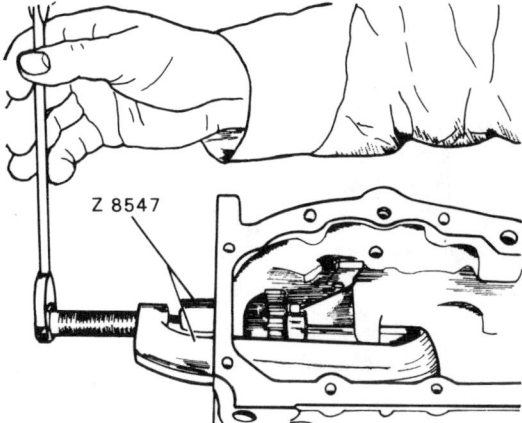

FIG 6:12 Removing reverse pinion shaft

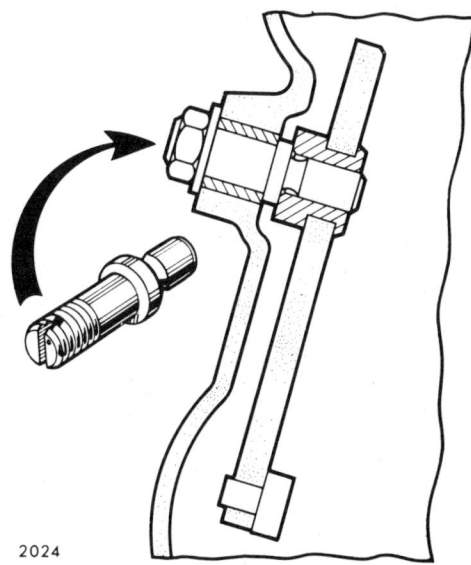

FIG 6:13 Reverse fulcrum pin is fitted with centre punch mark uppermost

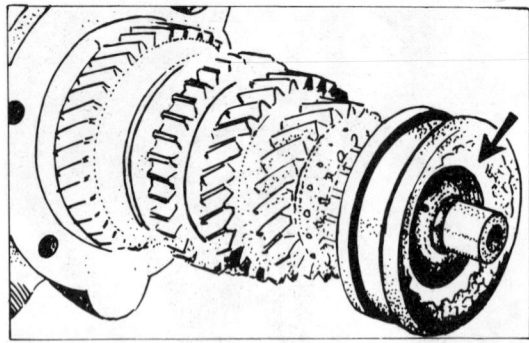

FIG 6:14 When installing mainshaft, ensure that slots in the synchronizing ring (arrowed) engage sliding keys and that clutch hub is located well forward

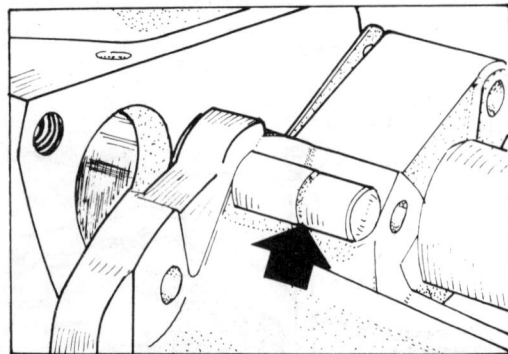

FIG 6:15 Fitting selector rail

6:7 Speedometer drive. Reverse light switch

To remove the speedometer driven gear from the gearbox with the gearbox in the car:

1 Disconnect the speedometer cable from the gearbox and remove the oil seal.
2 Place a tray to catch the oil from the rear cover.
3 Using a brass drift as shown in **FIG 6:17** drive out the gear and shaft together with the end cap.

To install the speedometer driven gear:

1 Lubricate the gear before installing.
2 Smear a new cap with jointing compound and install by using a suitable lever and distance piece. If the gearbox is out of the car the cap can be driven in using a brass drift.
3 Assemble the oil seal and reconnect the speedometer cable.
4 Run the engine a few minutes to circulate oil from the gearbox casing into the rear cover. Stop the engine and top up the gearbox to the bottom of the filler plug hole.

Note that the number of teeth on the speedometer driven gear is dependent on rear axle ratio and tyre size. Details are given in Technical Data.

To remove the speedometer cable, remove the five Phillips screws securing the instrument assembly to the facia and withdraw the assembly just sufficiently to disconnect the speedometer cable. Disconnect the cable from the gearbox and withdraw the cable and grommets

through the dash panel. Examine the outer casing for kinks and fractures and the inner cable for broken strands. Check for wear on the squared ends of the cable. When installing the cable, the lower two-thirds only should be lubricated with high melting point grease. Any bends in the outer casing must be not less than 5 inch radius.

FIG 6:18 shows the method of assembling the reverse light switch where fitted. Before installing, smear the threads of the switch with jointing compound. Do not allow compound to run on to the switch plunger or it may stick in ON position. Screw the switch into the gear-lever housing until dimension A is .20 inch, then tighten the locknut.

6:8 Fault diagnosis

(a) Jumping out of gear

1 Weak or broken detent ball spring
2 Excessive slackness between a synchronizer clutch and hub
3 Slack bearings causing mainshaft float
4 (Forward gears only) Wear or damage at ends of gear clutch internal splines and mainshaft gear or drive pinion.
5 (Top gear only) Bolts holding gearbox to crankcase loose or foreign matter between mating surfaces
6 (Top gear only) Slack main drive pinion bearing
7 (Reverse only) Incorrectly adjusted reverse striking lever.

(b) Noisy gearbox

1 Insufficient oil
2 Excessive end play in layshaft gear
3 Worn or damaged bearings
4 Worn or damaged gear teeth

(c) Difficulty in engaging gear

1 Clutch drag or spin (see **Section 5:8**)
2 Worn, damaged or incorrectly adjusted gearchange mechanism
3 (Reverse only) Incorrectly adjusted striking lever
4 Faulty synchromesh action

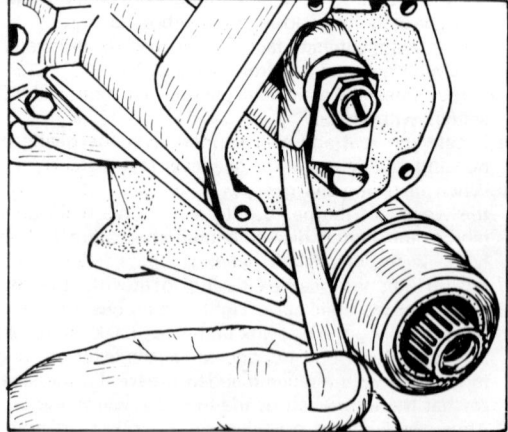

FIG 6:16 Checking clearance between longer leg of gear lever and selector shaft

(d) Faulty synchromesh action

1 Worn or damaged synchromesh cone or ring
2 Weak, broken or displaced key springs
3 Worn or damaged teeth on synchronizing ring

(e) Oil leaks

1 Damaged joint washers
2 Front rear or top covers loose or faces damaged
3 Worn or damaged rear cover oil seal

(f) Gearlever rattle

1 Loose cap
2 Weak cap spring
3 Worn rubber bush
4 Worn lever ball

AUTOMATIC TRANSMISSION

6:9 Construction and operation

The G.M. automatic transmission is available on the high performance versions of the Viva HC as an alternative to the manual synchromesh gearbox and consists of a fluid torque converter coupled to a hydraulically operated planetary gear set having three forward speeds and reverse (see **FIG 6:19**).

The torque converter which is shown diagrammatically in **FIG 6:20**—transmits or disconnects the drive between engine and gearbox according to engine speed and provides a smooth take-off from rest. It also multiplies the engine torque under certain conditions of input and output speed. The converter consists of the impeller 3 which is coupled directly to the engine crankshaft, the turbine 1 which has no mechanical connection with the impeller but is splined to the transmission input shaft and the stator 2 which is situated between the two and mounted on a one-way clutch.

When the engine is started the impeller rotates with it and the fluid is discharged from the impeller blades into the turbine and returns through the stator as shown. The shape and disposition of the stator blades is so designed that when the turbine and impeller are rotating at different speeds the angle at which the oil flow strikes the impeller blades from the stator is such as to assist in driving the impeller. Under these conditions a degree of torque multiplication is obtained varying from about 2:1 to 1:1 when the impeller and the turbine are rotating at the same speed.

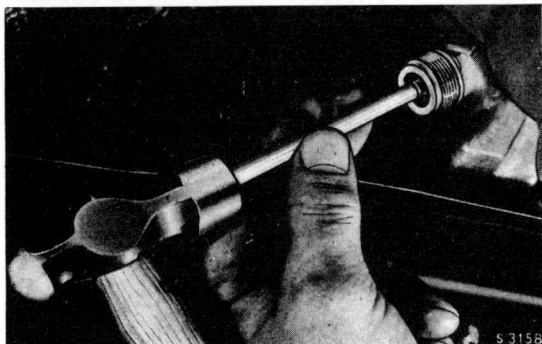

FIG 6:17 Removing speedometer driven gear

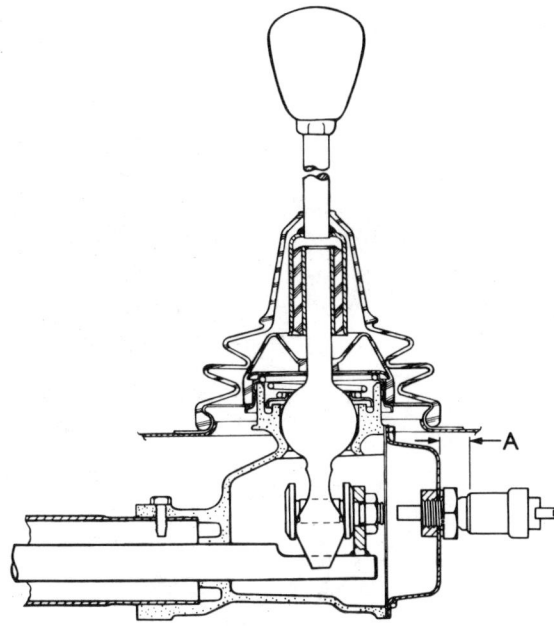

FIG 6:18   Section view of gear lever   **A**=.20 inch

At this point the stator freewheels and all three elements rotate together and the converter becomes a fluid coupling.

The planetary gear set utilizes two sets of planet pinions, two sun gears and one ring gear, and is shown diagrammatically in **FIG 6:21**. Control is effected through three disc clutches, a band brake and a sprag or one-way clutch, which are all operated by hydraulic pressure generated by a built-in oil pump and regulated by valves and a centrifugal governor. Six operating ranges are provided and are selected by a lever operating in a floor-mounted quadrant on which the six ranges are indicated by the following letters P, R, N, D, I and L. To prevent the accidental engagement of L, I, R or P a two-stage safety stop is incorporated in addition to the usual inhibitor switch which ensures that the starter will operate only when P or N have been selected.

P or Park:

In this position the engine may be started and run without any drive being transmitted to the road wheels. There is also a parking pawl or mechanical lock engaged which prevents the car from moving. The P position should never be selected while the car is in motion.

R or Reverse:

Is as its name implies for driving the car backwards and must not be selected when moving forwards. An exception to this rule is its use with very light throttle, for rocking the car out of mud, sand or snow.

N or Neutral:

Conditions are the same as in P except that the parking lock is not applied. In this position the handbrake should be applied when the car is at rest to ensure that it does not creep when engine speed is allowed to rise above idling speed.

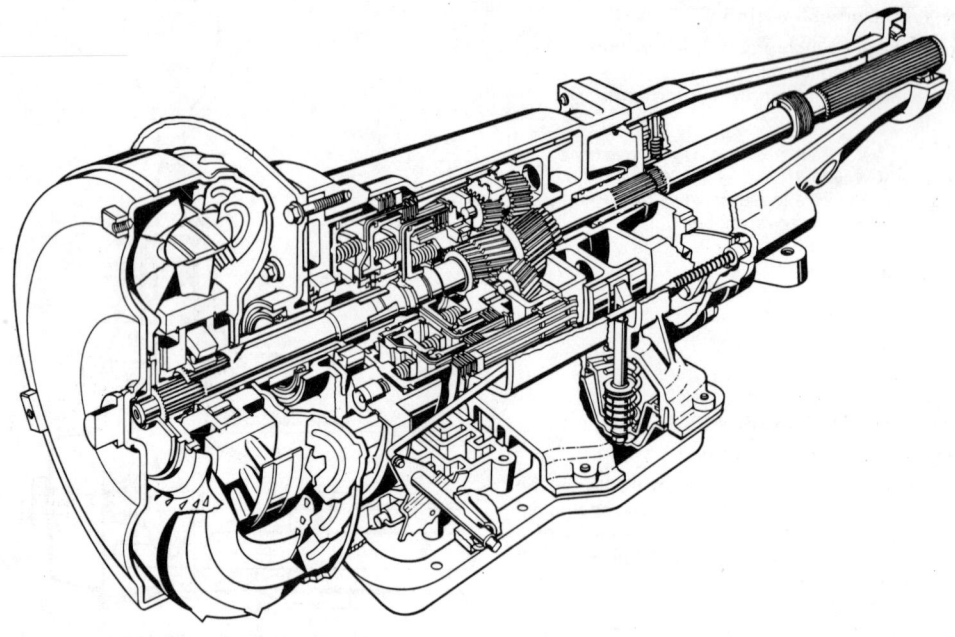

FIG 6:19   Cutaway view of GM Automatic Transmission

D or Drive:

This is used for all normal running. The transmission starts in first gear and shifts up automatically into second and third gears and down again depending upon road speed and throttle position. When accelerating away from rest upchanges will be made at higher speeds as the accelerator pedal is pressed lower. Similarly downshifts will be made at higher road speeds at wider throttle openings. The sudden depression of the accelerator pedal to its limit when travelling in high gear will cause the transmission to change down to second gear and so provide the extra power required for overtaking. This forced downshift is known as 'kick-down'.

I or Intermediate:

In this position the transmission starts in first gear and changes up to second as in D but does not move on into third. Selecting I when in D range causes an immediate downshift to second gear. To avoid over-speeding the engine this should obviously not be done at speeds in excess of those possible in the lower gear.

L or Low:

When this range is selected from rest the car will move off in first gear and remain in that ratio until the selector is moved.

Selecting L when in D or I ranges will cause the transmission to change down into first gear as quickly as road speed permits and remain in that range regardless of road speed and throttle position after engagement.

This position is most valuable in providing full engine braking when descending steep hills.

6:10 Maintenance

The fluid level in the transmission should be checked every 6000 miles or 3 months as follows:

Drive the car on to a level floor, apply the handbrake and allow the engine to idle and bring the fluid up to normal operating temperature. Move the selector lever through each position and then select N or P. With the engine still idling measure the fluid level on the dipstick and if necessary, add sufficient to bring the level up to the FULL mark. The quantity required to bring the level from ADD to FULL is approximately one pint and it is important that this level is accurately maintained. Only the recommended grade of oil may be used, and no additions or compounds included without serious risk of damage to the transmission.

At intervals of 24,000 miles the oil should be drained off and renewed. Raise the car or drive it onto a ramp to gain access to the underside and place a suitable container in position to catch the liquid. Remove the oil pan and gasket, then take out the oil strainer and its joint washer. A warning may be necessary to draw attention to the fact that at working temperatures the oil is hot enough to cause serious burns if allowed to contact the flesh and adequate precautions should be taken to prevent this.

Fit a new strainer and washer. Clean the oil pan before refitting it with a new gasket. Lower the car and refill the transmission. Start the engine and bring the transmission up to working heat by allowing it to idle with a drive range selected for **not more than two minutes.** For reasons of safety an assistant should be seated in the car to ensure that the brakes are held on at this time.

Before making a final check on the oil level move the selector lever through each position to ensure that all internal channels are filled.

In order to prevent the temperature of the oil from rising to excessive values an oil cooler is included in the radiator for the engine coolant and it should be remembered that if the radiator is removed for any reason it will be necessary to disconnect the oil supply hoses. Make sure that these pipes are sealed to avoid loss of oil and also that the level in the transmission is checked after re-installation.

Towing:

Provided that the transmission is working satisfactorily the car may safely be towed with N selected for distances up to 30 miles at speeds not exceeding 30 mile/hr.

For longer distances, higher speeds or if the transmission is damaged the propeller shaft should be removed or the car towed on its front wheels.

6:11 Adjustments

In view of the specialised knowledge and extensive equipment required for adequately testing and servicing this automatic transmission, it is strongly recommended that any servicing should be entrusted to a qualified service station. There are however, a few adjustments and tests which a reasonably competent owner can make for himself and they are described for his guidance.

Starter inhibitor and reverse light switch (see FIG 6:22):

Remove the selector lever console from the floor to gain access to the switch, then with the selector lever in the P position adjust the location of the switch so that the upper roller 1 is depressed by the rear cam 2. This closes the starter circuit contacts in the switch.

On some cars a combined starter inhibitor and reverse lamp switch is used.

On later models adjustment is by movement of the mounting bracket secured by two nuts. Set the selector lever in N, the selector plungers 1 (see FIG 6:28) should align with the cutout 2. Slacken the bracket nuts and move the bracket until the line 3 is aligned with line 4 and re-tighten the nuts. Check that starter will only function in N or P. Check reverse lamps only light when R is selected.

Selector lever and linkage (see FIGS 6:23 and 6:24)

Reference to FIG 6:23 will show that the selector lever 1 pivots in the housing 2 while the lower lever 3 is connected to the transmission selector lever by an adjustable rod. The plunger 4 engages in the selector plate 7 to prevent accidental selection of certain range positions.

Partial depression of the spring-loaded button 5 is necessary before I or R can be selected while full depression of the button is required to displace the plunger sufficiently to move into the L or P positions.

To adjust the linkage put the selector lever in the P position and the transmission lever also to Park, then set the adjuster (see FIG 6:24) so that the pip 1 is aligned with the lever notch 2 by adjusting the length of

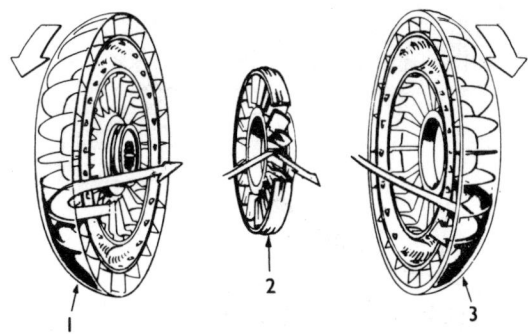

FIG 6:20   Torque converter operation

Key to Fig 6:20   1 Turbine   2 Stator   3 Impeller

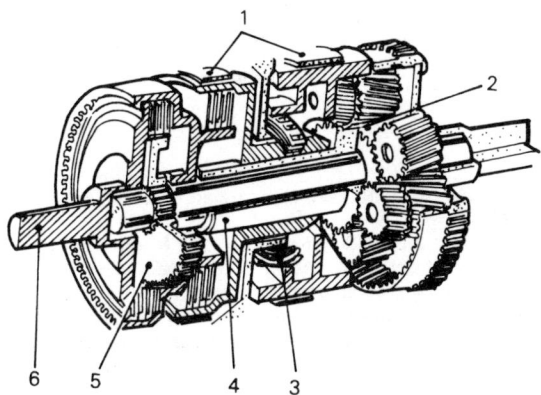

FIG 6:21   Clutches and planetary gear set

Key to Fig 6:21   1 Front and rear brake bands   2 Forward sun gear   3 One-way clutch   4 Reverse sun gear   5 Front clutch hub   6 Input shaft

the control rod using the screwed end and locknut as shown. Lubricate well with Duckhams Keenol before refitting the rubber boot.

Detent valve (see FIG 6:25):

The purpose of the detent valve is to cause the transmission to shift into a lower gear when the throttle pedal is fully depressed.

To check that the solenoid has the correct .25 inch clearance, place a steel ball of this diameter 3 in position as shown and install the solenoid temporarily in the transmission case. Make a mark 1 on the casing in line with the notch 2 on the mounting bracket. Remove the solenoid and take out the steel ball. Refit the solenoid in the position just indicated and tighten the securing nut.

The controlling switch is mounted on the carburetter and operated by the throttle lever when moved into the 'kick-down' position. It must be adjusted on its mounting bracket so that the contacts are closed at full throttle and open when the throttle stop is .040 inch from its abutment on the carburetter body.

On later models a detent valve operating cable is connected by a yoke to the accelerator pedal linkage. The outer cable is secured to the housing by a locknut. The

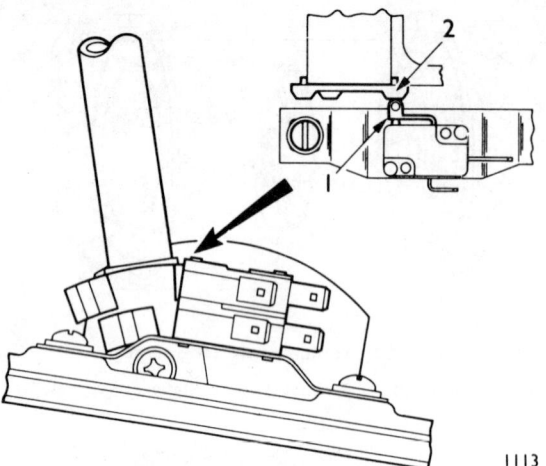

FIG 6:22 Setting the inhibitor switch

cable is in two parts connected by an adjuster (see **FIG 6:27**).

To adjust the cable, unscrew locknut 6 screw adjuster 1 onto the front cable casing 2 until the casing 2 protrudes through the adjuster 1, ensure that the cables 3 and 4 are properly connected. Holding the accelerator in the full throttle position pull the cable casings apart until the detent valve bottoms against the stop, in this position screw the adjuster 1 up to the flange 5, then back off half a turn and lock with lock nut 6.

6:12 Testing

The following tests are made with test equipment D1121 and Adapter VR2082, or any other suitable pressure gauge reading from 0 to 250 lb/sq in, connected to the low servo pressure check point on the lefthand side of the transmission as shown in **FIG 6:26**.

Run the engine at idling speed with D range selected and brakes applied. The pressure should read 47 to 53 lb/sq in. Move the selector lever to I and then to L and again note the pressure readings. In each case it should be between 78 and 87 lb/sq in.

Disconnect the vacuum modulator line, select D range and run the engine at 1000 rev/min and check that the pressure is 116 to 139 lb/sq in. With the engine speed still at 1000 rev/min select I and then L. The pressure in each case should be between 191 and 215 lb/sq in. Reconnect the vacuum modulator line and prepare for testing on the road.

With D range selected the pressure should read 47 lb/sq in at idle and 130 lb/sq in when running at full throttle.

Reduce speed and select I range. Close the throttle and allow the speed to fall to 30 mile/hr and note the pressure reading. Select L and still at 30 mile/hr and with the throttle closed note the reading again. In each case a minimum of 78 lb/sq in should be shown.

On completion of these tests, remove the gauge and tighten the check point plug to a torque of 6 lb ft.

6:13 Transmission removal

Both removal and installation of the transmission are generally straightforward, but it may be of assistance to mention a few points to be observed.

Remember that the transmission and torque converter, which *must* be removed as one assembly, weigh about 110 lb and a suitable cradle should be used to take the weight before disconnecting or when refitting.

Before disconnecting the cooler pipes and dipstick tube, clean carefully around the connections and plug any apertures to prevent the entry of any foreign matter.

In order to permit the rear of the engine to be lowered a number of items on the engine will have to be released, such as carburetter controls, exhaust pipes and starter motor. To facilitate the removal of the converter housing front cover the transmission braces must be removed.

The removal of some of the converter housing bolts which are reached from the engine compartment will be assisted by the use of a special angled wrench which is available.

Installation:

Before commencing to install the transmission, make sure that the flexplate to crankshaft bolts are correctly tightened to a torque of 47 lb ft.

Line up the painted balance marks on the rim of the torque converter and the rear of the flexplate as closely as possible, then tighten up the converter to flexplate bolts to 42 lb ft.

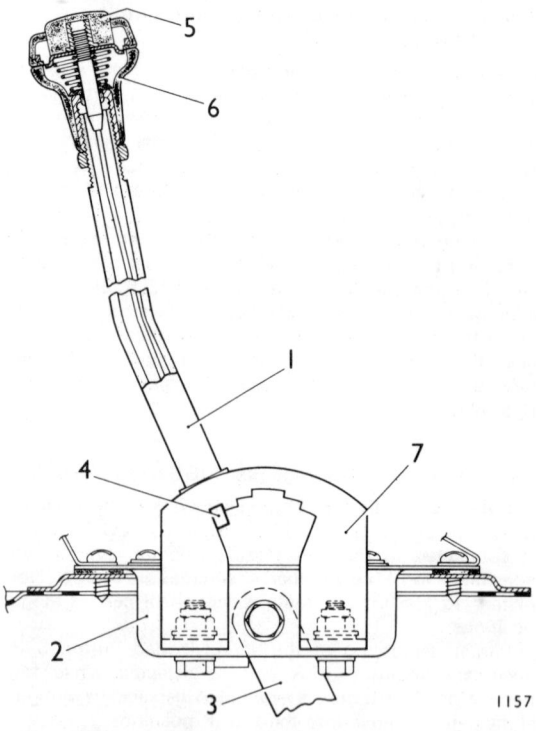

FIG 6:23 Section through selector lever assembly

Key to Fig 6:23   1 Selector lever   2 Housing
3 Lower lever   4 Plunger   5 Spring button   6 Knob
7 Selector plate

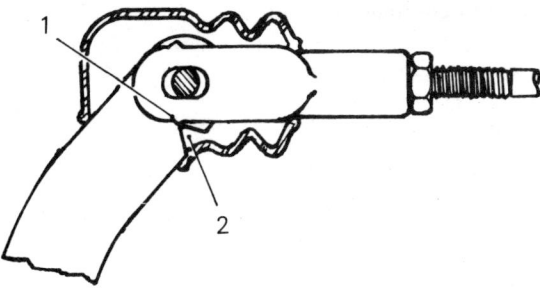

FIG 6:24 Adjusting the linkage

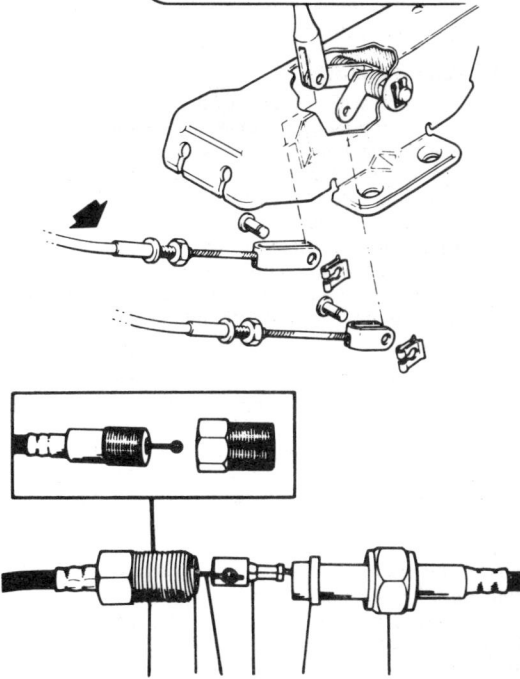

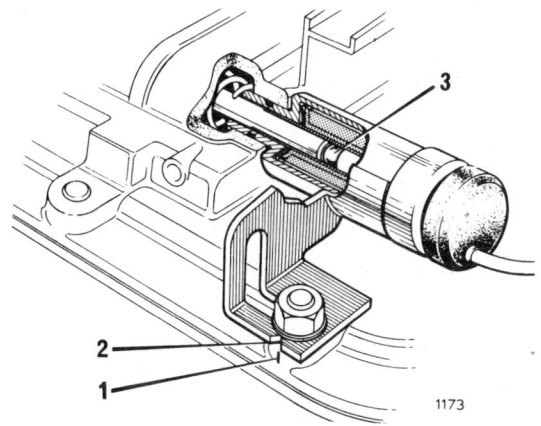

FIG 6:25 Detent valve solenoid and mounting

Key to Fig 6:25   1 Mark   2 Notch   3 .25 inch steel ball

FIG 6:27 Detent valve operating cable connection at top and adjustment at bottom

Key to Fig 6:27   1 Adjuster   2 Front cable casing
3 Cable   4 Cable   5 Flange on rear casing   6 Locknut

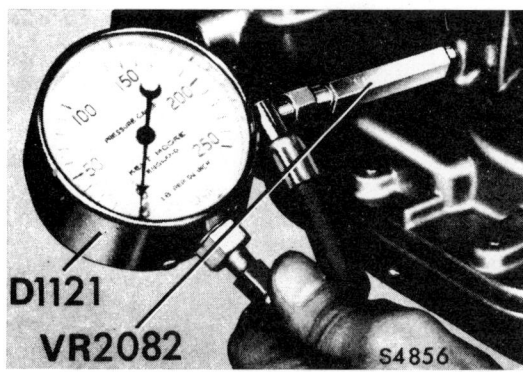

FIG 6:26 Low pressure check

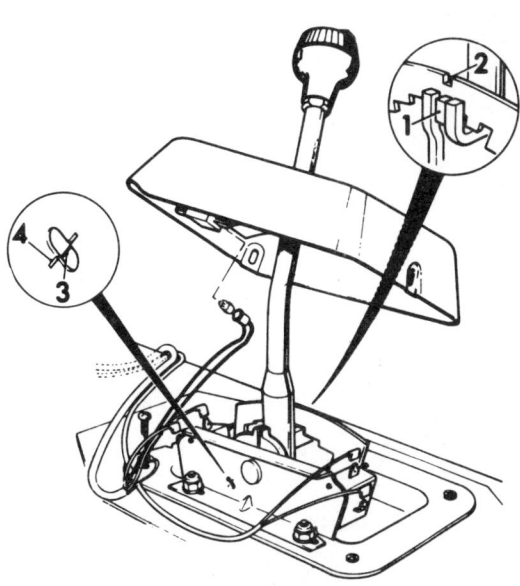

FIG 6:28 Adjusting the starter inhibitor and reverse lamp switches on later models

Key to Fig 6:28   1 Selector plunger   2 Cut-out
3 Line on bracket   4 Line on casing

Remember to tighten the bolts securing the transmission brace to the converter housing before the bolts securing the braces to the oilpan.

6:14 Fault diagnosis

In this section will be found a list of faults which may develop in the automatic transmission together with a list of possible causes. Very few of these faults will be within the scope of the home operator to rectify, but the information may help him to decide whether to attempt to do so or not, and perhaps to save the service station some valuable time spent in testing.

Before attempting to diagnose faults, ensure that the transmission is filled with a recommended grade of fluid and that all controls are correctly adjusted.

Fault	Possible cause
No drive in any selector position	1, 2, 3, 4, 5, 6
No drive in D or I	7
No gearchange at any speed	16, 17, 18
Gearchange only at full throttle	11, 12, 15
Gearchange only at part throttle	13, 14
No 3-2 part throttle downchange at low speed	19
No 2-3 upchange	20
Slipping 1-2 upchange	21, 22, 23
Slipping 2-3 upchange	21, 24, 25, 26
Abrupt 1-2 upchange	22, 27
Abrupt 2-3 upchange	27
Abrupt 3-2 'kick-down' at high speed	28
Abrupt 3-2 closed throttle downchange	29
Engine flare on high speed 'kick-down'	21, 24
Engine flare on low speed 'kick-down'	21, 24, 30
No 'kick-down'	14
No engine braking in L	31, 33
No parking lock in P	32, 33
Low oil pressure	1, 2, 8, 9, 10

Key to possible causes:

1 Low fluid level
2 Clogged air strainer
3 Inner manual valve broken or disconnected
4 Input shaft broken
5 Pressure regulator valve not functioning correctly
6 Oil pump defective
7 Sprag clutch slipping or incorrectly fitted
8 Leak in oil pump suction circuit
9 Leak in oil pump pressure circuit
10 Priming valve stuck
11 Broken vacuum line
12 Leak in vacuum system
13 Detent pressure regulator valve sticking
14 Detent cable broken or incorrectly adjusted
15 Vacuum modulator failed
16 Governor valves sticking or leaking
17 1-2 change valve sticking in first gear position
18 Bad leak in governor oil circuit
19 3-2 change valve sticking
20 2-3 change valve sticking
21 Low fluid pressure
22 1-2 accumulator valve sticking
23 Second clutch piston or seals damaged, or ball stuck open
24 Band adjustment loose
25 Third clutch piston or seals damaged or ball stuck open
26 Input shaft, bush worn
27 High fluid pressure
28 High speed downchange timing valve stuck open
29 Low speed downchange timing valve stuck open
30 High speed downchange timing valve stuck closed
31 Manual low control valve sticking
32 Parking pawl, gear or spring broken
33 Selector linkage incorrectly adjusted

CHAPTER 7

PROPELLER SHAFT, REAR AXLE, REAR SUSPENSION

7:1 Description of layout
7:2 Dismantling and servicing universal joints
7:3 Description and construction of axle
7:4 Lubrication. Servicing parts without axle
   removal
7:5 Axle removal
7:6 Refitting axle

7:7 Description of rear suspension system
7:8 Rear spring removal and refitting
7:9 Rebushing upper and lower rear suspension
   arms
7:10 Rear dampers
7:11 Fault diagnosis

7:1 Description of layout

The layout of propeller shaft, rear axle and suspension can be seen in **FIGS 7:2** and **7:13**. The open tubular propeller shaft incorporates two universal joints of the trunnion and needle roller type. The yoke of the front universal joint carries an internally splined sleeve which can slide on the splined mainshaft of the gearbox to compensate for movement of the rear axle. The rear universal joint is bolted to a flange attached to the pinion shaft of the rear axle.

The rear axle is of the semi-floating type with a hypoid final drive enclosed in a one-piece axle housing with detachable rear cover. The rear suspension is of the four-link coil spring type with longitudinal lower arms and diagonal upper arms. A full description is given in **Section 7:7**.

7:2 Dismantling and servicing universal joints

Two makes of propeller shaft are used, namely Hardy Spicer and BRD, identified by the name cast on the propeller shaft yoke. Replacement shafts, yokes and complete journal assemblies are interchangeable and the following instructions apply to both makes.

To remove the propeller shaft:
1 Have ready a spare sliding sleeve to insert in the gear-box rear cover to prevent oil loss.
2 Mark the relationship between the rear universal joint flange and the rear axle pinion shaft flange with quick drying paint. Remove the locking nuts and bolts securing the flanges.
3 After withdrawing the sliding sleeve from the gearbox protect the outer ground surface of the sleeve by binding with tape to prevent damage. Burrs or scratches on this surface may cause premature wear to the gearbox rear cover bush and oil seal.

To dismantle the universal joints, clean all dirt and paint from around the snap rings (see **FIG 7:1**). Mark the yokes with paint to ensure reassembly in the same relationship. Tap the end of one of the bearings with a brass drift to relieve the pressure on the snap ring which can then be removed using circlip pliers. Hold the shaft in the left hand with the bearing to be removed uppermost and tap the yoke downwards with a lead or copper hammer. Reaction should jar out the bearing upwards. When it projects far enough to be gripped, invert the joint and pull the bearing cup out downwards so that the needle rollers come out with it.

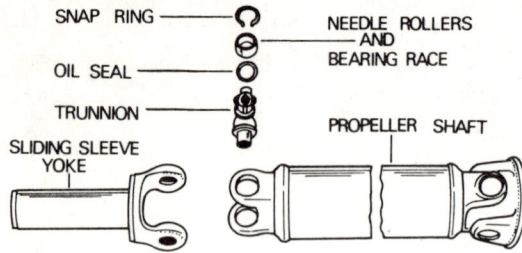

FIG 7:1 Exploded view of propeller shaft and universal joint

Remove the opposite snap ring and bearing, then the yoke can be detached from the trunnion. Remove the other two bearings and dismantle the other universal joint in the same way. An alternative method of dismantling is to use the special tool D.1093. Note that trunnion, bearings and oil seals are serviced only as an assembly. If the yoke bores are worn note that a complete propeller shaft can be supplied on an exchange basis.

When reassembling universal joints, coat the needle rollers with petroleum jelly to hold them in the races. Ensure that each bearing is one-third filled with the recommended grease before assembly, as no grease nipples are used. Tap home the races using a flat-faced drift slightly smaller in diameter than the yoke bore and ensure that the snap rings seat correctly. When installing the propeller shaft note that the heads of the rear flange coupling bolts are towards the propeller shaft. Tighten the bolts to a torque of 18 lb ft with clean dry threads. Run the engine for a few minutes to circulate oil from the gearbox casing into the rear cover. Stop the engine and top up the gearbox.

7:3 Description and construction of axle

FIG 7:2 is an exploded view of the rear axle components. The axle housing consists of a cast differential carrier with pressed-in tubular assemblies, to the ends of which are welded the axle shaft bearing housings (see **FIG 7:4**) which also provide attachment for the brake backplates. The suspension lower arm mountings are welded to the tubular assemblies, while the suspension upper arm mountings are integral with the differential carrier.

The differential case or cage incorporates two differential pinions and side gears and is bolted to the hypoid gear. Thrust washers are used against spherical faces on the differential pinions and graded spacers are assembled to the side gears to control backlash. The differential and hypoid gear assembly is carried by two taper roller bearings secured to the housing by caps and bolts. Lateral location of the assembly and preload of the bearings are controlled by graded spacers and shims.

The hypoid pinion is overhung mounted in the axle housing in two preloaded taper roller bearings and is located in correct mesh with the hypoid gear by spacers and shims between the front face of the rear bearing outer race and the housing. A distance washer is assembled between a compressible spacer and the front bearing. A spring-loaded oil seal is pressed into the front of the axle housing and operates directly on the pinion shaft.

To prevent oil leakage from the axle into the hubs and brakes each hub bearing embodies inner and outer oil seals, a description of which will be found in the following Section.

Complete dismantling of the rear axle and differential is not recommended as the work of reassembly entails the use of special jigs and equipment. The work should therefore be entrusted to a Vauxhall service agent. Complete replacement axles are available on an exchange basis, but take note that the 1256 cc models had a heavy duty type of axle assembly fitted (circa Sept. 71) and care must be taken when ordering spares. Procedure for removal and installation of axle is given in **Sections 7:5** and **7:6**.

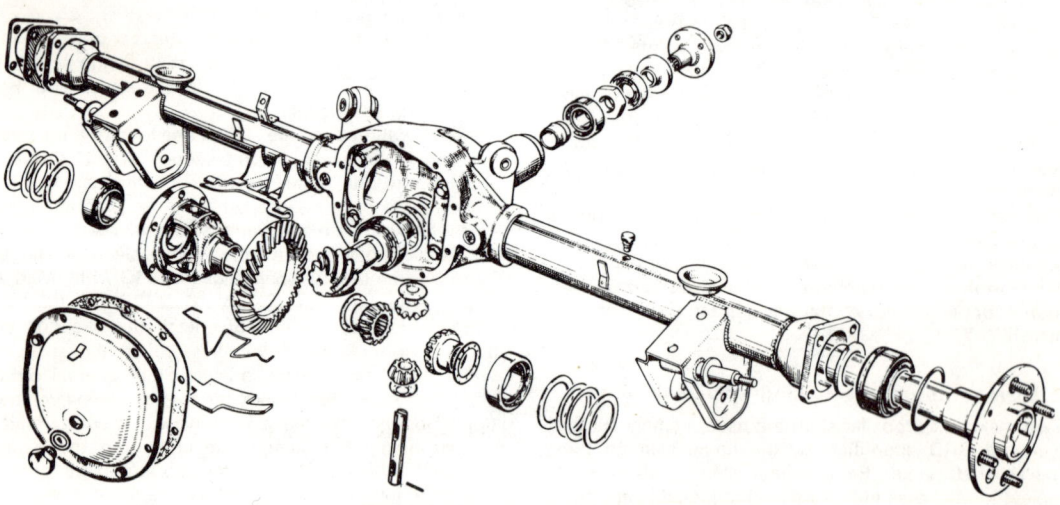

FIG 7:2 Components of rear axle

7:4 Lubrication. Servicing parts without axle removal

The rear axle requires special hypoid gear oil for its satisfactory operation. Ordinary high pressure gear oil even if of the same SAE number, must not be used. The combined oil level and filler plug is on the axle housing rear cover. Clean all dirt from around the plug before removing it. The oil level should be at the bottom of the filler plug hole, checked with the car unladen and on level ground. In other circumstances it is possible to put in far too much oil and the surplus may find its way past the seals and into the brakes.

The following operations can if required be carried out without removing the rear axle from the car:- Removal and refitting of axle shafts and hub bearings, renewal of hub oil seals and pinion shaft oil seal.

To remove an axle shaft proceed as follows:
1 Raise and support the vehicle.
2 Remove the road wheel and release the handbrake.
3 Remove the bolts securing the brake drum to the axle shaft flange and withdraw the drum. If necessary, slacken off the brake adjuster.
4 Remove the nuts securing the axle shaft bearing retainer plate (see **FIGS 7:4** and **7:5**) and withdraw the shaft. In case of difficulty, remove a bearing retainer plate bolt and use a drift inserted through the bolt hole to drive out the shaft. **Do not use levers on the flange** as this may cause distortion.
5 If the bearing and oil seal have to be renewed, the work of pressing off the old retainer ring and bearing and installing new parts can be more easily carried out by a Vauxhall service agent having the necessary special tools. The same applies to the work of pressing out and renewing hub flange bolts.

When installing the axle shafts note the following points:
1 Check that the oil drain hole in the brake flange plate is clear.
2 Fit a new outer seal in the groove in the periphery of the bearing and lubricate the outer oil seal and bearing housing to facilitate entry of the seal.
3 Coat the shaft from the bearing to the splined end with oil.
4 Tighten the bearing retainer plate nuts to 18 lb ft with clean dry threads.
5 Check the oil level in the axle as described at the beginning of this Section.

FIG 7:6 which is a section through the differential housing also shows the position of the spring-loaded seal which prevents oil leaking out round the pinion shaft. It can be renewed as follows:

Disconnect the rear end of the propeller shaft and tie it up to keep it from dropping to the ground.

Tap back the staking on the coupling flange nut and remove the nut using the tool Z.8307 as shown in **FIG 7:7** or a tool suitably fabricated for the purpose.

Mark the position of the coupling flange in relation to the pinion shaft and adapter plate and withdraw the flange.

Lever off the mud slinger, pierce the oil seal and remove it from the axle housing (see **FIG 7:9**).

Before installing the new seal, file a slot away from and similar to the existing slot in the pinion shaft to provide

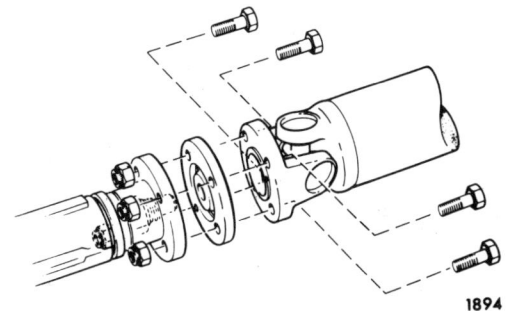

FIG 7:3 Coupling flange adaptor plate

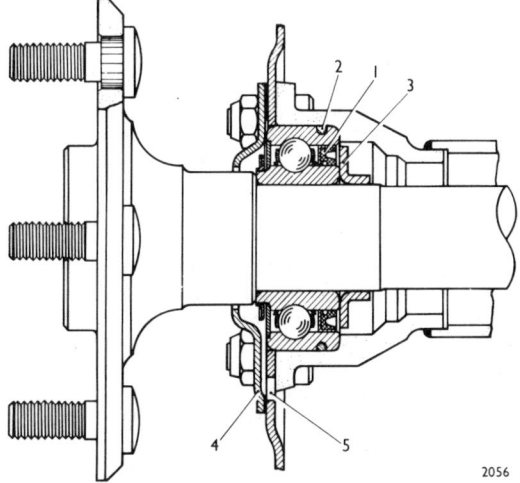

FIG 7:4 Axle shaft and wheel bearings

Key to Fig 7:4   1 Oil seal   2 Sealing ring   3 Flange
4 and 5 Oil drain

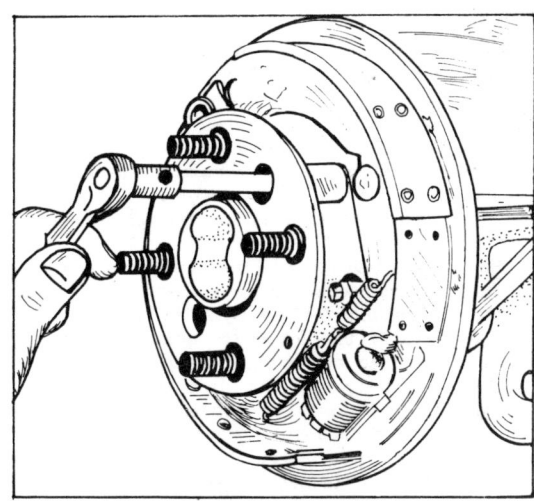

FIG 7:5 Axle shaft removal

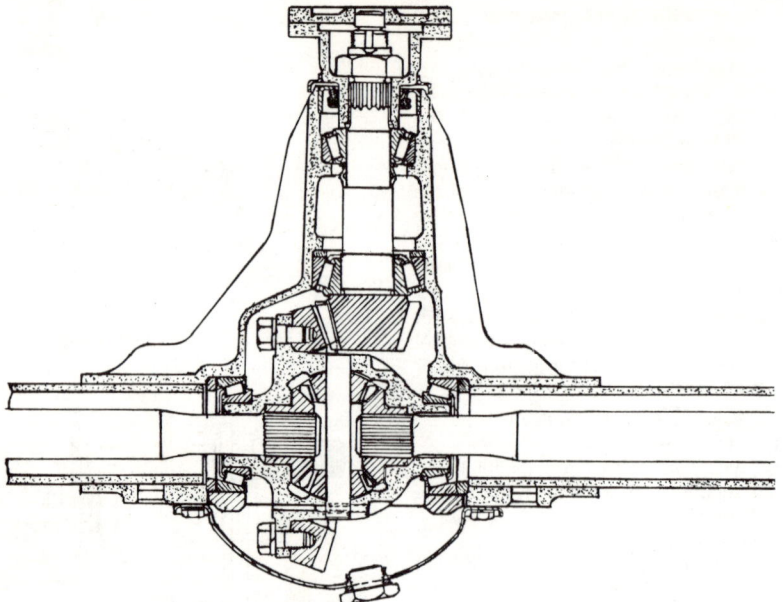

FIG 7:6 Section through differential assembly

a new location for staking the nut then insert the seal, open side first until it contacts the shoulder in the housing or is flush with the end of the housing. Smear well with the recommended grease. Drive on a new mud slinger.

Tighten up the coupling flange nut so that the original nut staking and pinion shaft slot are aligned, then stake the nut into the slot. The torque loading on the nut should be approximately 75 lb ft.

When fitting the propeller shaft, note that the adaptor plate between the rear axle coupling flange and the propeller shaft flange must be a snug fit on the pinion shaft and have the register towards the propeller shaft.

Top up the axle with the recommended gear oil as described earlier in **Section 7:4**.

7:5 Axle removal

Removal of the rear axle is only likely to be called for if a replacement unit is to be fitted. As already stated, dismantling of the axle and differential is best undertaken by a Vauxhall service agent. To remove the axle:

1 Disconnect the handbrake cable from the axle by slackening the adjuster, removing the cable ends from the slotted clevises on the brake shoe levers and removing the two splitpins from the cable guide on the axle.

2 Remove the bolt securing the hydraulic brake pipe three-way connector to the axle. Disconnect the two brake pipes from the rear wheel cylinders. Tie the brake pipes up out of the way of further operations.

3 Remove the rear dampers (see **Section 7:10**).

4 Disconnect the rear end of the propeller shaft only (see **Section 7:2**) and tie it up to a suitable component to prevent the front sliding sleeve being disconnected from the gearbox.

5 It is not necessary to lower the axle before removing it. The weight of the car must be firmly supported on stands under the lower suspension arms as shown in

FIG 7:11. Reference to **FIG 7:2** will show the method by which the axle is located.

6 Remove the road wheels.

7 Remove the bolts and nuts **from the rear ends** of the upper and lower suspension arms indicated at 1 and 2 in **FIG 7:12** and lower the axle to the ground. **If other work is to be carried out on the car while the arms are disconnected, stands should be placed under the body as an additional safety measure.**

7:6 Refitting axle

Refitting the rear axle entails a reversal of the removal procedure, but the following points should be noted:

1 Referring to **FIG 7:12**, the weight of the car must rest on the rear springs before tightening the upper arm mounting bolt nuts 1 and the lower arm bolt nuts 2 to a torque of 38 lb ft.

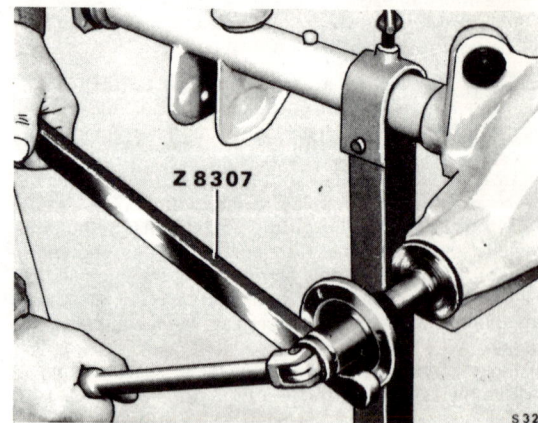

FIG 7:7 Holding bar for coupling flange

2 Bleed the braking system (see **Section 10:8**), reconnect the handbrake cable and adjust the brakes.

3 Connect the propeller shaft (see **Section 7:2**).

4 Check the level of oil in the axle (see **Section 7:4**).

7:7 Description of rear suspension system

The rear suspension is of the four link coil spring type, incorporating longitudinal lower arms and diagonal upper arms. The layout and an exploded view of the components of the suspension system may be seen in **FIG 7:13**. The lower arms (see **FIG 7:14**) are rubber bushed at each end and are clamped between brackets on the underbody sidemembers and brackets welded to the tubular portions of the axle housing. They provide fore and aft location of the axle. The coil springs (see **FIG 7:17**) are mounted between the lower arms and rubber-insulated seats on the sidemembers. The upper arms (see **FIG 7:15**) are also rubber bushed at each end. At their front ends they are clamped between brackets on the inner sides of the underbody sidemembers. The rear ends of the upper arms are bolted to sleeved bushes pressed into lugs formed on the axle housing. The upper arms prevent lateral movement of the axle while driving or braking torque is taken on the upper and lower arms.

7:8 Rear spring removal and refitting

If weakness of the rear springs is suspected, check the rear standing height as shown in **FIG 7:16.** This must be measured with the car standing on a level floor and at kerb weight, that is unladen but with a full petrol tank or equivalent weight placed on the tank. All tyre pressures must be correct. Bounce the rear end of the car, then allow it to settle and measure from the floor to the centre of the lower arm front mounting bolt. Take this measurement on both sides of the car. If the results are outside the specified limits given under Technical Data, check front standing height (see **Section 8:4**) to determine whether rear height is being influenced by the condition of the front springs, before renewed rear springs.

FIG 7:17 shows a spring assembly in section. The spring is serviced as an assembly complete with upper

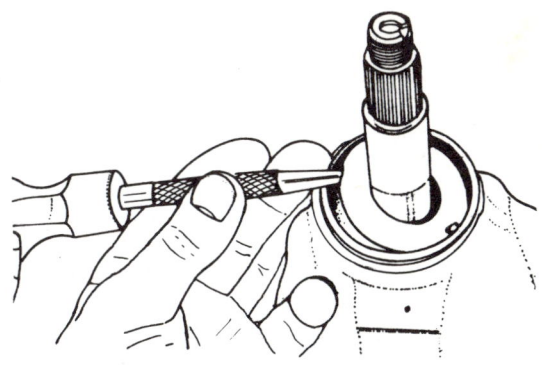

FIG 7:9 Removing pinion shaft oil seal

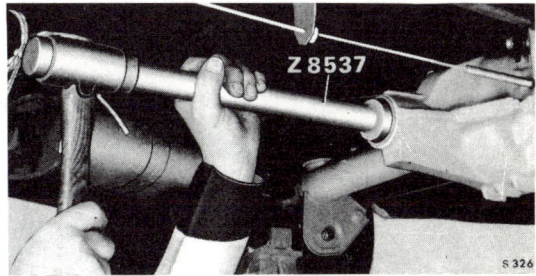

FIG 7:10 Fitting pinion shaft oil seal

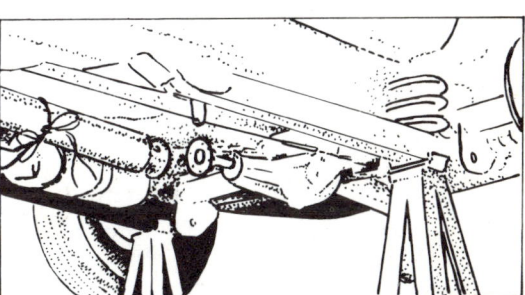

FIG 7:11 Rear axle removal. Car supported under suspension lower arms. Propeller shaft disconnected and tied up

FIG 7:8 Showing alignment marking on coupling flange and pinion shaft

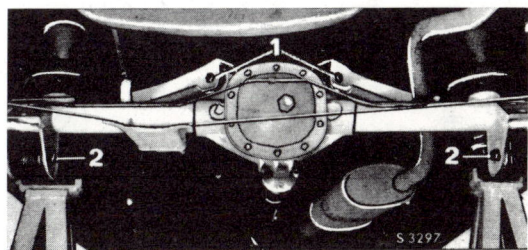

FIG 7:12 To release axle the four mounting bolts 1 and 2 are removed

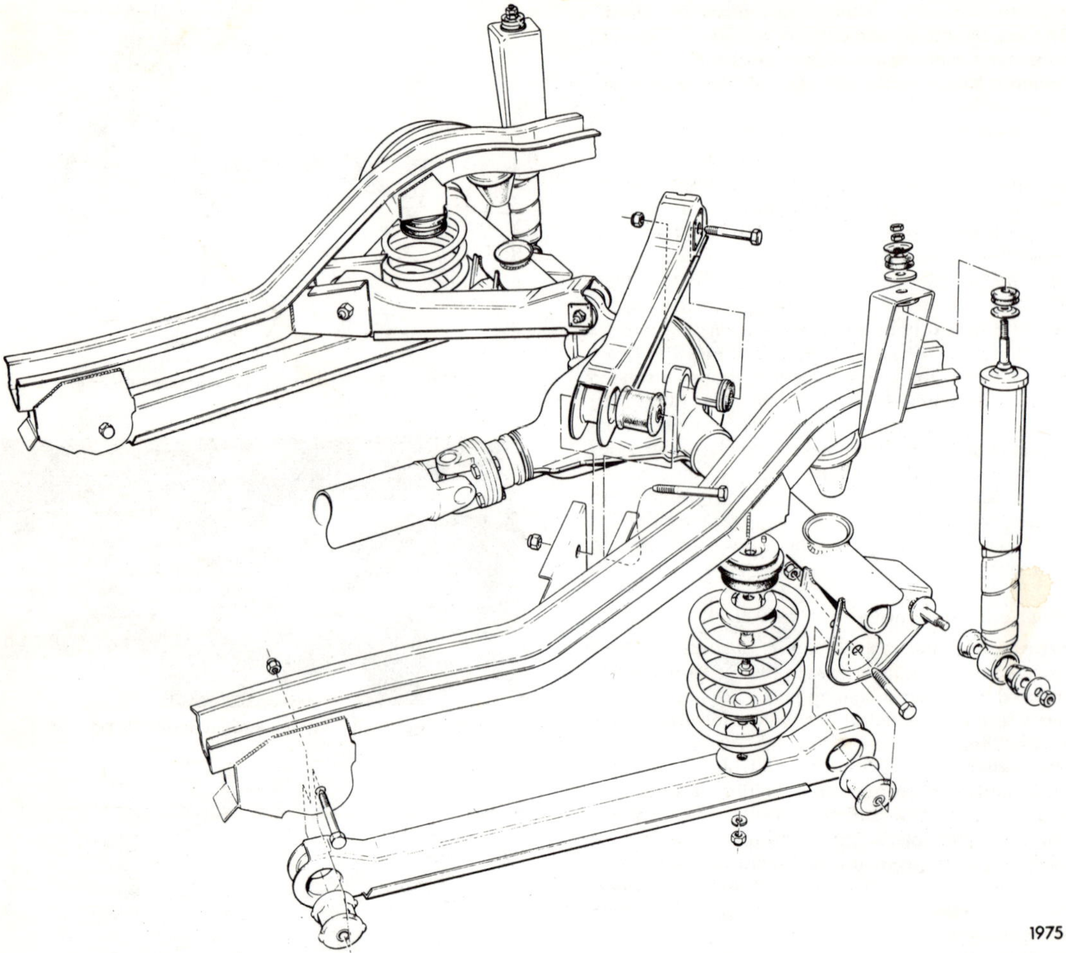

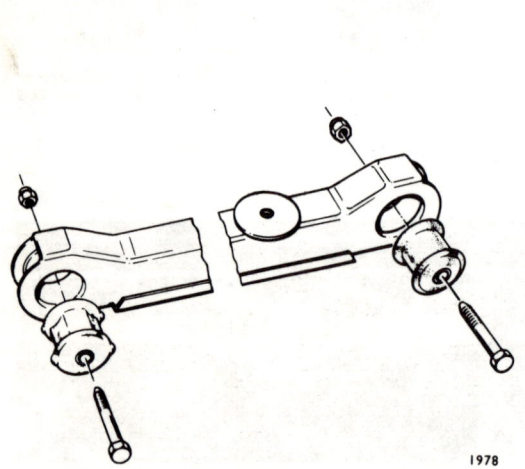

FIG 7:13 Components of rear suspension

1975

FIG 7:14 Rear suspension lower arm and bushes

1978

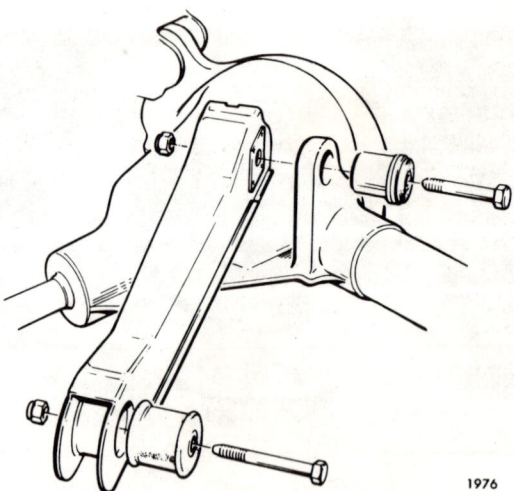

FIG 7:15 Rear suspension upper arm and bushes

1976

seat, insulator and retainer, held together by a peened bush. The upper seat is located by a dowel and bolted to a mounting on the underbody sidemember. The bottom of the spring is secured by a retainer with a stud and nut to the suspension lower arm.

To renew a rear spring:

1 Support the rear of the body firmly on stands. Take the weight of the axle on jacks or a hoist. Remove the rear wheel.
2 Remove the nut from the bottom end of the spring. Lower the axle.
3 Remove the spring upper seat bolt and withdraw the spring.
4 When installing a new spring, ensure that the upper seat dowel engages in the hole in the underbody mounting before tightening the upper bolt.

7:9 Rebushing upper and lower rear suspension arms

To remove the upper suspension arms remove the nuts and bolts at each end of the arm as shown in **FIG 7:15** and withdraw the arm.

To remove suspension lower arms:

1 Support the rear of the body firmly on stands.
2 Take the weight of the rear axle on jacks or on a hoist. Remove the road wheels.
3 Remove the nut from the bottom end of the spring only.
4 Lower the jack supporting the axle. Remove the bolts from the front and rear ends of the lower arm and withdraw the arm.

Special removal and installation tools are available for rebushing the upper and lower arms, three types being necessary in all, namely:

Suspension upper arm front bush—Tool VR.2023
Suspension upper arm rear bush—Tool VR.2026
Suspension lower arm front bush—Tool VR.2023
Suspension lower arm rear bush—Tool VR.2023
For installation of lower arm front bush—Tools VR.2023 and VR.2015

FIG 7:18 shows the removal of a lower arm rear bush. Note that when removing and installing any of the bushes, except the upper arm rear which is pressed into the axle casing lug, the bushes must be removed and installed in the direction indicated by the arrow in **FIG 7:19**. This is to prevent the edge of flange 'A' from cutting into the bush. Use liquid soap to assist in

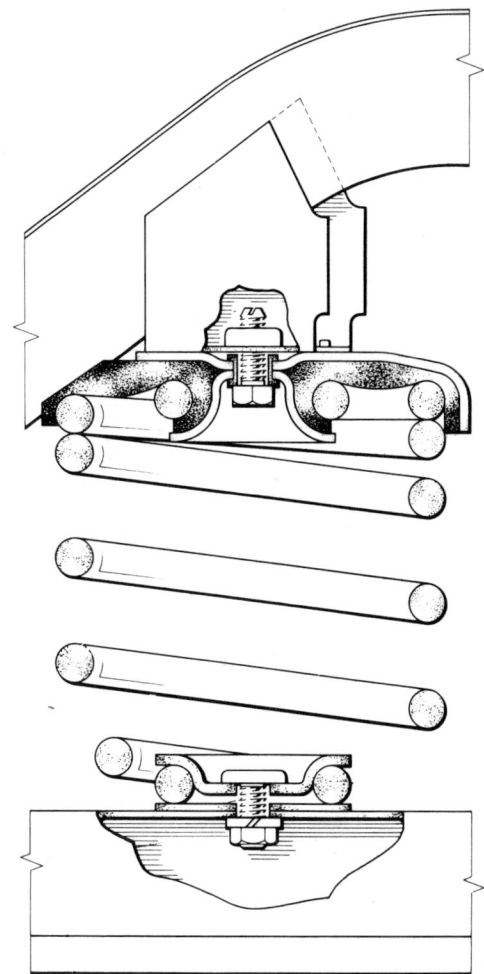

FIG 7:17 Section through rear spring and mounting

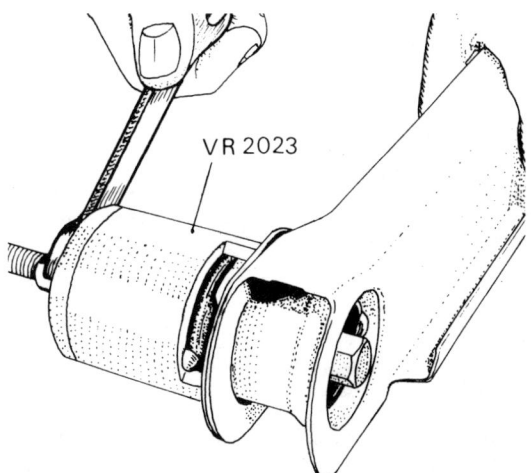

FIG 7:18 Withdrawing lower arm bush

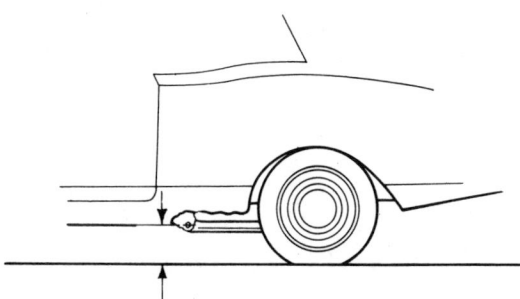

FIG 7:16 Rear standing height check

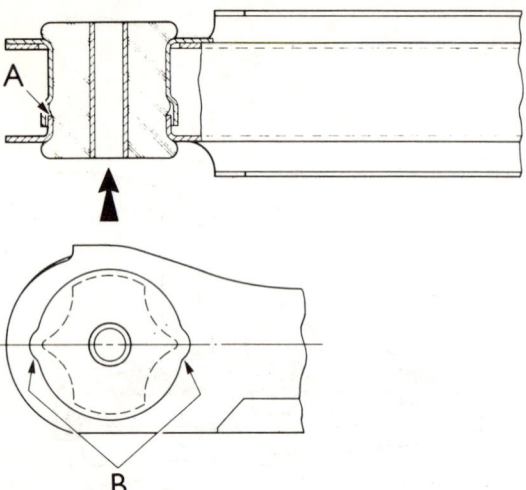

FIG 7:19 Direction of withdrawal or installation of lower arm bushes and upper arm front bush indicated by arrow. Lower arm front bush must be installed with location tabs **B** in position shown

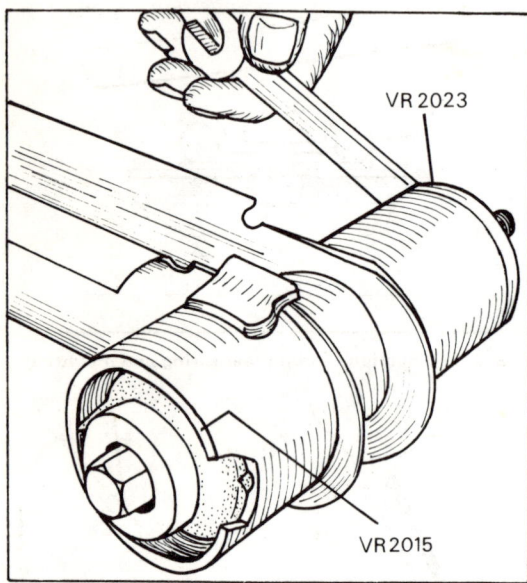

FIG 7:20 Installation of lower arm front bush, showing use of Tool VR.2015

installation. The lower arm front bush must be installed with the location tabs 'B' positioned as in **FIG 7:19**. The additional installer VR.2015 is supplied for this purpose, and is shown in use in **FIG 7:20**.

When refitting the rear suspension arms to the car, it is essential for the weight of the car to rest on the springs before tightening the arm mounting bolts to a torque of 38 lb ft.

7:10 Rear dampers

Double-acting telescopic dampers are fitted to the rear suspension. These cannot be topped up or serviced and if found defective should be renewed. **FIG 7:21** shows details of the damper mounting, which can also be seen in **FIGS 7:3** and **7:13**. Rubber-bushed studs at the top of the dampers are secured to brackets on the underbody, and rubber-bushed eye-mountings at the bottom of the dampers are carried on studs attached to the suspension lower arm mounting brackets on the axle.

If the car is raised to facilitate damper removal, it must be supported under the rear axle. Access to the upper mounting locknuts and securing nuts is obtained by removing the rubber plugs inside the luggage boot. When installing dampers, ensure that the upper mounting washers are correctly assembled as shown in **FIG 7:21**. Fit a steel washer to each bottom bush. The securing nuts should be tightened to the bottom of the stud threads to ensure correct compression of the rubber bushes.

7:11 Fault diagnosis

(a) Noisy axle

1 Insufficient or incorrect lubricant
2 Worn bearings
3 Worn gears

(b) Noises which can be mistaken for axle noise

1 Tyre and road surface noises
2 Defective hub bearings
3 Gearbox noises transmitted through propeller shaft

(c) Excessive backlash

1 Worn gears or bearings
2 Worn axle shaft splines
3 Worn universal joints or loose coupling flange bolts
4 Loose wheel studs

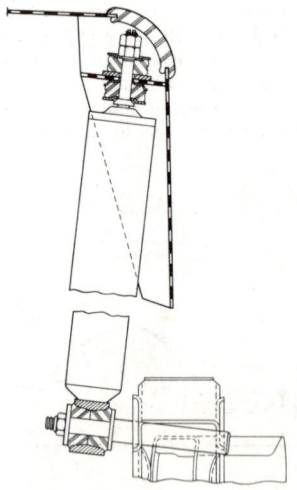

FIG 7:21 Rear damper mountings

(d) Oil leakage

1 Defective pinion shaft oil seal
2 Defective hub oil seals

(e) Vibration

1 Propeller shaft out of balance
2 Worn universal joints

(f) Rattles

1 Worn damper bushes
2 Loose spring seat bolts
3 Defective upper spring seat insulator
4 Worn suspension arm bushes

(g) 'Settling'

1 Weak or broken coil spring(s)

NOTES

CHAPTER 8

FRONT SUSPENSION AND HUBS

8:1 Description of system
8:2 Routine maintenance, lubrication points
8:3 Front hub bearings and seals
8:4 Checking, removing and refitting front springs
8:5 Suspension arm ball joints

8:6 Suspension arm bushes
8:7 Control rods
8:8 Front dampers
8:9 Suspension geometry
8:10 Fault diagnosis

8:1 Description of system

The independent front suspension is of the short and long arm type with coil springs and is shown in **FIG 8:1**. The wishbone type upper arms and single lower arms are rubber bushed at their inner ends and pivot on fulcrum bolts attached to a crossmember bolted to the underbody. At the outer ends of upper and lower arms ball joints carry the steering knuckles (or stub axles). The coil springs and telescopic dampers are fitted between the crossmember and the lower arms. Adjustable control rods are bolted to the lower arms and rubber mounted in the crossmember braces. Bump and rebound stops are incorporated in the dampers. Reference to the illustration will show that up and down movement is controlled by the coil springs and dampers, while fore and aft rigidity is provided by the triangulated upper arms and the control rods attached to the lower arms.

8:2 Routine maintenance, lubrication points

There are only four points which require lubrication on the front suspension system, these being the upper and lower suspension arm ball joints, two grease nipples being placed on each side of the vehicle. Inject sufficient lubricant of the recommended grade to ensure the rubber boots are filled, but do not over-lubricate as this will damage the rubber boots. On disc brake models the utmost care must be taken not to allow grease to find its way on to the disc or friction pads. Lubrication of hub bearings is dealt with in the following Section.

8:3 Front hub bearings and seals

The front hub bearings are of the taper roller type and are packed with grease during assembly to the hub. The grease is retained by a steel grease cap on the outer side of the hub and by an oil seal on the inner side. On cars fitted with drum brakes this is of felt, while on those with disc brakes a spring-loaded neoprene seal is fitted. The hubs are shown in section in **FIG 8:2** and **FIG 8:3** is an exploded view showing the bearings and seals. It is essential that only the recommended grease is used and that only the rollers are lubricated. The hub itself must not be packed with grease.

When checking the adjustment of front hub bearings note that it is possible to rock a front wheel when jacked

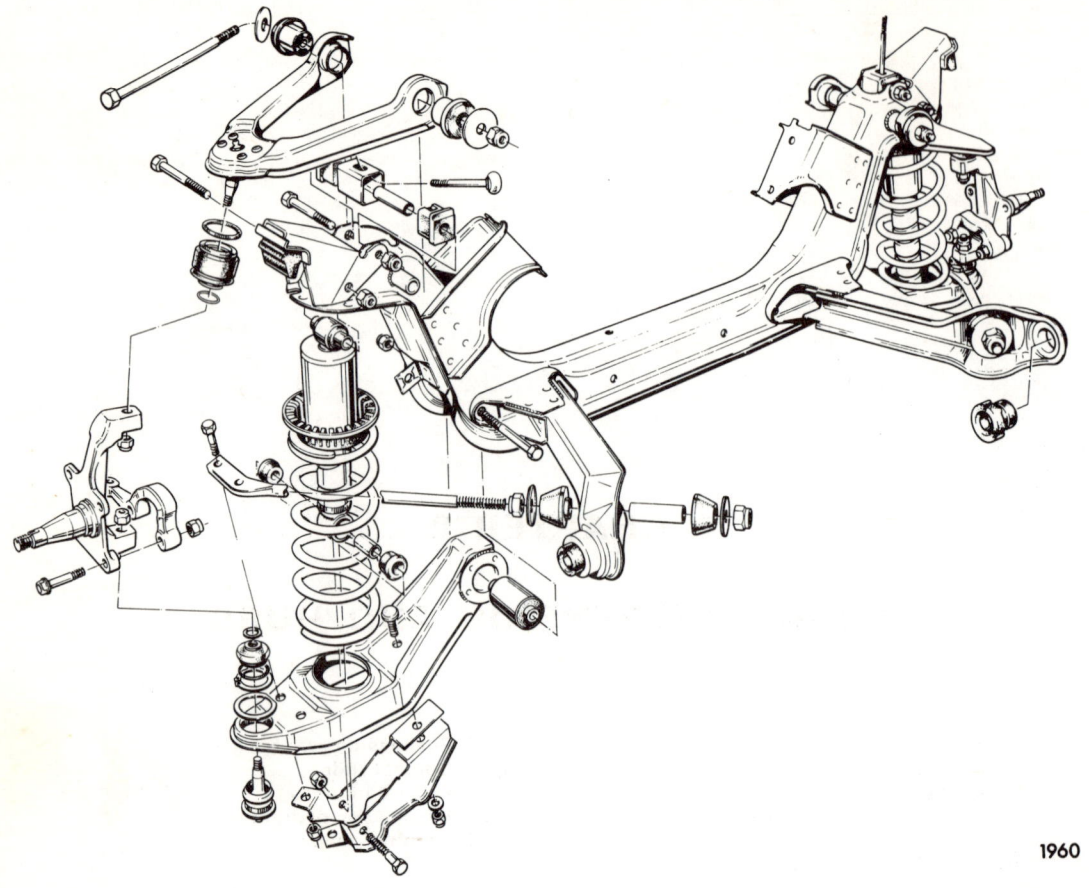

FIG 8:1   Components of front suspension (lefthand side)

1960

up owing to the clearance in the suspension lower arm ball joint when free of load. To eliminate possible errors proceed as follows:

1 Jack up the front wheel.
2 Check that the brakes are not binding.
3 Eliminate play in the lower ball joint by levering with a bar between the steering knuckle and the control rod bolts as shown in **FIG 8:4.** While holding the ball joint firm, rock the wheel to test for slackness in bearings.

If only slight play is perceptible, adjust the bearings · as follows:

1 Remove the wheel disc and the hub grease cap.
2 Remove and discard the splitpin, then tighten the nut using a tubular box spanner with an 8 inch tommy bar.
3 Slacken the nut and remove the tommy bar, then gripping the spanner by hand only, retighten the nut.
4 Insert a new splitpin, turning the nut **back** if necessary to align the splitpin hole. The final end float should be .002 to .005 inch.
5 Refit the grease cap and wheel disc.

If the preliminary check shows excessive slackness or roughness in the bearings, or if there is any sign of contamination of the grease by water or grit, it is essential to remove the hub for examination of the bearings as follows:

1 Remove the wheel.
2 (Drum brakes) Slacken brake shoe adjustment. (Disc brakes) Remove the caliper. For details refer to **Chapter 10.**
3 Remove the grease cap, splitpin, hub nut and keyed washer (see **FIG 8:3**).
4 Remove the hub complete with brake drum or disc.

To remove the outer races of the inner and outer bearings, drive them out by means of a drift from the opposite end. The oil seal will be driven out with the inner bearing outer race. On disc brake models care must be taken not to damage the surfaces of the disc. (To remove the disc undo the bolts with tab washers at the back of the hub.) For general notes on inspection and cleaning of bearings reference should be made to the Hints on Maintenance in the Appendix.

Examine the wheel bolts and if these have damaged threads or are loose in the hub flange new ones should be fitted. This work can be more conveniently carried out by a service agent using a hydraulic press.

To reassemble and install the hub:

1 Assemble the bearing outer races, wide end first, squarely into the hub and ensure that each race is fully home against the shoulder (see **FIG 8 : 2**).
2 Pack the inner bearing inner race and rollers with the recommended grease and install in the hub. Do not pack the hub itself with grease.
3 (Drum brakes) Press the felt oil seal on to the hub. (Disc brakes) Press the neoprene oil seal into the hub with the lip facing into the hub.
4 Fit the drum or disc to the hub. (Disc brakes) If all the locking tabs for the disc bolts have been used, fit new tab washers. Tighten and lock each bolt with one tab (see **FIG 8 : 3**).
5 Pack the outer bearing inner race with grease. Refit the hub, outer bearing, keyed washer and hub nut. Adjust the bearings as already described.
6 (Drum brakes) Adjust the brakes. (Disc brakes) Before installing the caliper refer to the Section on installation in **Chapter 10**.

8 : 4 Checking, removing and refitting front springs

If weakness of the front springs is suspected, check the front standing height as shown in **FIG 8 : 5**. This must be measured with the car standing on a level floor and at kerb weight, that is unladen but with a full petrol tank or equivalent weight placed on the tank. All tyre pressures must be correct. Bounce the front end of the car, then allow it to settle and measure from the floor to the centre of each lower fulcrum bolt. If the results are outside the specified limits given under Technical Data, check the rear standing height (see **Section 7 : 8**) to determine whether front height is being influenced by the condition of the rear springs before renewing the front springs.

To remove a front spring, proceed as follows:

1 Support the car firmly under the body. **Care must be taken to ensure the safety of the operator when working underneath the car.**
2 Remove the road wheel.

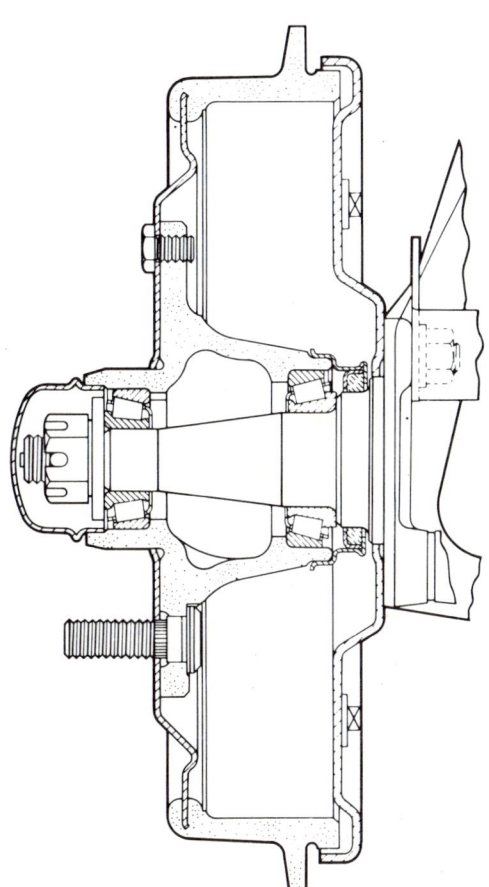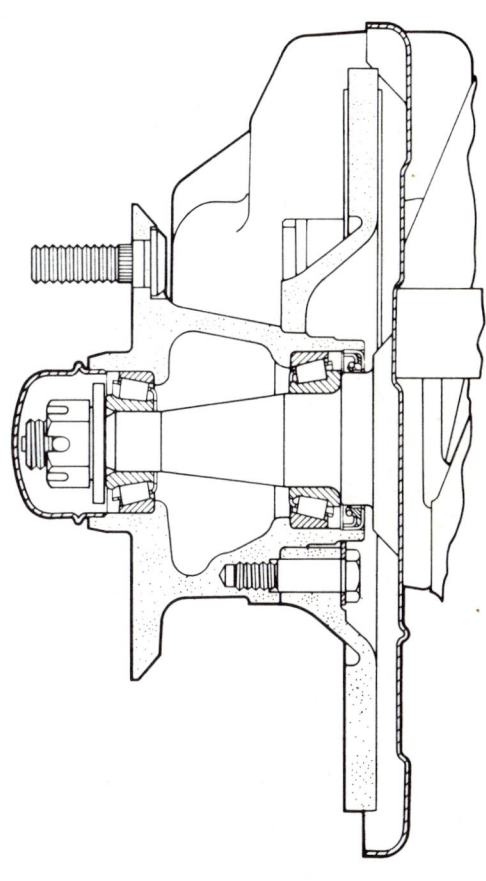

FIG 8:2 Sectional view of front hubs showing drum brakes on left, disc brakes on right

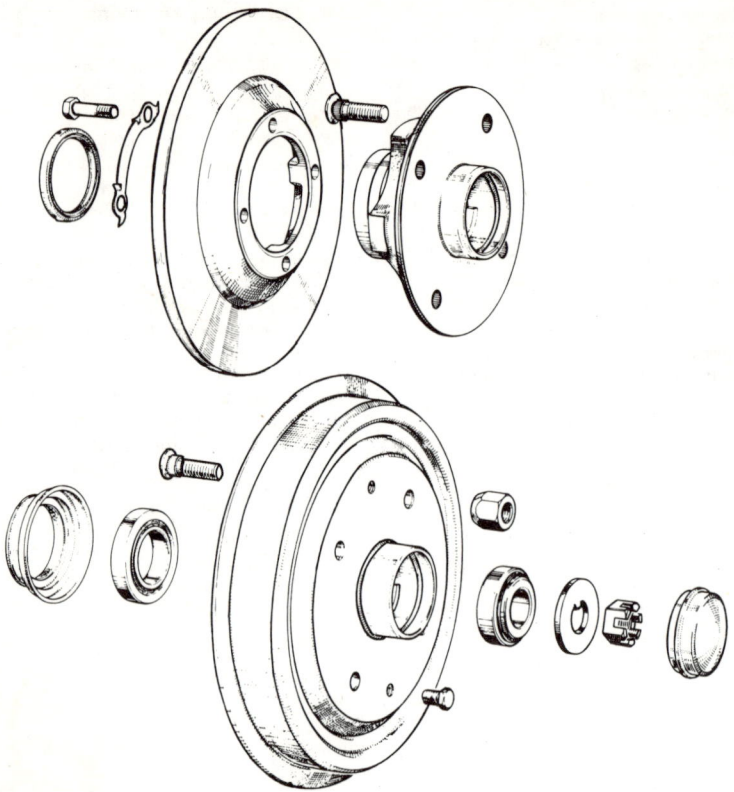

FIG 8:3 Hub bearing outer race removal. The upper illustration shows those parts which differ in the case of disc brakes

3 Remove the four nuts indicated by arrows in **FIG 8:6**. Detach the control rod from the lower suspension arm and slacken the lower arm fulcrum bolt nut.

4 Using the special Spring Compressor VR.2001 compress the spring as shown in **FIG 8:7**.

5 Remove the damper lower mounting bolt and brackets as shown in **FIG 8:8**.

6 Using the special Ball Joint Remover JWP.362, release the lower arm ball joint from the steering knuckle as shown in **FIG 8:9**. Before fitting the tool remove the splitpin and unscrew the nut sufficiently to protect the end of the thread.

7 Release the spring compressor and withdraw the spring as shown in **FIG 8:10**.

Note that the lefthand spring should be about $\frac{3}{16}$ inch longer than the righthand. Springs are therefore not interchangeable. There are three different spring lengths to cover the requirements of standard and heavy duty suspension.

Refitting of springs follows a reversal of the procedure for removal but the following points should be noted:

1 Ensure that the spring is correctly located on the lower arm seat.

2 Check that the rubber boot is correctly located.

3 Ensure that mating tapers are clean and free from grease before refitting the ball joint.

4 The lower arm fulcrum bolt should be tightened to a torque of 42 lb ft with the weight of the car on the tyres.

8:5 Suspension arm ball joints

The suspension upper arm ball joints can be checked for slackness with the wheels on the ground by attempting to rock the top of the wheel sideways while holding the ball joint. No play should be perceptible at this point.

To check the lower arm ball joints, raise the front wheels and tighten the hub nut (see **Section 8:3**) to eliminate slackness in the wheel bearings. Mount a clock gauge as shown in **FIG 8:11** to register on the wheel rim. Lift the wheel as shown to check vertical clearance in the joint, but do not use excessive force or the suspension arm will be raised and a false reading obtained. If the clearance exceeds .085 inch the joint must be renewed. On completion of the check readjust the wheel bearings.

An upper arm ball joint is shown in section in **FIG 8:12**. The joint has seatings which are internally loaded by a neoprene pressure ring (arrowed) and must not be compressed in a vice for assessment of wear. The joint must be renewed if there is any perceptible slackness of the ball in its seatings. To renew the joint proceed as follows:

1 Remove the suspension upper arm as described in **Section 8:6**.

2 Production joints are riveted to the upper arm as shown in **FIGS 8:12** and **8:16**. Replacement joints are secured by nuts and bolts. Drill and chisel off the rivet heads on the old joint and drill out the holes in the arm to $\frac{5}{16}$ inch diameter.

FIG 8:4 Checking for play in front hub bearings

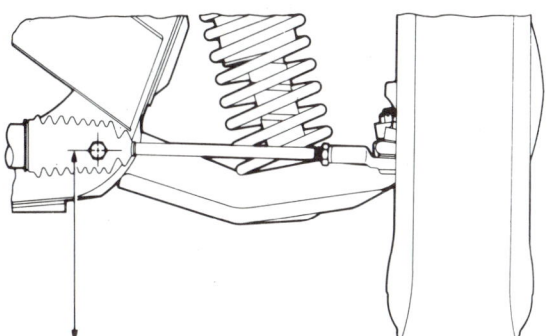

FIG 8:5 Front standing height check

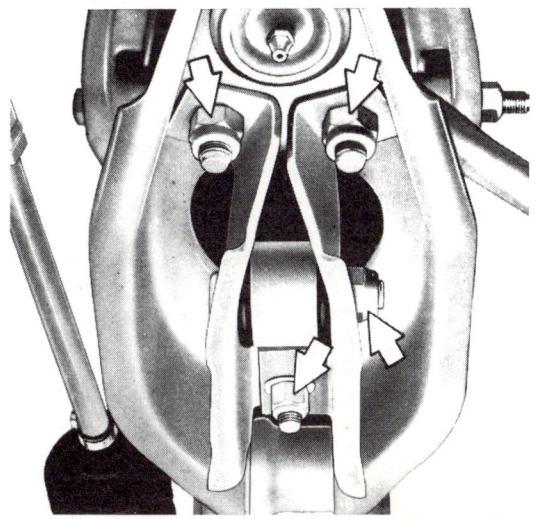

FIG 8:6 Front spring or damper removal. The four nuts (arrowed) must be removed before fitting spring compressor

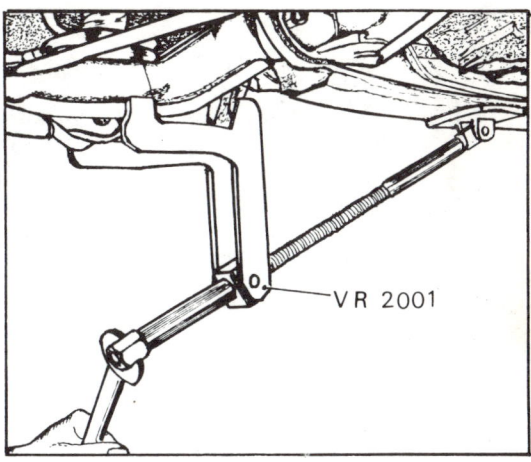

FIG 8:7 Showing use of Tool VR.2001, for spring or damper removal

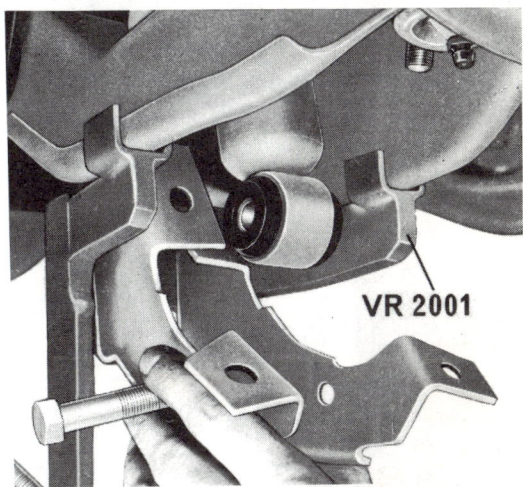

FIG 8:8 Removing damper brackets and lower mounting bolt

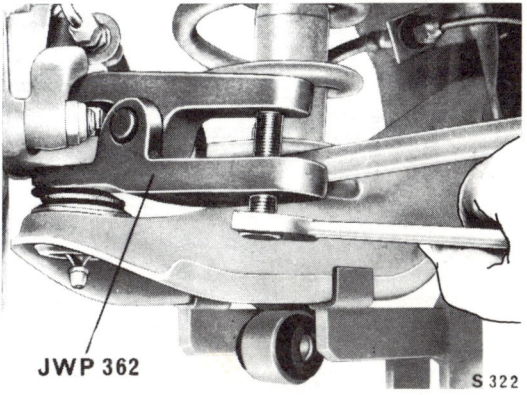

FIG 8:9 Releasing lower arm ball joint with Tool JWP.362

FIG 8:10 Withdrawing a front spring

FIG 8:11 Checking for play in lower arm ball joint

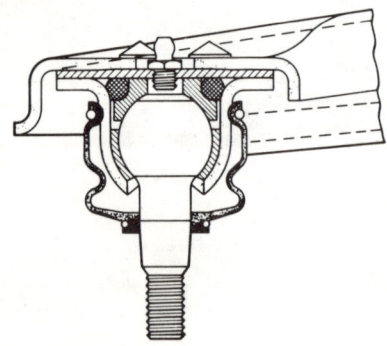

FIG 8:12 Suspension upper arm ball joint

3 Bolt the new joint to the arm and tighten the nuts to a torque of 22 lb ft with clean dry threads.

4 Refit the arm as described in **Section 8:6**.

A lower arm ball joint is shown in section in **FIG 8:13**. This is of the pendant type and the ball has a clearance of up to .053 inch in the socket when new. The joint is secured in the lower arm by a circlip and a special washer. It can be renewed without removal of the suspension lower arm as follows:

1 Support the car under the lower damper mounting bolt bracket, settling it firmly in the vee of an axle stand. **Care must be taken to ensure the safety of the operator when working underneath the car.**

2 Remove the road wheel.

3 Release the lower arm ball joint from the steering knuckle after removing the splitpin and nut, using the Remover JWP.362.

4 Slacken the upper arm fulcrum bolt and wedge the upper arm in the raised position.

5 Remove the circlip and the special washer.

6 Using a suitable piece of tube, drive out the joint as shown in **FIG 8:14**. Engage the splines of the new joint with those in the arm and drive the joint home.

7 Locate the special washer with the flat in the position shown in **FIG 8:15** and with the concave side upwards and install a new circlip.

8 Assemble the ball joint to the steering knuckle and tighten the nut to a torque of 33 lb ft. Where necessary tighten further to align the splitpin hole and secure with a new splitpin.

9 Refit the road wheel and with the weight of the car on the tyres tighten the upper arm fulcrum nut to a torque of 55 lb ft.

8:6 Suspension arm bushes

The wishbone type suspension upper arms are rubber bushed and secured to the front axle crossmember by long fulcrum bolts and nuts as shown in **FIG 8:16**. To remove the upper arms proceed as follows:

1 Support the car under the lower damper mounting bolt bracket, **settling it firmly in the vee of an axle stand.** Remove the road wheel.

2 Disconnect the upper arm ball joint from the steering knuckle, using the Special Remover JWP.362 (shown in use on the lower joint in **FIG 8:9**). Before fitting the tool remove the splitpin and unscrew the nut sufficiently to protect the end of the thread.

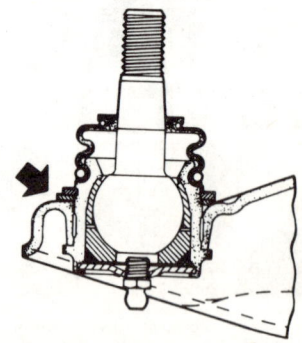

FIG 8:13 Suspension lower arm ball joint

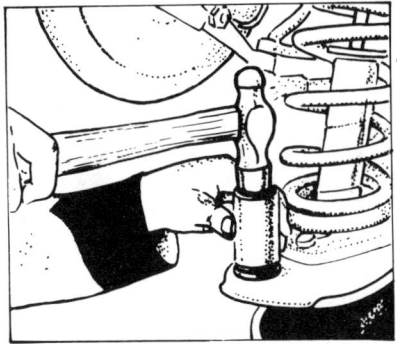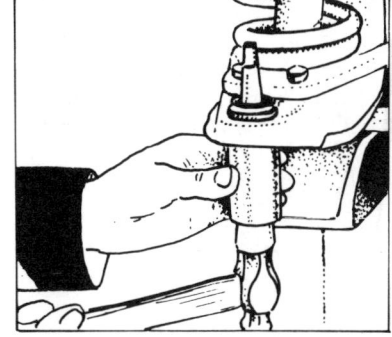

FIG 8:14 Suspension lower arm. (Left) Removing ball joint. (Right) Refitting ball joint

3 Remove the fulcrum bolt, if necessary bending the lashing eye to provide sufficient clearance.

To renew the bushes, remove the old bushes and install the new ones using the Special Remover and Installer VR.2023. This tool is used in the same manner as that described for the rear suspension bushes in **Section 7:9** and illustrated in **FIG 7:18**. It is also essential for bushes to be removed and installed in the direction of the arrow indicated in **FIG 7:19 (A)**.

When reassembling, ensure that the rubber boot is in good condition and correctly located and that the mating tapers are clean and free from grease before fitting the ball joint. Tighten the nut to a torque of 33 lb ft. Where necessary tighten further to align the next splitpin hole and fit a new splitpin. Retighten the upper arm fulcrum bolt to a torque of 37 lb ft with the weight of the car resting on the tyres.

Each front suspension lower arm (see **FIG 8:17**) is pivoted on the front axle crossmember by a single rubber bush clamped between the flanges by a fulcrum bolt and nut. To renew the bushes proceed as follows:

1 Remove the front spring as described in **Section 8:4, taking particular note of the safety precautions to be observed.**
2 Remove the fulcrum bolt and nut and withdraw the arm.
3 Cut off the flange of the old bush with a sharp knife to prevent distortion of the arm during removal of the bush.
4 Remove and install the bush using the special Remover and Installer VR.2023 as described and illustrated for the rear suspension bushes in **Section 7:9.**

8:7 Control rods

An adjustable control rod is fitted between each front suspension lower arm and a brace attached to the front axle crossmember. In addition to providing fore and aft stability for the lower arms, the control rods (see **FIG 8:18**) provide a means of adjusting and controlling the castor angle (see **Section 8:9**).

To facilitate removal and refitting of the control rod, the car should be supported under the suspension lower arm. After installing the control rod, the castor angle must be checked and the rod adjusted as required. The lower arm bolts and rear nut should be tightened to a torque of 32 lb ft.

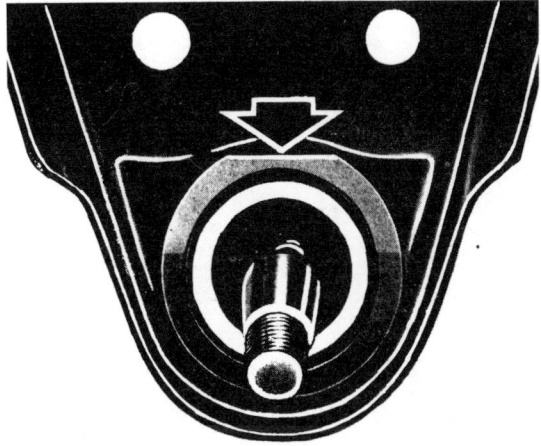

FIG 8:15 Lower arm ball joint showing location of special washer

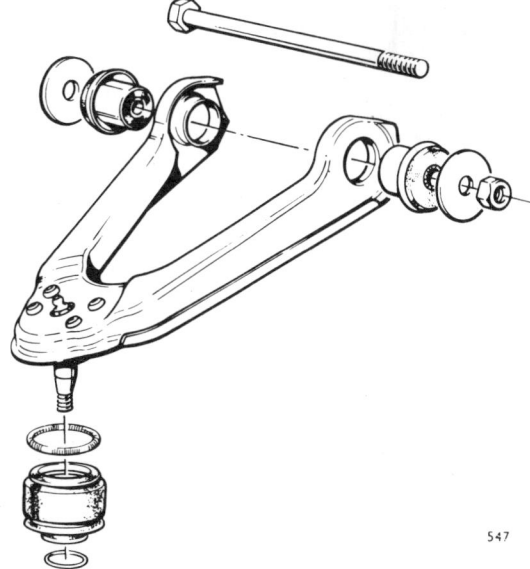

547

FIG 8:16 Upper arm showing fulcrum bolt and bushes

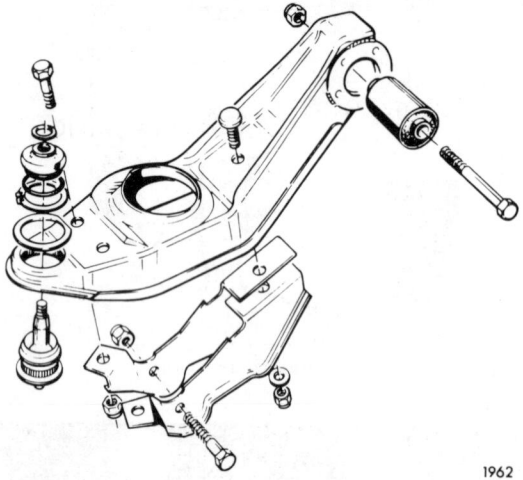

FIG 8:17 Lower arm showing ball joint, damper brackets, bush and fulcrum bolt

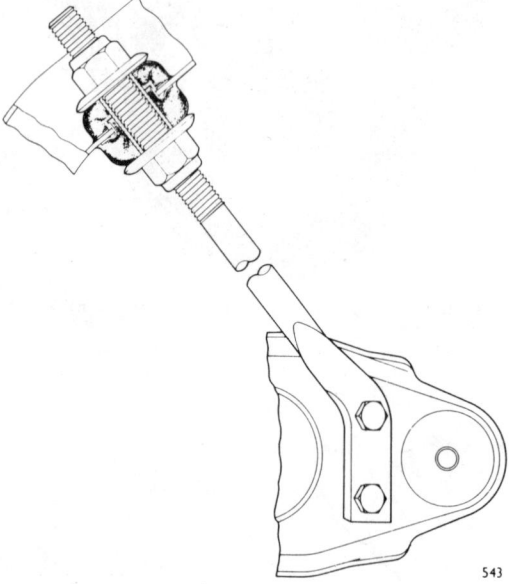

FIG 8:18 Front suspension control rod

8:8 Front dampers

The double acting telescopic dampers are not adjustable and no provision is made for topping up. If the dampers are defective they must be renewed. The upper mounting bush is not separately renewable and must be serviced with the damper. The lower eye bushes are renewable. Bump and rebound stops are incorporated in the dampers. To remove the dampers proceed as follows:

1 Support the car firmly under the body. **Care must be taken to ensure the safety of the operator when working underneath the car.**

2 Remove the nuts indicated by arrows in **FIG 8:6**.
3 Compress the spring using the special Spring Compressor VR.2001 as shown in **FIG 8:7**. **Note that the damper upper mounting bolt must not be disturbed when the front wheels are off the floor unless the car is supported under the suspension lower arm or the Spring Compressor is in place.**
4 After compressing the spring, remove the damper lower mounting bolt and brackets as shown in **FIG 8:8**.
5 Remove the damper upper mounting bolt and withdraw the damper.

Renew the lower eye bushes if necessary. These are fitted by hand. When installing the damper, loosely assemble the lower mounting bolt and brackets to the eye bushes before engaging the upper mounting. Tighten the top mounting bolt to a torque of 32 lb ft and the lower mounting bolt to 57 lb ft.

8:9 Suspension geometry

Although affecting the steering, castor angle, camber and steering pivot inclination are controlled by components of the front suspension system and are therefore dealt with in the present chapter. Toe-in and toe-out on turns will be covered in the section on adjustment of front wheel alignment in **Chapter 9**.

Professional equipments for checking suspension and steering geometry are unlikely to be available to the owner, so that unless the work is entrusted to a service agent, improvisation will be called for. Whatever type of

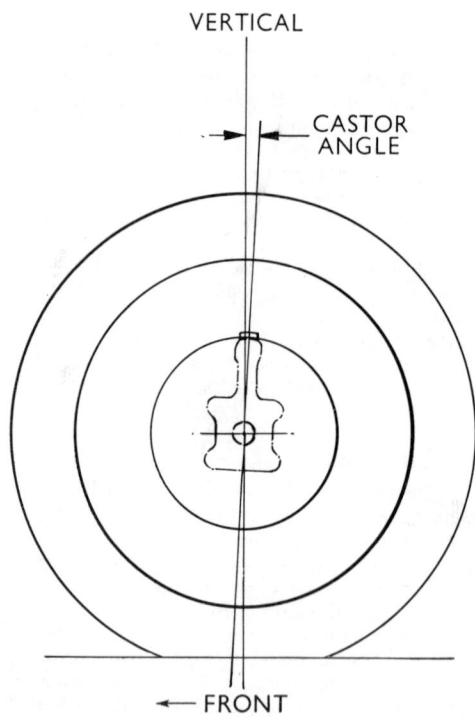

FIG 8:19 Diagram showing castor angle

measuring equipment is used, however, the car must be on a level floor and tyre pressures, front and rear standing height, front hub bearings and suspension joints must be in order.

FIG 8:19 shows castor angle, which can be adjusted by means of the control rod front nut as shown in **FIG 8:20**. To increase castor the control rod must be lengthened. To decrease, the rod must be shortened. Tighten the rear nut to 32 lb ft before rechecking the castor angle. After adjusting castor angle, the toe-in (see **Chapter 9**) must be checked and if necessary adjusted. The necessary dimensions for both will be found in Technical Data.

FIG 8:21 shows camber angle and pivot pin inclination. These should be checked in accordance with dimensions given in Technical Data. If camber angle is below the low limit and steering pivot inclination correspondingly greater, or if camber angle is above the high limit and steering pivot inclination correspondingly less, this will indicate distorted suspension arms or crossmember. If, however, steering pivot inclination is within the specified limits but camber angle is outside the limits, this indicates a distorted steering knuckle.

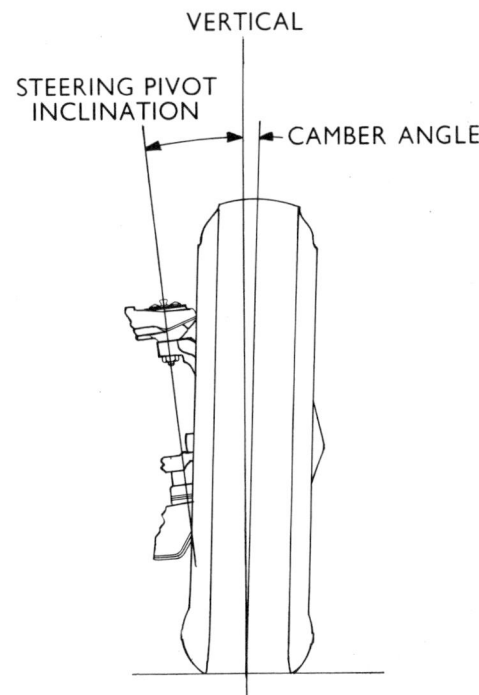

FIG 8:21 Diagram showing camber angle and steering pivot inclination

8:10 Fault diagnosis

(Reference should also be made to **Section 9:10**)

(a) Suspension hard

1 Tyre pressures too high
2 Suspension arm ball joints stiff
3 Dampers faulty

(b) Suspension soft (or 'bottoming')

1 Dampers faulty
2 Damper bump stops faulty
3 Weak spring(s)

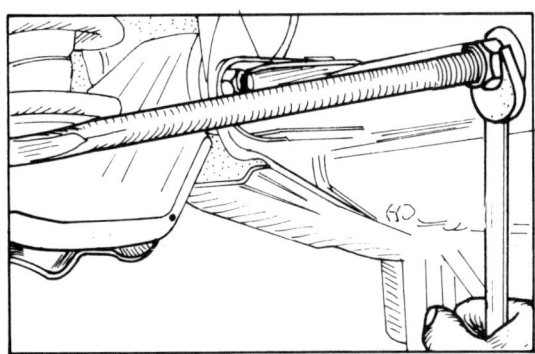

FIG 8:20 Adjusting castor angle with control rod

(c) Wheel wobble

1 Wheels and tyres out of balance
2 Suspension or steering geometry incorrect
3 Dampers faulty
4 Steering slack
5 Loose wheel nuts or bolts loose in flange
6 Worn hub bearings

(d) Heavy steering

1 Low front tyre pressures
2 Suspension or steering geometry incorrect
3 Suspension arm ball joints stiff

(e) Steering slack

1 Front hub bearings loose

(f) Steering wander

1 Low or uneven tyre pressures
2 Road wheel loose
3 Crossmember mountings loose
4 Steering geometry incorrect
5 Control rod loose

(g) Brake judder

Check 5 in (f)
(For other brake faults refer to **Chapter 10**)

NOTES

CHAPTER 9

THE STEERING GEAR

9:1 Description
9:2 Routine maintenance
9:3 Steering gear removal
9:4 Steering gear installation
9:5 Renewing inner ball joint rubber boots

9:6 Tie rod outer ball joints
9:7 Front wheel alignment
9:8 Steering shaft and column
9:9 Steering column lock
9:10 Fault diagnosis

9:1 Description

FIG 9:1 shows the layout of the steering gear and steering column. The rack and pinion type steering gear is secured to the front axle crossmember by three nuts and bolts. A tie rod is connected to each end of the rack by a ball joint enclosed in a concertina type rubber boot. The outer end of each tie rod is threaded into a ball joint attached to the steering arms. Steering lock is controlled by the inner ball joint housings contacting the steering gear housing.

A flexible coupling with riveted flanges is connected to the splined ends of the steering gear pinion shaft and steering shaft. The energy absorbing steering column is supported by brackets to the lower and upper dash panels. The column incorporates a combined steering lock and ignition switch.

The steering wheel is a push fit on the splined steering shaft and secured by a nut.

9:2 Routine maintenance

There are no grease nipples on the steering gear or connections. Maintenance is confined to a renewal of the rubber boots on the rack and pinion gear should these become defective, in which case the gear will be refilled with oil. This operation is described in **Section 9:5**. The tie rod outer ball joints are lubricated on assembly and the checking and renewal of these components is described in **Section 9:6**.

The rack and pinion steering gear should not be dismantled. If it becomes defective a replacement unit must be fitted. Instructions for removal and refitting are given in **Sections 9:3** and **9:4**.

9:3 Steering gear removal

To remove the rack and pinion steering gear for the purpose of fitting a replacement unit or for renewal of the concertina type rubber boots, proceed as follows:

1 Using the Extractor Z.8563 remove the cotter from the steering shaft coupling as shown in **FIG 9:2**.
2 Using the claw type Extractor JWP.362, detach the tie rod outer ball joints from the steering arms as shown in **FIG 9:3**.
3 Remove the three nuts and bolts securing the steering gear to the front axle crossmember and withdraw the steering gear complete with tie rods.

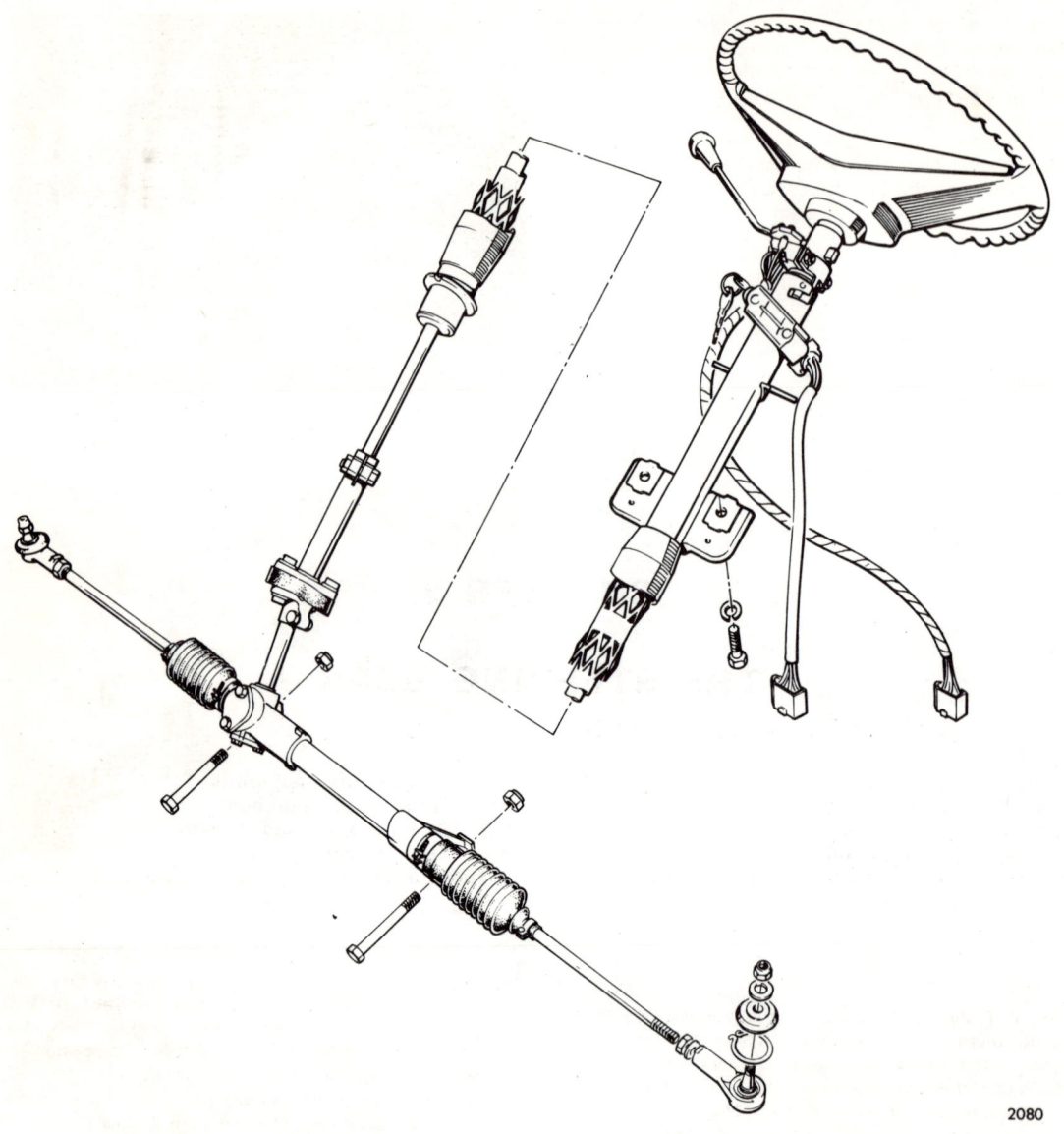

FIG 9:1 Layout of steering gear and steering column assembly

2080

9:4 Steering gear installation

Refit the rack and pinion gear as follows:

Secure the steering gear to the front axle crossmember and tighten the three nuts and bolts to a torque of 19 lb ft with clean dry threads. After ensuring that mating tapers are clean and free from grease, attach the outer ball joints to the steering arms. Tighten the nuts to 24 lb ft. Tighten the coupling flange cotter nut to a torque of 7 lb ft. Check that the nuts on the four bolts securing the upper and lower flanges of the coupling are tightened to 12 lb ft.

Check and if necessary adjust alignment according to the instructions given in **Section 9:7**.

9:5 Renewing inner ball joint rubber boots

The concertina type rubber boots on the rack and pinion steering gear (see **FIG 9:1**) not only protect the tie rod inner ball joints but are essential to retain the oil in the rack and pinion housing and to prevent entry of grit. If either or both of the boots is found to be defective, they should both be renewed as follows:

1 Remove the steering gear as described in the previous Section, but before removing the outer ball joints from the steering arms, slacken the locknuts at each end of the tie rod, leaving them in contact with the ball joints but only finger tight. This will greatly

88

facilitate the removal of the ball joints from the tie rod. Mark the position of the locknut on the tie rod with paint or count the number of threads visible to facilitate adjustment on reassembly.

2 Unscrew the ball joints and remove the locknuts.

3 Release the four boot clips and remove the boots.

4 Ensure that all oil is drained from the gear housing.

5 Fit a new boot at the end opposite the pinion shaft. Locate the boot clips so that when fitted to the car the screws will be in front and with their heads downwards.

6 Refill the steering gear by pouring in $\frac{1}{4}$ pint of SAE.90 gear oil at the pinion end as shown in **FIG 9:4**. **The specified quantity of oil must not be exceeded.**

7 Fit a new boot to the pinion end, also ensuring that the clips are located as under item 5.

8 Screw the tie rod locknuts and outer ball joints back into their original positions. Tighten the locknuts.

9 Refit the steering gear as described in the previous Section. Check and if necessary adjust alignment as described in **Section 9:7**.

9:6 Tie rod outer ball joints

The tie rod outer ball joints are of the spring-loaded type with nylon seatings and it is therefore possible to move the socket in line with the stud against compression of the spring when a load is applied. Check by attempting to move the joint up and down as indicated by the arrows in **FIG 9:5**. With a new joint, movement under a load of 50 lb can be up to .04 inch. The maximum permissible movement on a used joint is .08 inch. If this limit is exceeded, or if there is any free play which can be felt without applying pressure, the joint must be renewed.

Proceed as follows:

1 Slacken the locknut on the tie rod, leaving it in contact with the ball joint but only finger tight.

2 Slacken the ball joint stud nut sufficiently to protect the end of the thread and release the ball joint from the steering arm using the special Remover JWP.362 as shown in **FIG 9:3**. Remove the nut.

3 Unscrew the ball joint from the tie rod holding the locknut in position to facilitate adjustment on reassembly.

4 Screw the new ball joint on to the tie rod until it contacts the locknut. Ensure that the mating tapers are clean and free from grease and tighten the ball joint stud nut to 24 lb ft. Hold the ball joint by means of a spanner on the flats provided and tighten the locknut.

5 Check and if necessary adjust the toe-in as described in **Section 9:7**.

9:7 Front wheel alignment

Castor angle, camber and steering pivot inclination, although affecting steering, are determined by the condition and adjustment of the front suspension and have therefore been dealt with in the previous Chapter.

When the two front wheels of a car are viewed from vertically overhead it will be seen that they are not

FIG 9:2 Steering shaft coupling

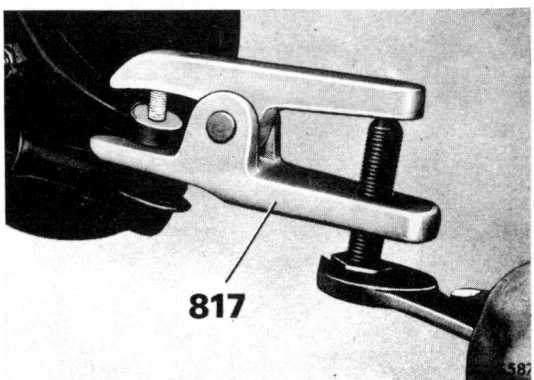

FIG 9:3 Removing tie rod outer ball joints

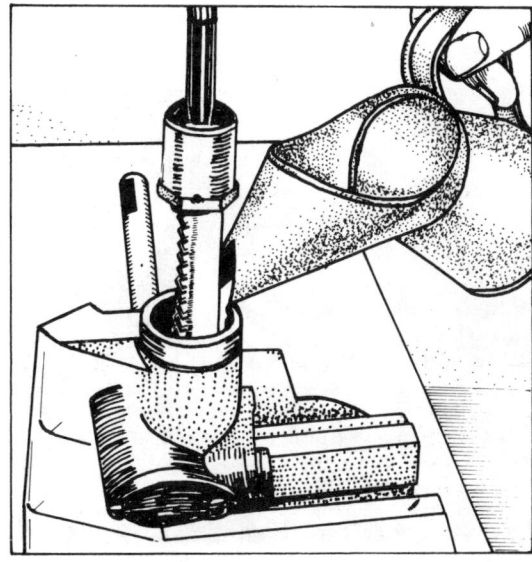

FIG 9:4 Refilling steering gear with oil

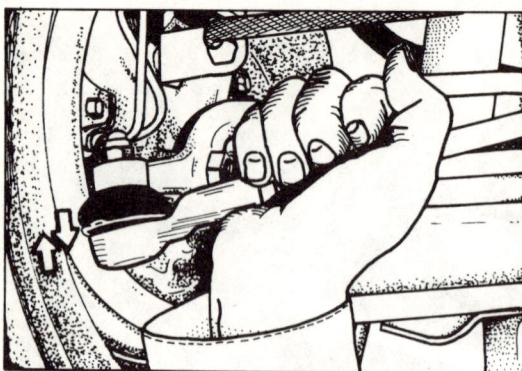

FIG 9:5 Checking outer ball joint for play

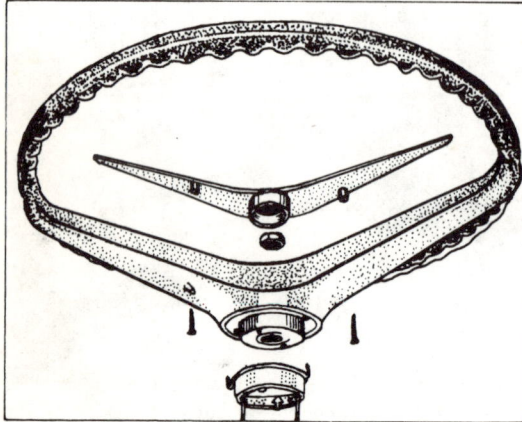

FIG 9:6 Steering wheel attachment

FIG 9:7 Showing steering wheel boss and turn signal switch

necessarily parallel but may either point in towards each other at the front or diverge a little according to the design and construction of the vehicle. These two conditions are known as toe-in and toe-out respectively.

In the case of the Viva HC the front wheels may be set with a tolerance of .045 inch on either side of straight-ahead and although this measurement is best made and the adjustment set by a qualified service station with the necessary equipment, an acceptable degree of accuracy can be obtained by using the following method:

Place the car on a level floor with the wheels in the straight-ahead position. Make sure that the tyres are correctly inflated.

Make a chalk mark on the inside of each wheel rim at the front and at wheel centre height and measure the distance between the two marks. Then roll the car forward by one half of a revolution of the road wheels so that the chalk marks are now at the back of the wheels and again measure the distance between them. If the second measurement is greater than the first, the wheels may be said to toe-in by the amount of the difference and vice versa.

If necessary, the front-wheel alignment should be adjusted as follows:

(a) Slacken the retaining clips securing the rubber boots on the steering gear, to prevent them being twisted when the tie rods are turned.

(b) Slacken each outer ball joint locknut and adjust the toe-in. Both rods have righthand threads. The rods must be adjusted by an equal amount, that is the same amount of thread must be visible each end.

(c) Tighten the locknuts and recheck the toe-in.

(d) Tighten boot clips so that the screws are in front with their heads downwards and readily accessible.

Toe-out on turns is a measurement which is not adjustable being controlled by the shape of the steering arms. Its purpose is to enable the wheels to be turned so that the inside front wheel on a turn can follow a path with a smaller radius than the outside wheel (the Ackerman Principle). It is not easy to check without specialized equipment, being expressed in degrees and minutes. If the measurements do not come within the specified limits given in Technical Data it indicates that the steering arms are distorted and must be renewed.

9:8 Steering shaft and column

To remove the steering wheel, first remove the two screws securing the medallion, which are accessible from below the wheel spokes as shown in **FIG 9:6**. The wheel is a splined fit on the steering shaft and sits on tapered collars. It can be lifted off after removing the centre nut. The steering wheel boss has two integral lugs which engage with slots in a turn signal switch cancelling sleeve on the steering shaft (see **FIG 9:7**). When installing the steering wheel check that the tapered collars are in position and are retained by the rubber ring. Set the road wheels in the straight-ahead position and the spokes of the steering wheel horizontal, then rotate the turn signal switch cancelling sleeve 1 so that its slots engage the lugs 2 on the steering wheel boss. Tighten the steering wheel nut to a torque of 45 lb ft with clean dry threads.

The component parts of the energy absorbing steering column assembly are shown in **FIG 9:8**. The top bearing housing has an extended spigot with two lugs which

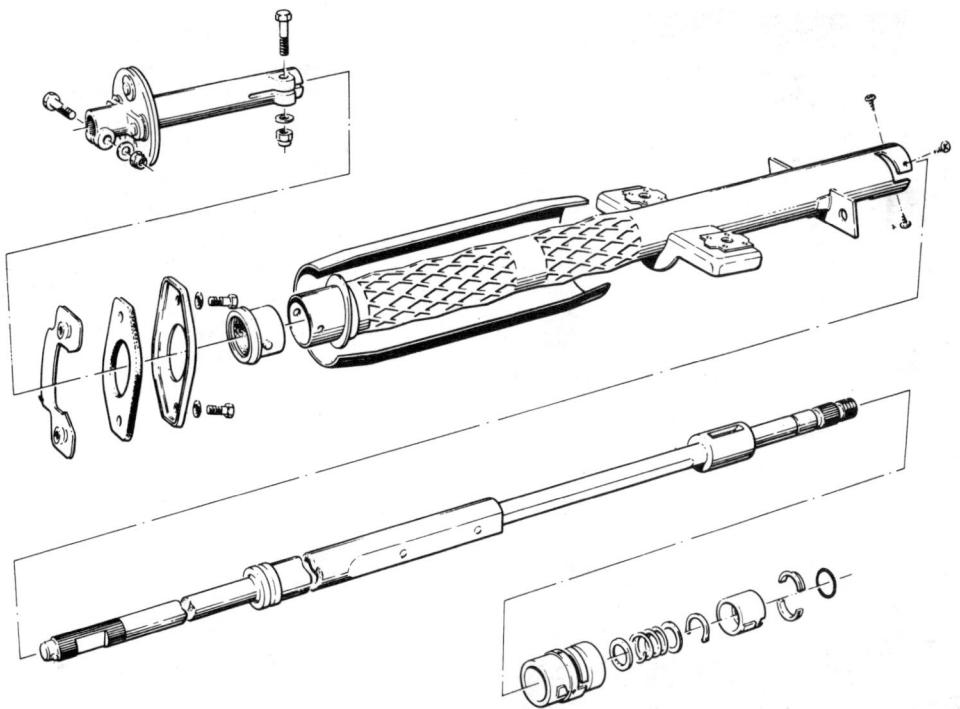

FIG 9:8 Components of energy absorbing steering column assembly

engage in slots in the column. The housing forms a mounting for the combined switch and horn push, and is secured by four self-tapping screws. The steering shaft is retained in the bearing by a spring, thrust washers and circlip. At the lower end a nylon bearing incorporates a felt lining for lubricant retention.

There are two mounting brackets, the upper being attached to a bracket bolted to the facia panel. The lower bracket incorporates two shear-type bosses bolted to a body bracket. A plate and insulator hold the column at floor level.

The canopy is removed in two halves. The upper half is unclipped from the lower half which is then unscrewed (see **FIGS 9:9** and **9:10**). The steering shaft and the upper bearing may now be withdrawn from the column after removing the screws and turning the bearing housing (see **FIG 9:11**). The lower bearing can be prised out of the column.

Reassembly:

It will be seen that the lower bearing of the steering shaft has two pips which must be located in corresponding holes in the column. Smear the felt bearing lining with grease before fitting the steering shaft.

If a new upper bearing, which is supplied complete with housing, is being fitted, it should be twisted into position with a 'C' wrench and four size 31 holes drilled as shown in **FIG 9:12**. Make sure that all drilling swarf is removed.

Before tightening the upper bearing housing, pack the bearing with the recommended grease and press the inner lower race against the shoulder of the steering shaft and fit the thick washer, spring, thin washer and circlip in that order.

Ensure that the ends of the steering column mesh cover are in close contact with the column and secure with a hot iron, as shown in **FIG 9:13** in five places.

Before installing the steering column, slacken off the bolts securing the plate and insulator to the floor and smear the insulator with soft or liquid soap.

Align the peg on the steering shaft with the slot in the upper flange of the coupling.

The column and shaft securing bolts may now be tightened in the following order and to the specified torque: Upper support bracket bolts 17 lb ft. Insulator to floor panel bolts 7 lb ft. Column brace bolts 7 lb ft. Coupling upper flange pinch bolts 14 lb ft (see **FIG 9:9**).

The rubber and fabric steering coupling is riveted to both upper and lower flanges which are splined to the steering shaft and steering gear pinion shaft and held in position by pinch bolts. To remove the coupling, the pinch bolts and the steering gear securing bolts must be withdrawn and the steering gear lowered.

When refitting, the peg on the steering shaft is aligned with the slot in the upper coupling flange. Fit the lower flange pinch bolt and tighten the steering gear bolts before tightening the upper pinch bolt.

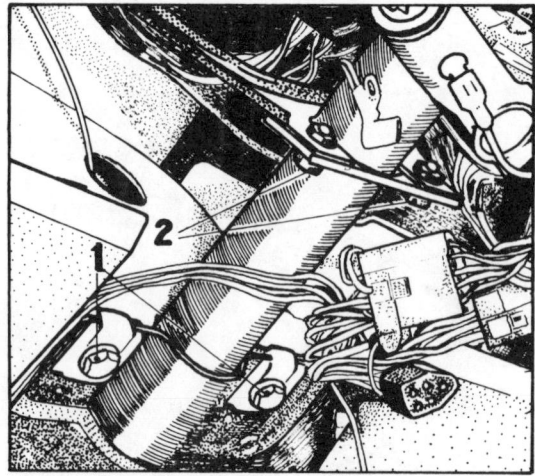

FIG 9:9 Remove canopy for access to upper support bracket bolts 1 and column brace bolts 2

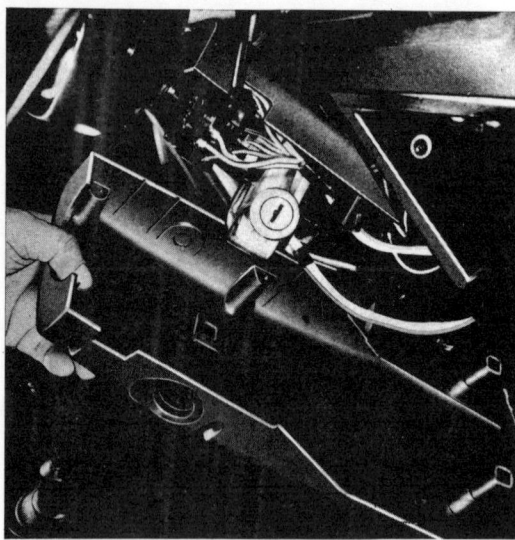

FIG 9:10 Lower half of canopy is secured by three screws

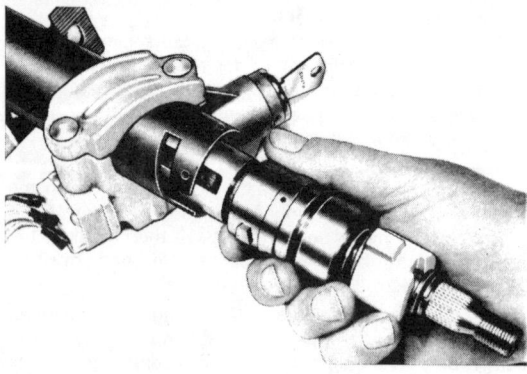

FIG 9:11 Removing steering shaft

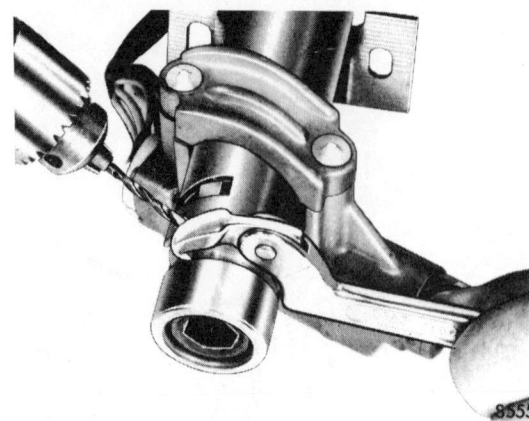

FIG 9:12 Fitting the upper bearing

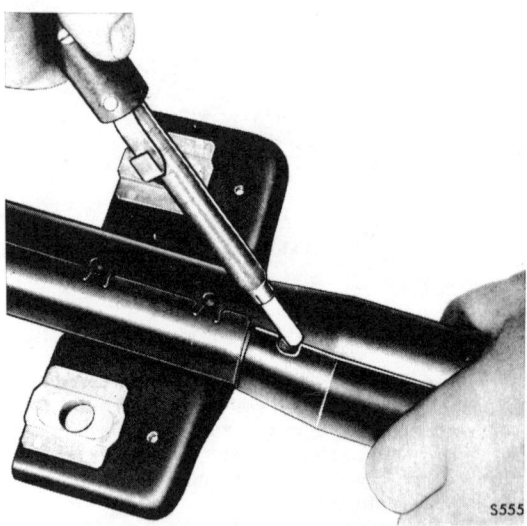

FIG 9:13 Fitting the steering column cover

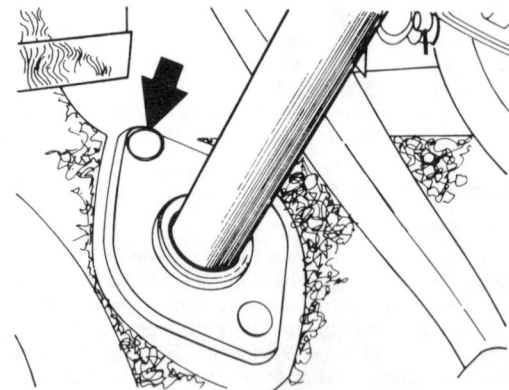

FIG 9:14 The insulator bracket is fitted to the toe board with the bolt nearest the edge uppermost. Later models have an improved insulator

FIG 9:15   Removing steering column lock

9:9 Steering column lock

The ignition and starter switch is incorporated in the steering column lock and includes four positions for the key which are marked 0, 1, 11 and 111 for the following services.

0   When the key is removed and the steering wheel turned to line up the locking bolt with the slot in the steering shaft, the lock will engage.

1   Accessory circuits energised and lock disengaged.

11   Ignition switched on.

111 Starter operation.

It will be noted that the key can be inserted and removed only in the 0 position. Before the key can be turned to 0 from 1 position the key must be pushed inwards.

Never turn the key to the 0 position and remove it when the car is in motion. If the car is to be towed, the key should be in 1 position.

On later models a safety button is incorporated which must be depressed before the steering can be locked.

Removal and refitting:

After removing the steering column assembly, the lock can be freed from the column after drilling each bolt (arrowed in **FIG 9:15**) with a $\frac{1}{8}$ inch high-speed drill and removing the bolts with an extractor.

When refitting the lock, tighten the break-head bolts sufficiently to hold the lock in position, then check the operation of the lock before finally tightening the bolts until the heads break off.

9:10 Fault diagnosis

(Reference should also be made to **Section 8:10** describing suspension faults, as these can often affect steering.)

(a) Wheel wobble

1 Unbalanced wheels and tyres
2 Slack steering connections
3 Incorrect steering geometry
4 Excessive play in steering gear
5 Steering gear loose in crossmember
6 Worn hub bearings

(b) Wander

1 Check 2, 3, 4 and 5 in (a)
2 Front and rear wheels not in line
3 Uneven tyre pressures
4 Uneven tyre wear
5 Defective dampers
6 Weak spring

(c) Heavy steering

1 Check 3 in (a)
2 Very low tyre pressures
3 Lack of oil in steering gear
4 Tie rod or suspension ball joints tight
5 Wheels out of track
6 Steering column out of line or strained
7 Steering shaft bent
8 Steering shaft bearings tight

(d) Lost motion

1 Play in steering shaft flange coupling
2 Loose steering wheel
3 Steering gear loose on crossmember
4 Play in steering gear (rack and pinion)
5 Worn tie rod ball joints
6 Worn suspension ball joints

(e) Irregular front tyre wear

1 Excessive toe-in produces feathered edges on inner side of tread
2 Toe-out produces similar effects on outer side of tread
3 Excessive positive camber causes wear on outer side of tread
4 Negative camber causes more wear on inner side of tread

NOTES

CHAPTER 10

THE BRAKING SYSTEM

10:1 Layout of drum brake system
10:2 Routine maintenance, brake shoe adjustment
10:3 Removing the master cylinder
10:4 Dismantling the brakes
10:5 Servicing hydraulic internals
10:6 Servicing master and wheel cylinders
10:7 Brake shoe linings
10:8 Bleeding the system

10:9 Handbrake cables
10:10 Fault diagnosis (drum brakes)
10:11 Disc brakes. Description of system
10:12 Vacuum servo unit
10:13 Discs, calipers and pads
10:14 Bleeding the system (disc brakes)
10:15 Fault diagnosis (disc brakes)

The standard equipment on early HC models consists of hydraulically operated drum brakes on all four wheels. Disc brakes on the front wheels, with vacuum-servo assistance on both front and rear, are an optional extra on standard models, but are fitted as initial equipment on cars with the extra performance engine and all later models after 1973. The rear drum brakes are the same in each case.

Either a Girling or Lockheed system may be used and there are slight differences in the construction, but not in the application.

The first part of this chapter deals with drum brakes and components common to all models. The second part covers disc brake systems.

10:1 Layout of drum brake systems

The master cylinder incorporates two pistons in a common bore with the primary piston operating the front brakes through two separate pipes, and the secondary piston operating the rear brakes. On some cars a pressure warning lamp switch is screwed into the lower face of the master cylinder body and actuated by a separate piston.

The master cylinder is bolted directly onto the brake pedal support with the pushrod attached without any adjustment for the pedal. The front brakes are of the two leading shoe type while those on the rear wheels are of the leading/trailing shoe type with a floating single ended hydraulic cylinder. The handbrake operates the rear wheels only through a system of cables.

Both Girling and Lockheed components are used, but they are similar to each other.

Later models have self-adjusting rear brakes and, in addition to the brake failure warning, there is also a warning to indicate that the handbrake has been left on.

10:2 Routine maintenance, brake shoe adjustment

The combined master cylinder and fluid reservoir is under the bonnet on the driver's side and has a screw-type filler cap. Clean the cap before removal and top up to .30 inch below the top of the filler. Use Castrol/Girling Universal Brake and Clutch Fluid. **It is essential that only the recommended fluid is used.** Do not use containers which have been used for mineral oils or other liquids as contamination can affect the rubber seals in the system and cause complete brake failure. If frequent topping up is necessary, check the hydraulic system for leaks. Lubricate the handbrake cable bridle, guides and clevises with the oil can.

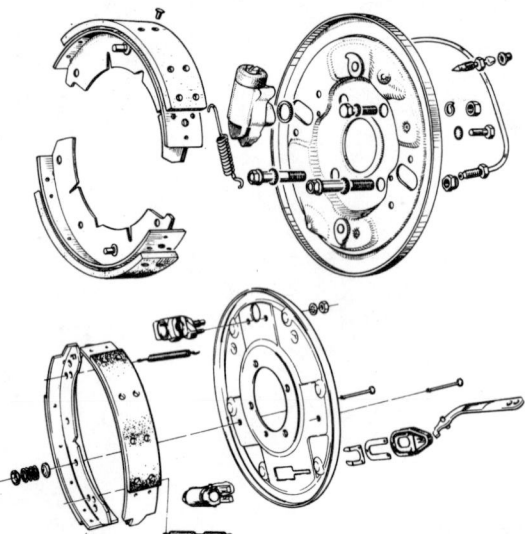

FIG 10:1 Brake components. (Top) Front brake. (Bottom) Rear brake (Both Girling type)

Adjusting brake shoes:

Excessive pedal travel indicates the need for brake shoe adjustment. The hydraulic system provides equalized pressure on all four brakes, but each shoe must be adjusted as near as possible to its drum in order to avoid lost movement. Each front brake has two adjusters, each rear brake has a single adjuster operating on both shoes.

When carrying out brake adjustments the handbrake must be in the off position and the car should be on a level floor. Jack up each wheel in turn to adjust its brake, chocking one of the other wheels to prevent rolling. All four wheels must receive attention. FIG 10:2 shows the method of adjusting a Girling front brake, using the special Girling Brake Spanner, Vauxhall Part No. VR.2102. Rotate each adjuster clockwise as viewed from the inside of the wheel until the shoe is hard on, then slacken off two notches. On Lockheed brakes the adjusters are turned in the direction of wheel forward rotation, both sides. Check that all brakes are free. The rear brakes are adjusted in a similar manner except that there is only one adjuster on each, situated near the upper edge of the brake backplate. If the adjusters are found to be very stiff they should be slackened right off and the threads lubricated with the recommended grease.

Normally the handbrake is automatically adjusted by the action of adjusting the rear brake shoes, but if there is still excessive travel of the hand lever, or if the cables have been renewed, adjustment should be carried out as follows:

1 Raise and support the rear of the car, with the handbrake in the off position.
2 If not already adjusted, adjust the footbrake as already described.
3 Referring to FIG 10:3, slacken the locknut 'A' and turn the sleeve 'B' to take up slack in the cable without causing the rear brakes to rub. When correctly adjusted, the rear brakes should be hard on when the hand lever is pulled on 5 or 6 clicks on the ratchet.

4 Tighten the locknut 'A' and recheck.
5 If there is insufficient adjustment at the sleeve 'B', the cables can be further adjusted by using the alternative holes in the slotted clevises at the brake shoe levers. If the inner hole in the clevis is used, the clevis must be positioned as shown in FIG 10:4 to avoid contact with the wheel rim. In either case the clevis pin must be fitted to the end hole in the brake shoe lever.
6 On later cars with the swivelling equaliser levers, adjustment is made at the cable connection to the equaliser.

Self-adjusting brake shoes:

Fine toothed ratchet plates are operated by application of the brake pedal or parking brake and position the shoes as necessary to maintain the correct brake clearance (see FIG 10:5).

Servicing is similar to previous types except that the brake shoe ratchet plate is retained against the shoe web by a long hook at the end of the longer return spring. Remove the shoe without the ratchet first to prevent straining this hook. On re-assembly lightly grease the ratchet pivot pin, the operating lever pin, and the contact surfaces of the flange plate. Do not lubricate the ratchet teeth.

10:3 Removing the master cylinder

Disconnect the three hydraulic supply pipes and hold a suitable container in place to catch the spillage which may be reduced by plugging the vent hole in the filler cap.

Detach the pushrod clevis pin from the brake pedal. Disconnect the lead to the warning lamp switch.

Remove the securing bolts and lift off the master cylinder assembly.

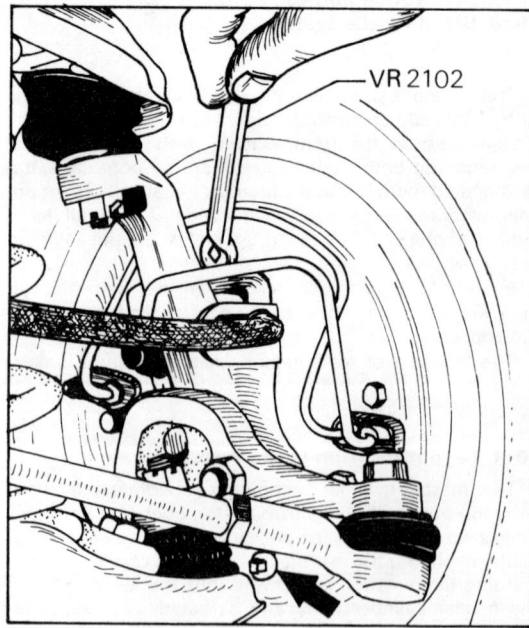

FIG 10:2 Adjusting a Girling front brake upper shoe. The arrow shows the adjuster for lower shoe. Rear brakes have a single adjuster.

10:4 Dismantling brakes. Note on flexible hoses

To identify the different types of systems between Lockheed and Girling, the Girling type has V-shaped slots cropped out of the edge of the shoe webs as shown in **FIG 10:13**. Furthermore, the shoe return springs in the front brakes differ in shape and location. On the Lockheed type the slimmer, longer springs are located with both their hooks registered in the webs of the shoes. The short, squat springs of the Girling have hooks that register in the web of each shoe but the remaining hook of each spring is located in the backplate. For further identification in the rear brakes, the Lockheed type has a double piston wheel cylinder that is fixed firmly to the backplate. The wheel cylinder of the Girling is the floating type incorporating a single piston. Before removing the shoes make a note of the position of the brake shoe return springs.

To remove the brake shoes:

1 Jack up and remove the road wheels. In the case of rear brakes the handbrake must be in the off position.
2 Remove the brake drums. The drums are located by the wheel bolts and secured to the hubs by single bolts. In the case of front brakes remove the hubs as described in **Section 8:3.**
3 Note that front drums are machined as an assembly with the hubs and must not be interchanged or renewed individually. Do not handle the inside of the drums or the brake shoe linings as oil or grease is detrimental to braking surfaces. Blow out the accumulation of dust with compressed air. Ensure that the brake pedal is not depressed when the drums are off.
4 Slacken the brake adjusters fully.
5 Remove the front brake shoes by prising the trailing end of each shoe in turn out of the slot in the end of the cylinder. Tie a length of wire round each brake cylinder and piston to prevent the pistons being forced out if the footbrake is applied while shoes are removed.

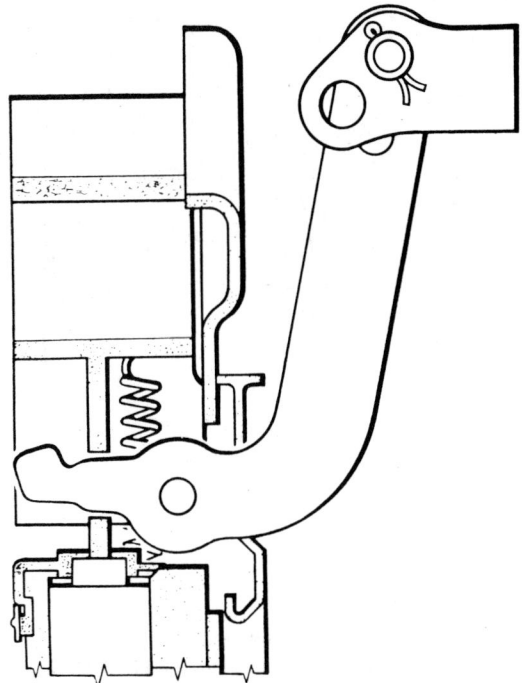

FIG 10:4 Handbrake shoe lever showing position of clevis pin attachment. The inner hole in the lever is not used

6 To remove the rear brake shoes, remove the retainer, guide spring and pin from each shoe. Prise the leading shoe out of the adjuster and withdraw both shoes and springs. Tie a length of wire round the brake cylinder and piston.

When removing brake hoses, note the following points:

1 To minimize fluid loss when a hose is disconnected, the air vent in the master cylinder cap should be temporarily sealed.
2 Hoses must not be twisted or permanent damage will result. Always unscrew the union nuts on the metal pipes first. Hold the hexagon on the flexible hose with a second spanner as a precaution against its turning when removing the hose locknut at a bracket.

10:5 Servicing hydraulic internals

The following instructions apply to the servicing of the internal parts of all hydraulic components. Absolute cleanliness is essential. Any traces of grit can damage the highly polished bores or seals. Brake fluid or Girling Cleaning Fluid should be used for cleaning internal parts as petrol and other solvents will cause damage to rubber cups and seals. Rubber seals are available in kit form, so that when master and brake cylinders are dismantled it is best to fit new seals throughout. Alternatively, complete cylinders are available as exchange units. Wet all internal parts with clean brake fluid during reassembly. Be very careful not to turn back the lips of piston seals when installing them in cylinder bores.

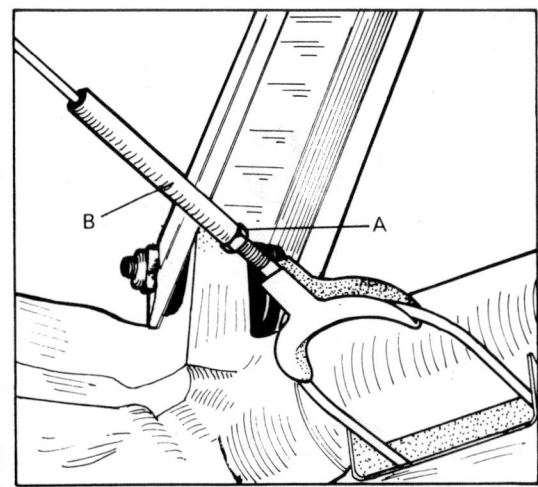

FIG 10:3 Handbrake adjustment showing A Locknut and B Adjusting sleeve

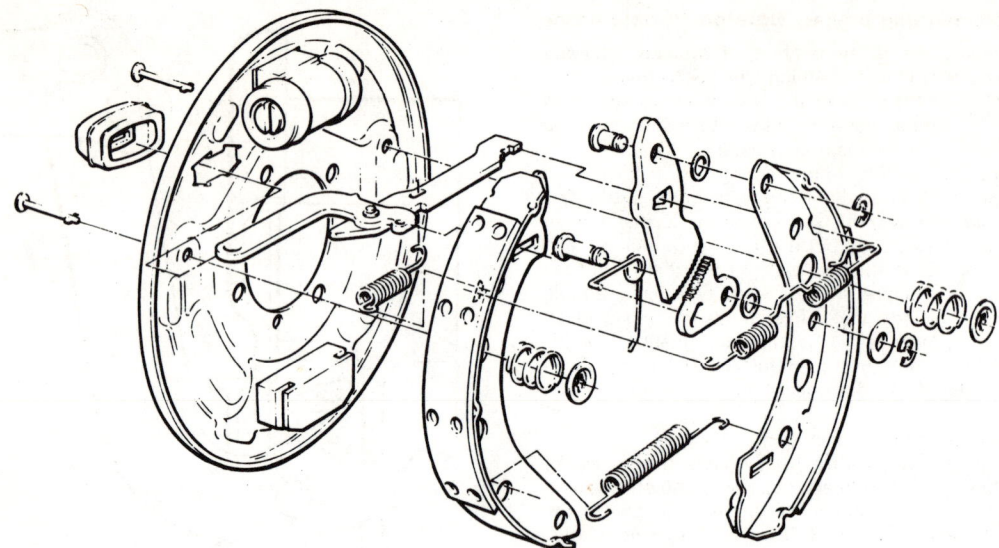

FIG 10:5   Lockheed self-adjusting rear brakes

10:6 Servicing master and wheel cylinders

To dismantle the master cylinder (see **FIGS 10:6** and **10:7**).

Remove the rubber boot and the circlip from the end of the cylinder and withdraw the primary piston 4 and its spring. Detach the fluid reservoir and take out the rubber seal 1 and stop pin 2 from the fluid inlet port. The stop pin is a loose fit but its removal will be assisted by pushing the piston against its spring to relieve pressure on the pin.

Withdraw the secondary piston 3 and spring.

Remove the plug 1 in **FIG 10:7** tap the assembly lightly and withdraw the pressure warning lamp actuator piston 2. Unscrew the actuator switch 3.

The piston return spring is retained by a circlip.

Thoroughly clean all parts with Girling cleaning fluid and examine carefully for wear or damage. If there is any doubt about the condition of the bore a new cylinder should be obtained. All rubber seals should be renewed.

Reassembly:

The master cylinder is reassembled in the reverse order to dismantling with particular attention to the following points:

Immerse all parts in the recommended grade of hydraulic fluid to assist assembly and ensure that the lips of the seals fitted to the two pistons are facing in the correct directions. Reference to **FIG 10:8** will show that the seals on the primary piston both face towards the

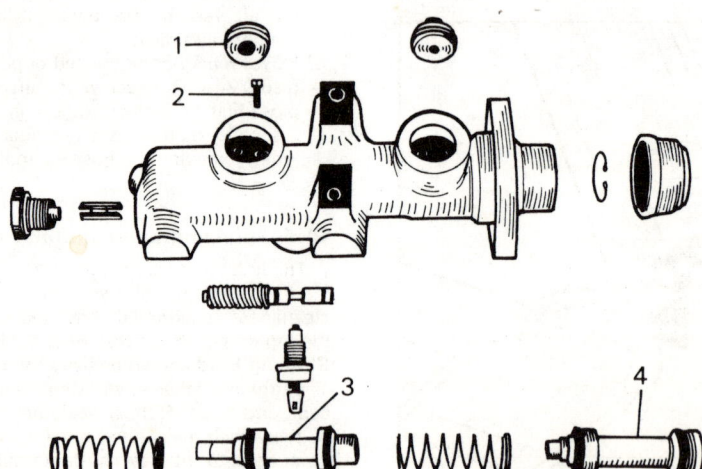

FIG 10:6   Exploded view of tandem master cylinder used with servo. The spring between pistons 3 and 4 is not used in non-servo models

Key to Fig 10:6   1 Rubber seal   2 Stop pin   3 Secondary piston   4 Primary piston

smaller end of the piston, while secondary piston seals face outwards from each other as in **FIG 10:9**. Both piston return springs have retainer washers at one end. These washers should be located over the spigot end of the piston.

When assembling the primary inlet port adaptor, ensure that the O-ring 2 and seal 1 are correctly located (see **FIG 10:10**).

Ensure that a plain washer is fitted at each end of the spring on the warning lamp actuator piston before fitting the circlip. Check that the O-rings are fully seated in the piston grooves. Use a new sealing washer on the end plug and see that the distance sleeve is securely attached to the spigot.

When reconnecting the brake pipes to the master cylinder, observe the following order: Pipe from rear brakes to the single port at the end of the cylinder, pipe from lefthand front brake to the upper of the other two ports and the pipe from the righthand front brake to the lower port.

Front brake cylinders (see FIG 10:11):

Remove the brake shoes as described in **Section 10:4** and detach the hydraulic pipe from the brake cylinder. Unbolt the cylinder and remove it from the backplate, taking care not to mislay the sealing ring 2.

Remove the rubber boot 8 and withdraw the piston 6 and seal 5 together with the spring 4. Remove the bleed nipple 1 when fitted.

Clean all parts, inspect and renew as mentioned above for the master cylinder.

Rear brake cylinders (see FIG 10:12)

Remove the brake shoes as previously described.

Disconnect the handbrake cable from the shoe lever seen in **FIG 10:4**. Detach the hydraulic pipe from the cylinder and seal the end of the pipe.

On the Girling type remove the external boot 1 from the cylinder boss and handbrake lever.

Depress the spring plate tags 2 sufficiently to free the retaining plate 3 which may then be prised out, also the distance piece 4 and the spring plate.

Withdraw the handbrake lever 9, then take off the clip 11 and the internal boot 10 and extract the piston 8 and piston seal 7. Remove the bleed nipple 5.

On the Lockheed type, remove the rubber boot and detach the E-clip that secures the cylinder at the rear of the backplate. Note the dowel in the cylinder body to provide positive location and also that a bleed screw is fitted only to the righthand cylinder.

Clean and inspect all parts, renewing any which are showing signs of wear or damage.

When reassembling front and rear brake cylinders, ensure that the new seal is fitted with the larger diameter towards the inner end of the piston.

Fit the internal boot over the piston, smear the bore with brake fluid, and insert the piston into the cylinder. Before fastening the clip over the boot, fill the boot with the recommended grease. Lubricate also both sides of the backplate where a cylinder slides and the fulcrum pin of the handbrake operating lever.

The remaining parts are fitted in the reverse order to dismantling.

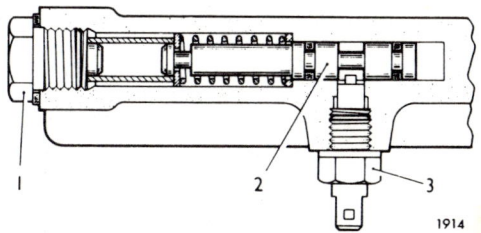

FIG 10:7   Pressure warning lamp actuator

Key to Fig 10:7   1 Plug   2 Piston   3 Switch

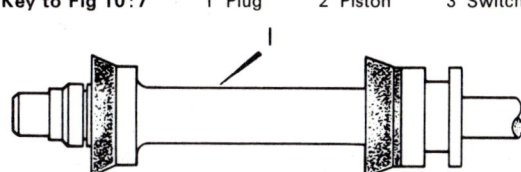

FIG 10:8   Primary piston seals

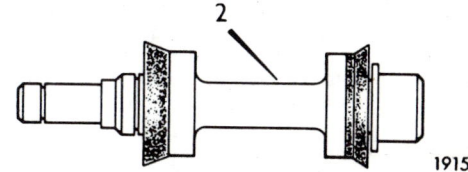

FIG 10:9   Secondary piston seals

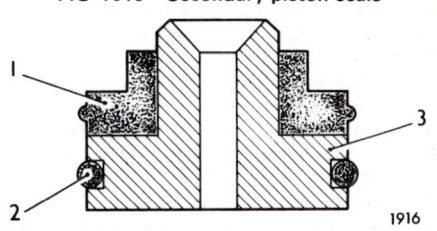

FIG 10:10   Primary piston inlet port adaptor 3 showing seal 1 and O-ring 2

10:7 Brake shoe linings

Brakes should be relined if the linings are worn down to the extent that the rivets are likely to contact the drums or if they show signs of contamination from grease or oil. It is strongly recommended that replacement shoes be obtained on an exchange basis rather than fit new linings to the old shoes, also that a complete set of the genuine makers replacement be fitted otherwise uneven braking is likely to result.

At the same time the brake drums should be checked for scoring or ovality and any fault remedied by machining provided that they are still within the limits given in Technical Data. If the front drums are to be machined, it must be done on their individual hubs to maintain concentricity. It is advisable to fit new shoes and linings after treating the drums.

When refitting the brake shoes a thin film of Keenol grease should be applied to the shoe contact pads. The position of the pull-off springs is important as described in **Section 10:4**.

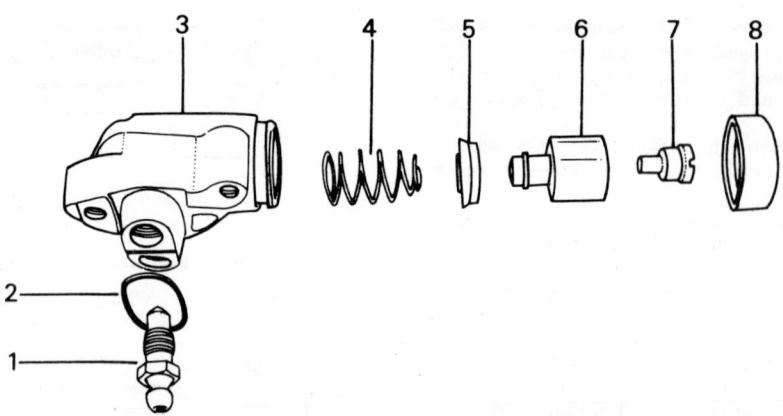

FIG 10:11   Components of front brake cylinder

Key to Fig 10:11   1 Bleed nipple   2 Sealing ring   3 Cylinder   4 Spring   5 Piston seal   6 Piston   7 Brake shoe guide
8 Rubber boot

If difficulty is found in adjusting the brake shoes on early models, it is possible that the adjustment mechanism is sticking. This is shown broken open in **FIG 10:14** and if all parts are cleaned and lubricated lightly no further trouble should be experienced.

10:8   Bleeding the system

This will be necessary if air has entered the hydraulic system owing to leakage or low fluid level or when any of the pipelines have been disconnected. The presence of air in the system usually produces the symptoms of a 'spongy' brake pedal and loss of braking power. In bleeding the brakes the pedal has to be operated, expelled fluid has to be watched for air bubbles and at the same time the reservoir must be kept topped up, so that an assistant is essential. Proceed as follows:

1 Slacken off the four front brake shoe adjusters to the limit by turning anticlockwise. Turn the two rear brake shoe adjusters clockwise until the shoes contact the drums. These operations reduce the capacity of the brake cylinders to the minimum.
2 Ensure that all hydraulic connections are secure and that the reservoir has been topped up. Use only the recommended fluids (see **Section 10:2**). **Unsuitable fluids, or the use of vessels contaminated with mineral oils, petrol or similar solvents can cause serious brake troubles.** Note also that the reservoir must be kept topped up throughout the process, or more air will enter the system and a fresh start will have to be made.
3 Bleed each brake in turn, starting with the one with the longest pipe run from the master cylinder and finishing with the shortest, i.e. righthand rear, righthand front, lefthand front. Remove the rubber cap from the bleed nipple on the first brake. If no cap is fitted clean the nipple first. Fit a rubber or plastic tube over the nipple and immerse the free end in a small quantity of fluid in a clean glass jar.
4 Unscrew the nipple a part of a turn only. Operate the foot pedal giving one sharp application to the limit of its travel followed by three short rapid strokes through the last third of pedal movement. Pause when the pedal is right back to allow the master cylinder to

refill and repeat the sequence until fluid is seen to emerge from the bleed tube free of air bubbles. Then on a downward stroke of the pedal, tighten the bleed nipple.
5 Repeat on the front brakes, still ensuring that the reservoir is kept topped up.
6 Readjust all brake shoes.
7 Check by applying foot pressure to the brake pedal, which should offer a firm resistance and hold it indefinitely. If the pedal feels 'spongy' there is still air in the system. If the pedal sinks gradually there is leakage. In either case the trouble must be located and the system bled once more.

10:9   Handbrake cables

FIG 10:15 shows the layout of the handbrake cables. The front cable is connected to the handbrake lever by a slotted clevis and passes through a rubber boot and two guides secured to the underbody. An adjuster and bridle are attached to the rear end of the cable. The rear cable is looped through the bridle and directed through a guide on the rear axle to the two brake shoe levers. On later cars the bridle is replaced by a pivoted equaliser bar.

To remove the front cable, raise the rear floor covering and detach the cable from the clevis. It can then be withdrawn towards the rear. To remove the rear cable, detach each end from its slotted clevis and remove the two splitpins from the guide on the rear axle. When installing the cables, lubricate the cables, guides and clevises with the recommended grease. Instructions for adjustment of the handbrake are given in **Section 10:2**.

10:10   Fault diagnosis (drum brakes)

(a)   Brakes ineffective (see also b, c and d)

1 Worn brake linings
2 Oily brake linings
3 Incorrect grade of linings
4 Scored brake drums
5 Incorrect brake fluid (leading to restricted hoses and swollen seals)

(b)   Excessive brake pedal travel

1 Brake shoes need adjustment

(c) Pedal gradually sinks to the floor

1 External leaks in hydraulic system
2 Master cylinder seals leaking
3 Leaking wheel cylinders

(d) Pedal 'spongy' or needs 'pumping'

1 Air in hydraulic system
2 Master cylinder seals defective

(e) Brakes bind

1 Shoe adjustment too close
2 Handbrake cable adjustment incorrect
3 Rear brake cylinder seized to backplate
4 Handbrake shoe levers seized
5 Weak pull-off springs
6 Slack hub bearings (brake drum tilting)
7 Reservoir overfilled or air vent restricted
8 Check 5 in (a)

(f) Brakes grab

1 Backplate loose
2 Hub bearings slack
3 Linings oily
4 Distorted brake drums
5 Incorrect grade of linings
6 Suspension worn or loose

(g) Brakes pull to one side

1 Unequal tyre pressures
2 Odd brake linings
3 One front brake hose restricted
4 Steering or front suspension worn
5 Front suspension control rod loose
6 Check also 1, 2, 3 and 4 in (f)

10:11 Disc brakes. Description of system

Self-adjusting disc brakes of either Girling or Lockheed are on the front wheels, with a servo-assisted hydraulic system, this set up is optional equipment on early standard models, but fitted as standard on extra performance and all later models. Drum brakes of the same type as those already described are fitted on the rear wheels, but of course have the benefit of the servo-assisted operation. Brake pedal details and handbrake layout are the same for all cars.

The master cylinder is the same as that described in **Section 10:6,** but where a servo-unit is included it is mounted directly on the servo pushrod.

On some later cars a reducing valve is fitted into the rear braking circuit whereby the hydraulic pressure to the rear brakes is restricted in order to prevent locking up under heavy pressure. This device may be pressure sensitive or load sensitive, in each case a faulty unit must be renewed as no servicing is possible.

10:12 Vacuum servo unit

This direct acting unit is bolted to brackets on the clutch and brake pedal support and is shown in the section diagram of **FIG 10:16.**

The movement of the servo pushrod is governed by the travel of a valve rod and plunger connected to the foot-brake pedal. In the 'brakes off' position the valve body and the rubber diaphragm are held by a spring against

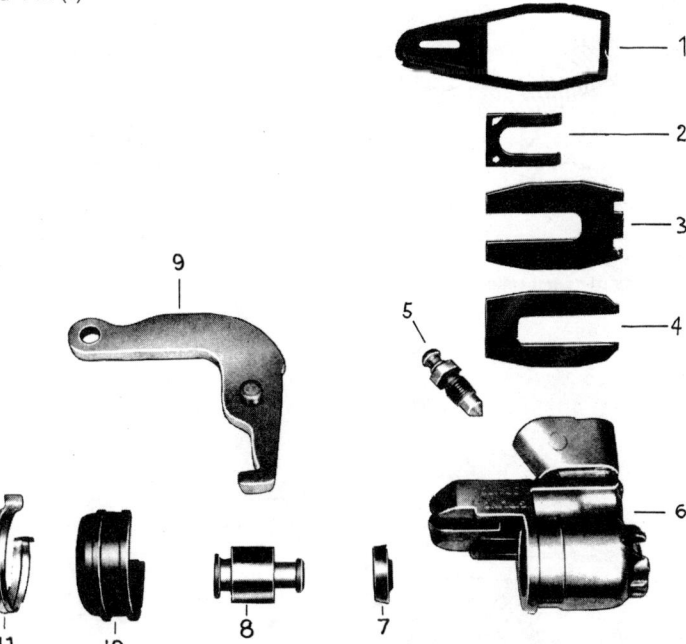

FIG 10:12 Components of rear brake cylinder (Girling) 9 inch brakes

Key to Fig 10:12   1 External boot   2 Spring tag   3 Retaining plate   4 Distance piece   5 Bleed nipple   6 Cylinder body
7 Piston seal   8 Piston   9 Handbrake lever   10 Internal boot   11 Boot clip

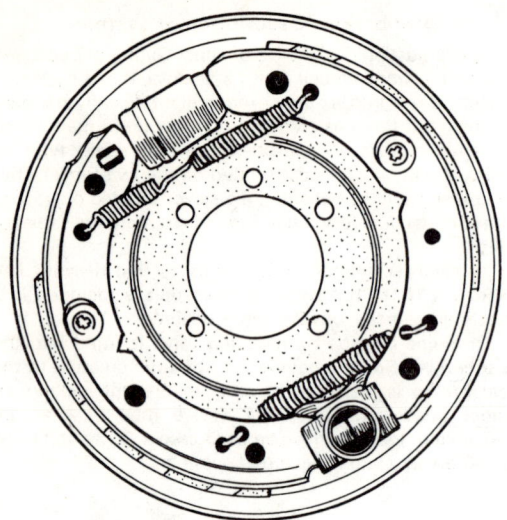

FIG 10:13 Rear brake assembly showing correct location of shoes and springs (Girling)

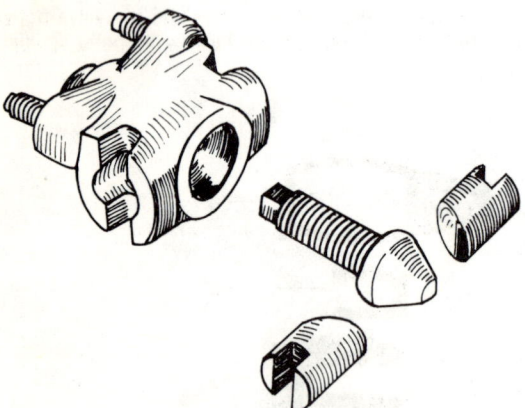

FIG 10:14 Components of rear brake adjuster

the end cover, as shown, in a state of suspended vacuum created by exhaustion of air through a non-return valve and hose connected to the engine inlet manifold.

On application of the brake pedal, controlled entry of air at atmospheric pressure to the rear chamber **B** moves the diaphragm, valve body and pushrod to the left, thus operating the piston in the master cylinder until such time as the pedal pressure is released when the chamber **B** is exhausted of air and the diaphragm and its associated components move back to the right and the 'brakes off' condition is restored.

In the event of a failure causing a loss of servo-assistance, the brakes can still be applied since there will be direct mechanical action on the pushrod.

Maintenance:

The home operator is advised not to interfere with the internal mechanism of the servo unit and in the event of a failure to take the car to a service station. He should however, examine the air filter occasionally and fit a new one when necessary.

Access to the air filter is gained after pulling back the rubber boot from the rear of the servo and withdrawing the filter retainer (see **FIG 10:17**). The old filter has to be cut to allow removal, as also does the new replacement to install it over the pushrod. After fitting, ensure that the retainer is pressed on the end of the valve bore and that the rubber boot is located over all five lugs on the end cover.

The distance that the pushrod stem projects from the shell, when the servo is at rest, is critical and can be checked by placing a gauge against the master cylinder mounting studs as in **FIG 10:18**. The correct pushrod projection is .408 inch and if the dimension as measured is more than .005 inch above or below the appropriate datum edge on the gauge, the pushrod should be removed and adjusted by turning the adjuster stem as required.

When the pushrod setting is correct press the retainer back into position with a metal tube and without using undue force. Insert the metal retainer in the end of the shell over the pushrod which should be smeared with grease and the rubber seal inserted, bedding it down and leaving the adjuster and threads exposed.

Check the condition of the vacuum hose occasionally and renew if it is damaged or deteriorated.

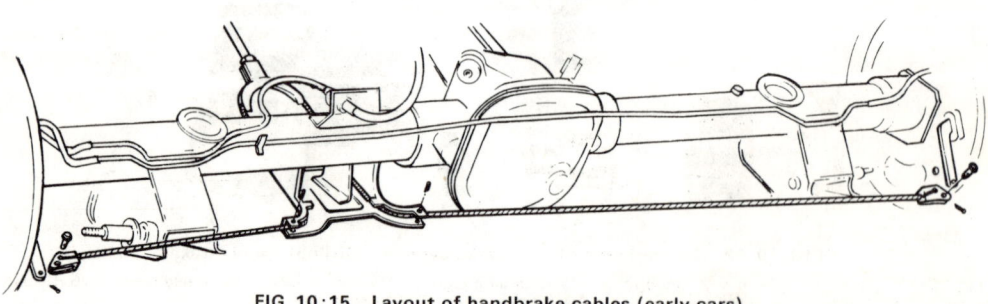

FIG 10:15 Layout of handbrake cables (early cars)

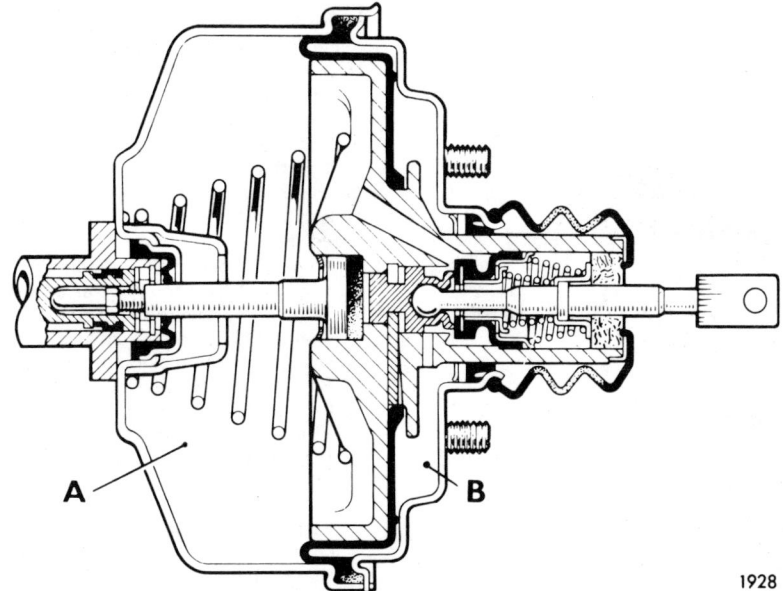

FIG 10:16   Sectional view of vacuum servo unit

FIG 10:17   Air filter removal

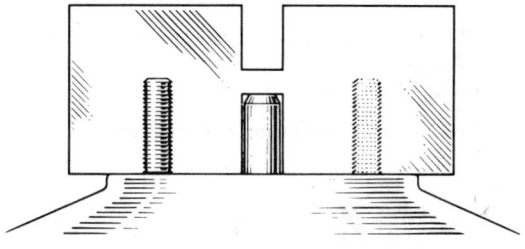

FIG 10:18   Checking projection of servo pushrod

10:13 Discs, calipers and pads

Wheel brake assemblies for Viva HC cars may be manufactured by either Girling or Lockheed. The principle of operation is the same in each case and the construction sufficiently similar for one set of instructions to cover the two types. Two exploded illustrations are given in **FIGS 10:19** and **10:20** which will show the differences.

Each brake disc is attached to the front hub by four bolts with locking plates as shown in **FIG 8:3**. The caliper and disc shield are attached to the steering knuckle by bolts having nylon inserts in the threads. On each side of the caliper the cylinders incorporate a groove housing a rubber sealing ring. The exposed ends of the pistons are protected by rubber boots. The friction pads are held in the caliper body by retaining pins with spring clips. An anti-squeal shim is interposed between each pad and piston. The caliper components are shown in exploded form in **FIGS 10:19** and **10:20,** one piston being shown in position in its cylinder. Hydraulic pressure is supplied equally to both cylinders so that the brakes are self-adjusting.

Disc brake pads must be renewed when the friction material has worn to a thickness of .06 inch. **Oil or grease must not be allowed to come into contact with the pads.** To renew pads:

1 Remove road wheel.
2 Withdraw spring clips from pad retaining pins and withdraw the pins. Details are shown in **FIG 10:19.**
3 Siphon off sufficient fluid from the master cylinder secondary tank to allow for displacement of fluid in the next operation.
4 Press each piston back into the caliper by applying finger pressure to the pad.
5 Lift the friction pads and anti-squeal shims out of the caliper. **Do not depress the brake pedal while the pads are removed.**
6 Install the new friction pads and the anti-squeal shims with the arrow in the shim pointing in the direction of forward rotation of the disc, as shown in **FIG 10:21**. Install the pad retaining pins using new spring clips.
7 Depress the brake pedal two or three times to reposition the pistons in the caliper. Top up the master cylinder with the approved fluid to within .30 inch of the top.
8 Refit the road wheel.

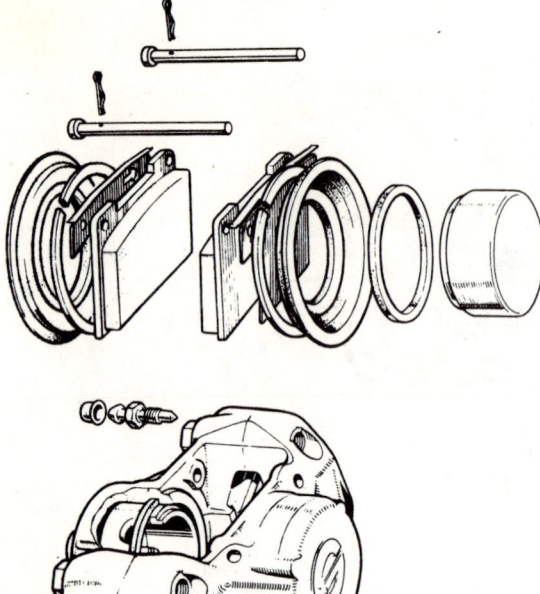

779

FIG 10:19 Components of Girling brake caliper

Lockheed brakes:

On later models the anti-squeal shims have two D-shaped cut-outs. These must always be fitted in the correct position, with the larger cut-out towards the lower end of the caliper, and must not be interchanged with the earlier type of shim.

A further method of reducing brake squeal on all models is to smear lightly the back and edges of the brake pads and the shims with a high melting point copper based grease.

To remove disc brake calipers:

1 Remove the friction pads as already described.
2 Temporarily seal the vent hole in the master cylinder filler cap to minimize fluid loss.
3 Disconnect the brake pipe from the caliper.
4 Remove the bolts and lockwashers securing the caliper to the steering knuckle and withdraw the caliper. **The bolts clamping the two halves of the caliper together must not be disturbed.**

To renew fluid seals in caliper:

1 Clean the outside of the caliper.
2 Ease the rubber boot (dust cover) out of the groove in each piston and off the caliper (see **FIG 10:19**).
3 Retain the piston in the inlet port side of the caliper by binding a cloth round caliper and piston as shown in **FIG 10:22**. Apply compressed air to eject the other piston. **Keep fingers clear of pistons as compressed air will eject these forcibly.**
4 Untie the cloth and place it inside the caliper to act as a cushion while applying air pressure to port to eject the other piston.
5 Using a small screwdriver remove the fluid seals, taking care not to damage the seal groove or bore.

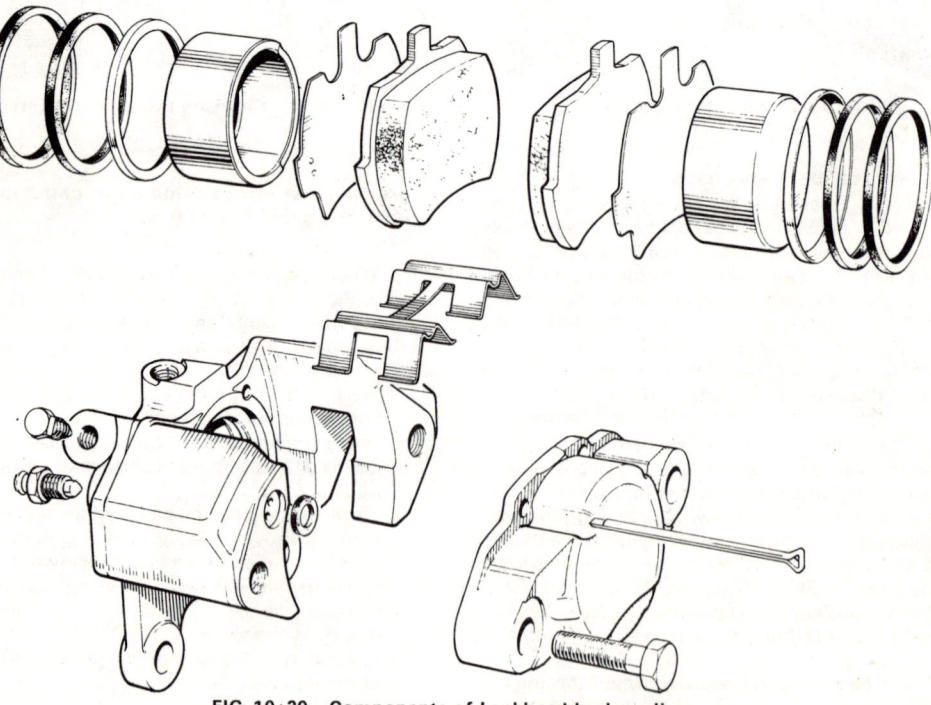

FIG 10:20 Components of Lockheed brake caliper

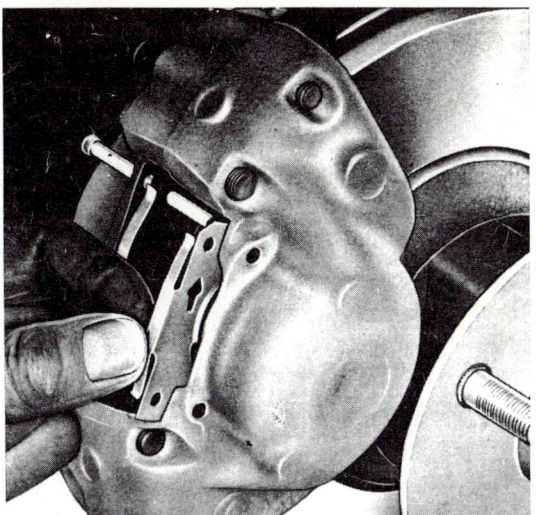

FIG 10:21 Anti-squeal shims should be fitted with the arrow pointing in the direction of forward rotation

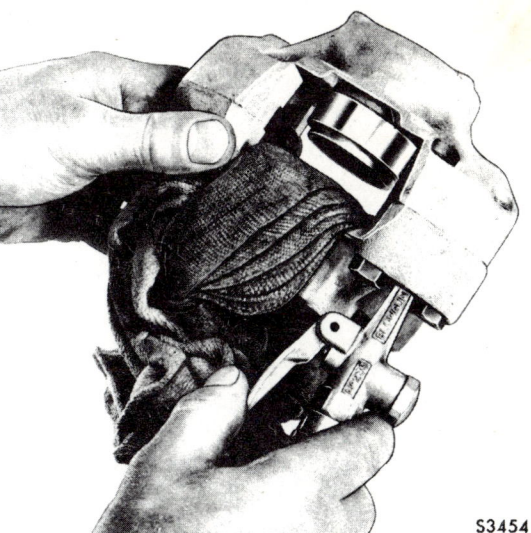

S3454

FIG 10:22 Removal of caliper piston

6 Examine bores and pistons for scuffing and corrosion. The bores from the seal recesses outwards may be cleaned with fine steel wool but care must be taken to remove any particles of steel wool afterwards.

7 Thoroughly flush out caliper bores and clean the pistons with Girling Cleaning Fluid.

8 Ensure that the new seals are seated correctly in the caliper bore grooves.

9 Lubricate seals, caliper bores and pistons with rubber grease and push the pistons squarely into the bores.

10 Install the boots (dust covers), ensuring that the outer lip engages in the groove in the caliper and the inner lip the groove in the piston.

When installing calipers, note that the attaching bolts have a nylon insert in their threads. If they have been removed more than twice they should be renewed. Tighten the bolts to a torque of 33 lb ft. Install friction pads as already described. Bleed the brakes (see **Section 10:15**) and unseal the master cylinder air vent.

Brake discs should be checked for runout, preferably using a suitably mounted dial gauge. If such equipment is not available, it may be possible to make the check using a fixed pointer and a feeler gauge. The measurement is taken .70 inch from the outer edge of the disc. The hub nut must first be tightened to eliminate play. The maximum permissible runout is .004 inch. If this measurement is exceeded the disc must be renewed. Readjust the hub bearings as described in **Section 8:3**.

10:14 Bleeding the system, disc brake models

The procedure for bleeding the hydraulic system where disc brakes are fitted is the same as that given in **Section 10:8** for drum brakes but the following points should be noted:

1 The engine must not be running whilst bleeding is carried out.

2 Before commencing operations, depress the brake pedal several times to eliminate residual vacuum in the servo system.

3 The bleed nipple is located on the mounting half of the caliper as shown in the diagrams.

10:15 Fault diagnosis (disc brake models)

Faults which are common to both systems have been described in **Section 10:10** which should be referred to in conjunction with the present Section.

(a) Pedal travel excessive

1 Brake disc runout excessive
2 Hub bearings slack
3 Defective caliper fluid seals or pistons
4 Defects in vacuum servo unit

(b) Excessive pedal pressure required

1 Collapsed, restricted or punctured vacuum hose
2 Vacuum non-return valve faulty
3 Servo air filter restricted
4 Defects in vacuum servo unit

(Note that similar symptoms occur if the engine is not running, e.g. when coasting, as soon as the residual vacuum in the servo unit has been exhausted. The braking system will then function, but without the benefit of servo assistance.)

(c) Brakes bind

1 Caliper piston seized
2 Caliper fluid seals defective
3 Defects in servo unit

(d) Brakes grab or pull to one side

1 Brake disc distorted
2 Caliper mounting bolts loose
3 Friction pads contaminated by fluid leaks
4 Friction pads contaminated by lubricant from hubs or ball joints

NOTES

CHAPTER 11

THE ELECTRICAL SYSTEM

11:1 Description
11:2 The battery
11:3 The alternator
11:4 Starter motor M35G/1
11:5 Servicing the starter
11:6 Starter motor M35J/1
11:7 Fuses

11:8 Lamps
11:9 Windscreen wipers
11:10 Instruments
11:11 Combined switch and horn push
11:12 Pre-engaged starter motors
11:13 Fault diagnosis

11:1 Description

The 12-volt electrical system is quite conventional, but includes an alternator as its source of supply in place of the more common DC generator and it is earthed to the negative side.

A description of most of the components used on the car will be found in this chapter, but it must be stressed that unless the operator has some electrical knowledge and suitable testing equipment he would be advised to take his car to a qualified service station in the event of electrical failure, either for servicing or replacement under the very comprehensive scheme available.

It will be found that most of the vehicles wiring is included in multiple harnesses with multi-way plug adapters for making connections. A comprehensive system of fuses protects the various services and a thermal circuit breaker protects the lighting circuits. In addition there is a fusible link in the main battery feed.

A warning must be given with regard to working on this, or any other, system employing an alternator.

To avoid damage to any diodes and transistors in the system, strict polarity must be observed at all times.

Do not disconnect any wires while the engine is running.

It is advisable to disconnect the battery before boost charging, and the engine should not be started at this time.

Do not attempt to polarize the alternator.

11:2 The battery

The battery is of the lead/acid type using dilute sulphuric acid as an electrolyte. As on all modern cars, the battery has an enormous amount of work to do and its life will be shortened by abuse or lack of regular maintenance. The outside of the battery should be kept

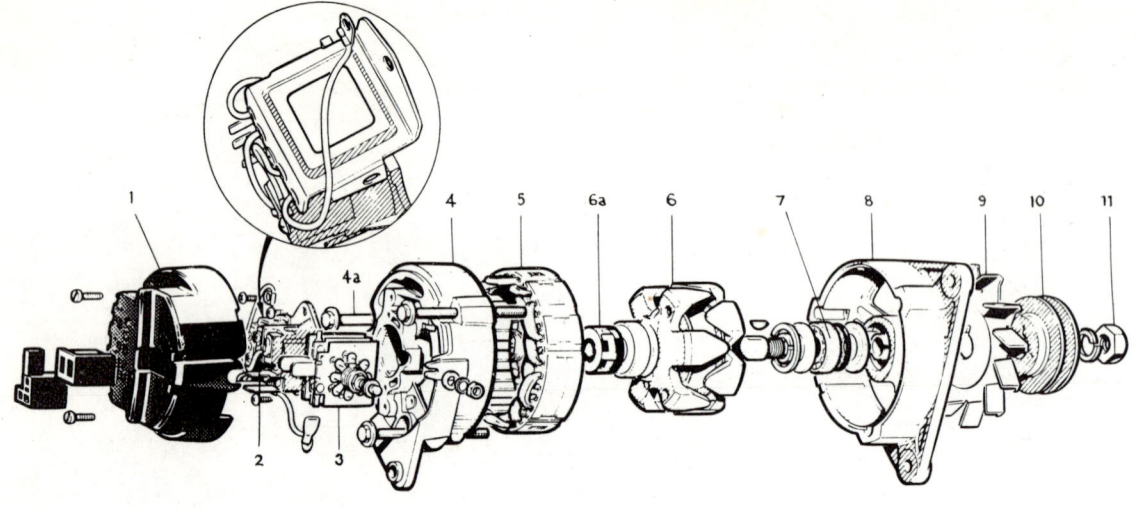

FIG 11:1 Components of Lucas 15ACR alternator

Key to Fig 11:1   1 Plastic cover   2 Brushgear   3 Rectifier   4 Slip ring end bracket   4a Long bolt   5 Stator   6 Rotor
6a Slip ring moulding   7 Bearing   8 Drive end bracket   9 Fan   10 Pulley   11 Pulley

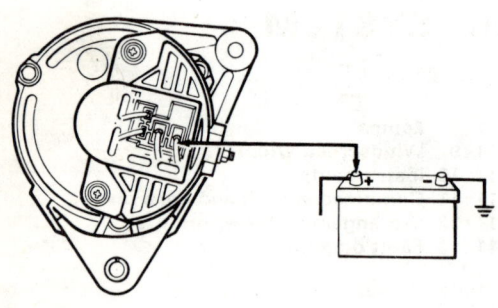

Live Side

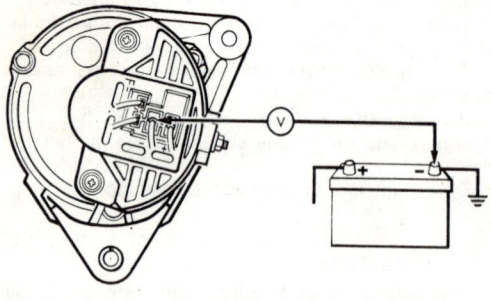

Earth Side

FIG 11:2 Voltage drop tests on alternator

clean and dry and any corrosion at the terminals should be eliminated. All affected parts, including the battery support and clamp, should be cleaned with dilute ammonia and then washed with clean water. The support and clamp should be painted with acid-resisting paint and the terminals and lugs smeared with petroleum jelly before reconnecting. Ensure that the battery is connected with its negative terminal to earth, as a reversal of polarity can cause serious trouble.

The level of the electrolyte in the cells should be checked regularly. Losses due to normal evaporation should be made up by adding distilled water only, though losses due to spillage or leakage will call for the addition of dilute sulphuric acid at the correct specific gravity. This can be obtained ready diluted, but if strong sulphuric acid is used, remember when diluting it to **add acid** to water. **On no account must water be added to the strong acid.**

The specific gravity of the electrolyte in each cell should be checked by using a hydrometer. This gives an indication of the state of charge as follows:

Fully charged—Specific Gravity 1.270 to 1.290
Half discharged—Specific Gravity 1.190 to 1.210
Discharged—Specific Gravity 1.110 to 1.130

These figures apply at a temperature of 16°C (60°F). Add or subtract .002 for a rise or fall respectively of 3°C (5°F). If the battery is unused for long periods it should be recharged at least once a month. It will deteriorate rapidly if left in a discharged condition. Also, on vehicles left in the open in severe winter conditions, it should be noted that while a fully-charged battery will withstand a temperature of minus 30°F, one that is completely discharged could freeze at a temperature only a few degrees below the freezing point of water.

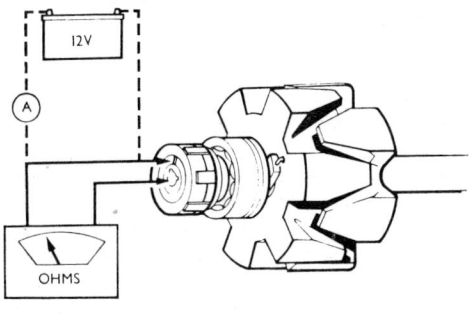

Measuring Rotor Winding Resistance

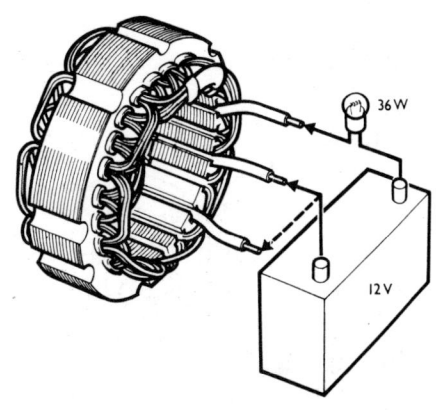

Stator Winding Continuity Test

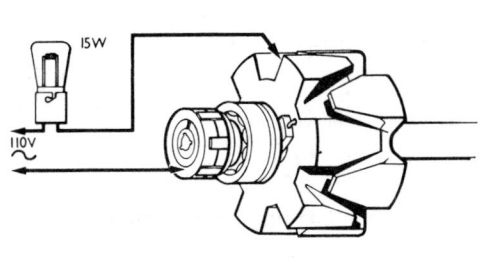

Rotor Insulation Test

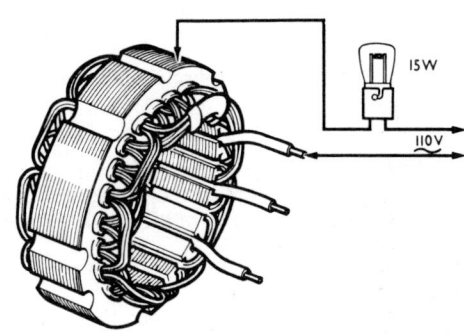

Stator Winding Insulation Test

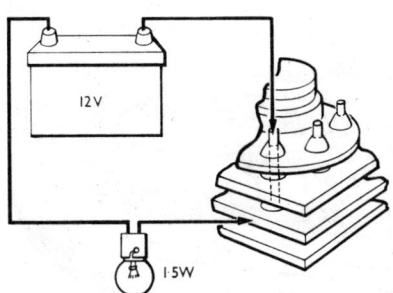

Diode Test

FIG 11:3 Alternator tests. (Left) Checking rotor winding resistance and insulation. (Right) Checking stator continuity and insulation. (Centre) Checking diode assembly

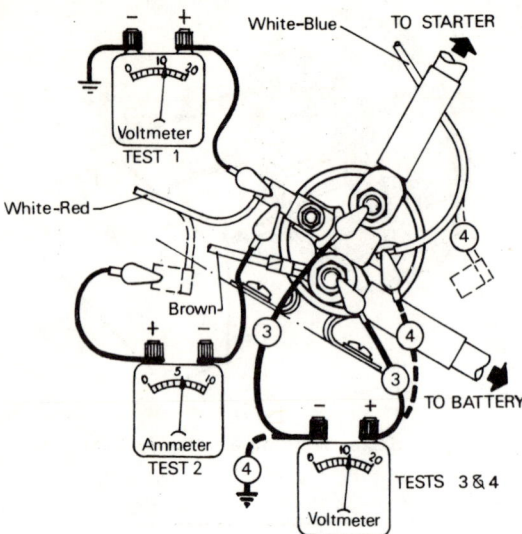

11:3 The alternator

This is either Lucas type 15.ACR or 17.ACR or Delco-Remy DN460, but a description of the first will cover all types.

To remove the alternator: Disconnect the battery and the cables from the alternator.

Slacken the mounting bolts and nuts and disengage the drive belt from the pulleys. Remove the bolts and lift off the alternator.

Dismantling:

Refer to **FIG 11:1** and proceed as follows:

1 Remove nut 11, lockwasher, pulley 10 and fan 9. Remove cover 1 (two screws).

2 Note connections then remove regulator from brush-gear 2 (two screws). Remove lead from brushgear to rectifier 3 and detach brushgear (two screws).

3 Remove through-bolts 4a. Press drive end bracket 8 off shaft, retaining spacer, but first remove key from shaft.

4 Remove rectifier 3 by loosening nut and unsoldering leads, after noting connections. Prevent heat reaching pack by holding tags with thin-nosed pliers, to act as heat sink.

5 Press rotor 6 out of slip ring end bracket 4. Use metal tube 3 inch long with outer diameter of 1.32 inch and bore of 1.24 inch. Slide tube over slip ring moulding 6a and use it to drive the outer race of the bearing from its housing.

6 If necessary, unsolder field connections from slip ring moulding and withdraw moulding. Pull off bearing if renewal is required.

7 Carefully prise stator 5 out of bracket 4. Remove circlip from bracket 8 to remove bearing 7. Note order of grease seal assembly.

Testing and adjusting charging circuit:

When the charging circuit appears to be faulty, first check that the fan belt is not slipping. Ensure that the battery is in good condition as outlined in **Section 11:2**. Carry out further tests as follows:

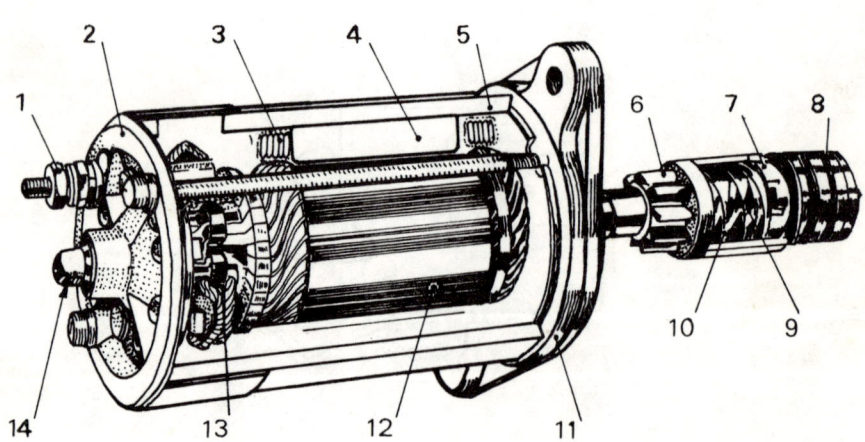

FIG 11:5   Cutaway view of starter M35G/1

Key to Fig 11:5   1 Terminal   2 Commutator and bracket   3 Field coil   4 Pole shoe   5 Yoke   6 Pinion   7 Sleeve nut   8 Thrust spring   9 Screwed sleeve   10 Anti-drift spring   11 Drive end bracket   12 Armature   13 Brush   14 Squared end armature shaft

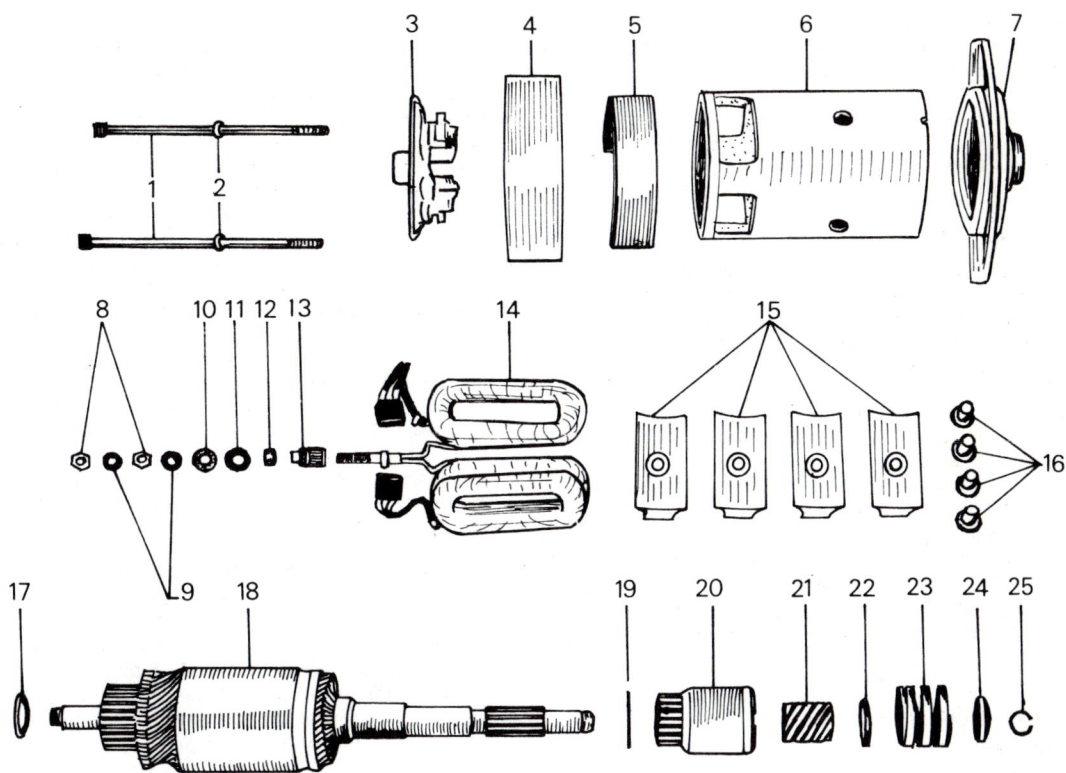

FIG 11:6   Exploded view of starter M35G/1

Key to Fig 11:6   1 Through-bolts   2 Lock washers   3 Commutator end bracket and brushgear   4 Commutator cover band
5 Insulator   6 Yoke   7 Drive end bracket   8 Terminal nuts   9 Lock washers   10 Plain washer   11 Insulating washer
12 Spacer   13 Insulating sleeve   14 Field coils   15 Pole shoes   16 Pole shoe screws   17 Thrust washer   18 Armature
19 Thrust washer   20 Pinion   21 Screwed sleeve   22 Thrust washer   23 Thrust spring   24 Spring collar   25 Circlip

Voltage drop test:

1 Refer to **FIG 11:2**. Connect a low-range voltmeter to positive terminal of battery and positive terminal on alternator (top view). Voltmeter must be high-grade moving coil instrument with a scale suitable for readings of .25 volt.

2 Switch on headlamps (main beam) and start engine. Run at about 3000 rev/min. If meter reads in excess of .5 volt, there is a high resistance in the positive side of the charging circuit.

3 Repeat test with negative connections (lower view). If meter reading exceeds .25 volt there is a high resistance in the negative side of the charging circuit.

4 Check for high resistance due to loose, dirty or corroded connectors. These must be clean and tight.

Rotor tests:

1 Refer to both lefthand views in **FIG 11:3**. Connect ohmmeter between slip rings of rotor (top view). Resistance should be 4.3 ohms. Alternatively, use a 12-volt battery and ammeter in series. Reading should be approximately 2.8 amp.

2 Test insulation with 110-volt AC supply and 15 watt lamp (lower view). Connect between one of slip rings and a rotor pole. Coil is earthed to rotor if lamp lights. Fit new rotor.

Stator tests:

1 Refer to righthand views in **FIG 11:3**. Test continuity of windings as in top view. Connect any two of the three stator cables across a 12-volt battery and test lamp taking not less than 36 watts. Repeat, replacing one of the two cables with the third. Failure of lamp to light means a break in part of the stator winding. Renew the stator.

2 Test insulation with 110-volt AC supply and 15 watt test lamp. Connect between one of stator cables and laminations (lower view). Lamp will light if coils are earthed. Renew stator.

Diode tests:

1 Refer to single view in centre in **FIG 11:3**. If alternator output test indicates a fault in one or more of the diodes, remove the rectifier from the alternator (see under 'Dismantling').

2 Connect each of the nine diode pins in turn, in series with a 1.5 watt test bulb and one side of a 12-volt battery. Connect the other battery terminal to the particular heat sink into which the diode is soldered.

3 Now reverse the connections to the diode pin and the heat sink. The bulb should light in one test only.

4 If the bulb lights in both tests, or not in either, fit a new rectifier.

Reassembling:

This is mainly a matter of reversing the dismantling instructions. Having fitted the brushgear, check the brush springs by placing new brushes in their holders. Press down until the brushes are flush with the holder, using a spring compression scale. The scale should read 7 to 10 oz.

When soldering the leads onto the rectifier, use thin-nosed pliers as a heat sink to prevent soldering heat from reaching the rectifier.

Fit the drive end bearing after packing with suitable grease. The slip ring end bearing is fitted to the rotor shaft with its shielded side facing the rotor. Then re-engage the slip ring moulding with the slot on the rotor shaft and resolder the field connections.

Fit the stator into the slip ring end bracket, ensuring that the slots in the stator line up with the through holes for the bolts.

11:4 Starter motor M35G/1

Testing in the car:

When the starter switch (ignition key) is turned fully to the right a small current operates a solenoid and closes its contacts. These contacts, which are capable of handling a heavy current, connect the battery direct to the starter by heavy cables. An additional contact on the solenoid feeds current to the ignition coil, without passing through the resistor (see **Section 3:8**) to provide a more powerful ignition current when starting.

When checking starter troubles, first ensure that the battery is in good condition and that all battery and starter connections are in good order. A corroded battery terminal or bad earth connection may have sufficient electrical resistance to make the starter inoperative, though it may pass enough current for lamps and accessories.

To check the solenoid, operate the starter switch, when a click should be heard from the solenoid indicating that the contact bridge is moving. If no click can be heard, carry out the following tests using a 0-20 range voltmeter and a 0-10 range ammeter as shown in **FIG 11:4**.

1 Connect the voltmeter positive terminal to the solenoid small terminal carrying the white/red wire and connect the negative of the voltmeter to earth. On operating the starter switch a reading of 12 volts should be obtained. If no reading, current is not reaching the solenoid owing to a faulty starter switch or wiring.

2 If test 1 is satisfactory, disconnect the voltmeter. Disconnect the white/red wire from the solenoid terminal and connect the ammeter between the wire and the terminal as shown. Operate the starter switch when a reading of 4 to 6 amperes should be recorded if the solenoid winding is in good condition. If no reading, renew the solenoid.

3 Connect the voltmeter across the main solenoid terminals as shown. A reading of 12 volts should be obtained. Operate the starter switch and if the solenoid contacts are closing the voltmeter should return to zero. If it fails to do so, renew the solenoid. Disconnect the voltmeter after completing this test.

4 Disconnect the white/blue wire from its terminal and connect the voltmeter as shown between the terminal and earth. On operating the starter switch a reading of 12 volts should be obtained. If no reading, the solenoid should be renewed, as although the starter should still operate, the 'cold-start' coil contacts in the solenoid are not functioning.

11:5 Removing, servicing and refitting starter

The starter is shown in a cutaway view in **FIG 11:5** while the components are shown in exploded form in **FIG 11:6**. To remove the starter:

1 Disconnect both battery cables.

2 Remove the exhaust manifold. On some cars it is necessary to remove the alternator.

3 Disconnect cable from starter. Remove the two bolts and lockwashers securing the starter to the crankcase and withdraw the starter.

Inspect and test the starter as follows:

1 Remove the cover band 4 and examine the brushes and their spring. The brushes should move freely in their holders and should be renewed when they are

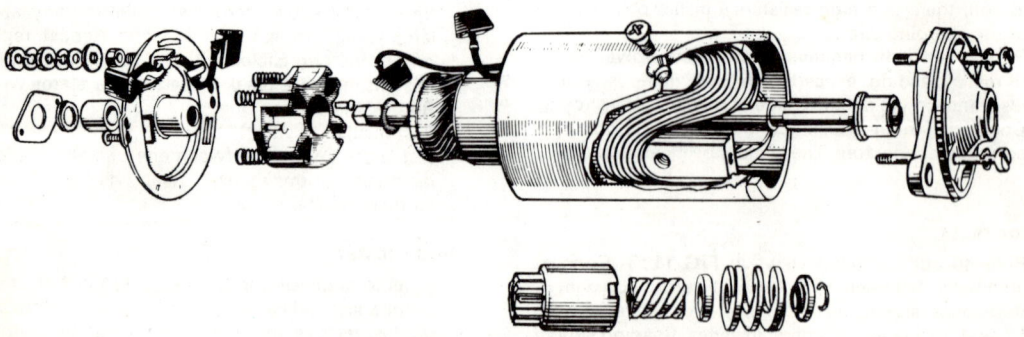

FIG 11:7 Exploded view of starter M35J/1

worn down to a minimum length of .38 inch, and if a spring balance is available the spring tension should be measured and the spring renewed if it is less than 28 oz.

2 Clean the commutator with a petrol moistened cloth while rotating the armature. Do not saturate as petrol is injurious to the windings.

3 Hold the starter body firmly in a vice and connect to a 12-volt battery by heavy cables, one cable going to the starter terminal while the other is earthed to the yoke 6.

The starter should now 'motor' at high speed. If it does not, it should be dismantled as follows, referring to **FIG 11 : 6** for identification of parts:

1 If not already removed take off cover band 4 and insulator 5.

2 Remove through-bolts 1. Tap the drive end bracket 7 away from the yoke 6 and withdraw armature 18 complete with starter drive 19 to 25 and drive and bracket 7. Note washer 17.

3 Remove the two insulated brushes from the holders on bracket 3. Remove terminal nut 8, lockwasher 9, plain washer 10 and insulating washer 11 from terminal post. Remove spacer 12 from insulating sleeve 13.

4 Remove commutator end bracket 3 and withdraw the plastic insulating sleeve 13 from the terminal post.

If the starter drive is in good condition it need not be dismantled but should be washed in petrol. Oil must not be used as this will collect grit and cause the starter to fail to engage. If the drive has to be dismantled either for servicing or for removal of the drive end bracket 7, proceed as follows:

1 Compress the thrust spring 23. This operation is facilitated if the special spring compressor No. JWP.376 is used. Remove the circlip 25. Release the spring.

2 Remove the spring collar 24, spring and thrust washer 22.

3 Withdraw the pinion assembly 20 and screwed sleeve 21 from the armature shaft. If necessary, rotate the pinion slightly so as to line up the splined washer (not shown in illustration) inside the pinion barrel with the splines on the shaft. Check that the light control spring (or anti-drift spring) which is also inside the barrel is not damaged. The pinion assembly 20 should not be dismantled being only serviced as an assembly. The thrust spring 23 can be checked by comparison with a new spring.

After cleaning the commutator as already described, any further attention to the commutator, or renewal of the sintered bronze bearings, should be carried out by a service agent. The earthed brushes can be renewed by unsoldering the brush leads at the tags under the brush holders and soldering the new leads in position. Renewal of insulated brushes however should be left to a service agent as the leads cannot be soldered direct to the aluminium field coils and the work entails removal and refitting of polepieces.

To reassemble the starter, also referring to **FIG 11 : 6** for identification of parts:

1 If the starter drive and drive end bracket have been removed, assemble the thrust washer 19 and drive end bracket 7 on the shaft. Install the pinion assembly

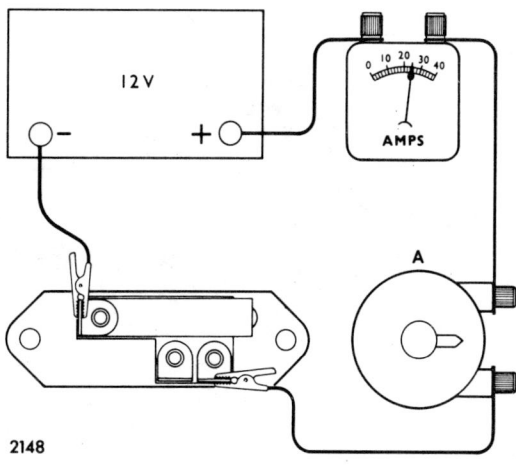

FIG 11 :8   Testing thermal circuit breaker

20 and screwed sleeve 21 on the shaft, rotating the pinion to engage its splined washer and the screwed sleeve with the splines on the shaft. Now assemble thrust washer 22, spring 23 and collar 24 to the shaft. Compress the spring as when dismantling and assemble circlip 25 to the groove in the shaft. Release the spring slowly.

2 Fit the insulating sleeve 13 over the field coil terminal post with the extension located between the post and the yoke and install commutator end bracket 3, ensuring that the dowel in the bracket engages the recess in the yoke and the brush leads are not trapped.

3 Retract and wedge the two earthed brushes.

4 Install thrust washer 17 on the commutator end of the armature shaft. Insert the armature between the pole shoes and engage the shaft in the commutator end bracket brush. Locate the dowel in the drive end bracket with the recess in the yoke.

5 Release the two earthed brushes to their working positions. Lift the springs of the insulated brush holders and insert the brushes, ensuring that the leads do not foul the armature.

6 Test the tension of the brush springs with a spring balance. The tension should be 34 to 46 oz with a new brush or 25 oz with a brush worn to the minimum length of .30 inch. If necessary, withdraw armature and renew springs.

7 Install the through-bolts 1 with lockwashers 2 and when tightened check that the armature rotates freely.

8 Fit spacer 12 over insulating sleeve 13, and the insulating washer 11, plain washer 10, lockwashers 9 and nuts 8 on the terminal post. Tighten securely but do not over-tighten.

9 Test the starter as previously described.

10 Before installing the starter ensure that the starter pinion rubber boot is serviceable and is correctly installed in the clutch housing.

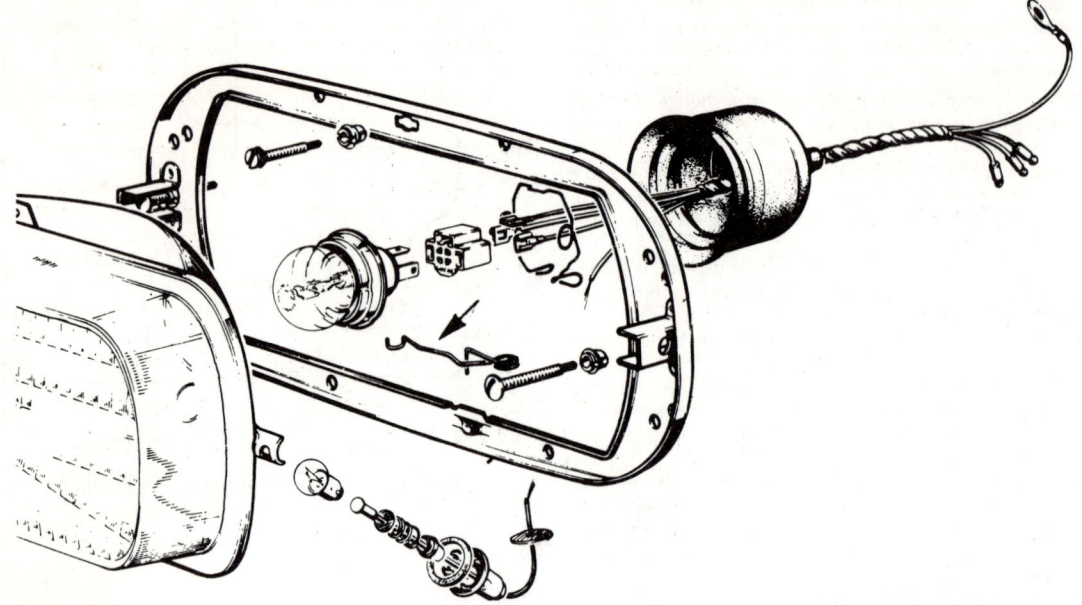

FIG 11:9   Components of headlamp unit. Single system

11:6 Starter motor M35J/1

This also is an inertia type unit and may be fitted in place of the type M35G/1 which was described earlier. It varies from the earlier type in that it has a face type moulded commutator, but has the same type of starter drive components and can be serviced in the same manner.

A cut-open diagram is given in **FIG 11:7**.

11:7 Fuses

Four 35 amp fuses are contained in the bulkhead connector and the circuits protected by them are as follows:

1 Horn, interior lamp, headlamp flasher.
2 Stoplamps, turn signal lamps, oil and alternator warning lamps, fuel and temperature gauges, heater motor, reverse lamps.
3 Wipers, radio, cigarette lighter.
4 Instrument lamps, rear lamps, number plate lamps, boot interior and cigarette lighter lamp.

Note that fuse No. 4 is fed via the thermal interruptor and lighting switch. From 1974, in order to accommodate the heavy loading particularly when a heated rear window is fitted, No. 2 fuse is rated at 50 amp. If a heated rear window is fitted to earlier cars, No. 2 fuse should be replaced by an uprated element.

Thermal circuit breaker:

This is a self-contained unit attached to a bracket on the scuttle side panel. It incorporates a bi-metal strip and a pair of contacts and is provided with a detachable cover.

The operation can be tested after removal by wiring up the circuit shown in **FIG 11:8** when the contacts should remain closed with a current of 25 amps but should open within 30 to 180 seconds with a current of 33 amps. If results of the test are not within these limits, the unit must be renewed.

Fusible link:

This is connected into the main battery feed and protects the entire system apart from the starter. The link consists of a length of copper wire which will burn out in the event of a heavy overload. The insulation will not burn or disintegrate.

One end of the link is connected to the bulkhead connector assembly through a terminal block on the battery tray and the other end to the main feed terminal on the starter solenoid.

1974 models have two links. One protects the lighting circuits, the other the remainder of the electrical circuits with the exception of the starter.

11:8 Lamps

Headlamps:

De luxe models of the Firenza coupé and Viva HC models are fitted with rectangular light units of the Unified European pre-focus type as illustrated in the exploded diagram of **FIG 11:9**. This unit houses a twin filament bulb for main and dipped beams and also the bulb for the side or parking lamps.

Access to the headlamp bulb is from inside the engine compartment where a rubber cover must be pulled back to expose the securing spring clip. The holder for the side lamp bulb is a push fit and is released simply by pulling it out.

The removal of a complete light unit entails the removal of the radiator grille in order to gain access to the spring clip (arrowed). This clip should be released and then the bracket eased out of the top beam trimming screw and the unit withdrawn. Do not disturb the trim screws otherwise the alignment of the lamp will be upset.

SL models of the Firenza are fitted with a four-lamp system comprising either sealed beam units or the pre-focus type described above. A lamp of each type is shown in **FIG 11:10**. The two inner lamps have only a main beam filament whilst the two outer lamps have a dipped beam filament and a supplementary main beam filament.

When on main beam all four lamps are in operation. Dipping the lights extinguishes the inner pair and switches the outer pair from supplementary main beam to dip filament.

Access to the bulb and wiring adaptor on the pre-focus type is again from inside the engine compartment. The spring clip securing the bulb can be released after squeezing the sides of the plastic cover and withdrawing it from the lamp mounting ring.

To withdraw a complete light unit it is necessary first to remove the radiator grille insert. The retaining ring is removed by slackening three screws and turning the rim a few degrees in an anti-clockwise direction. The lamp unit is secured to the front panel by four screws and quick action nuts.

Beam setting:

The alignment of the headlamp beams on single lamp installations is carried out by adjusting the trim screws at the rear of the front body panel of which there are three to each lamp. This may conveniently be done with Adjusting Tool VR.2024 as shown in **FIG 11:11**.

To ensure accuracy, beam setting equipment should be used to aim the lamp, but if it is not available the beams may be projected on to a wall at a distance of 25 feet. The surface of the ground should be level, the car normally loaded and tyre pressures correct. With the car square to the wall, adjust the main beams by means of the trim screws so that the light spots projected on the wall are $2\frac{1}{2}$ inches below lamp centre height and the beams parallel to the car's centre line.

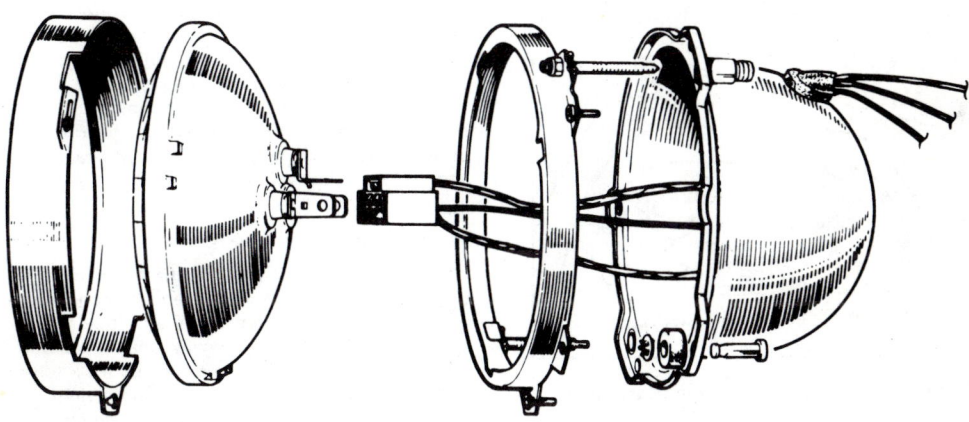

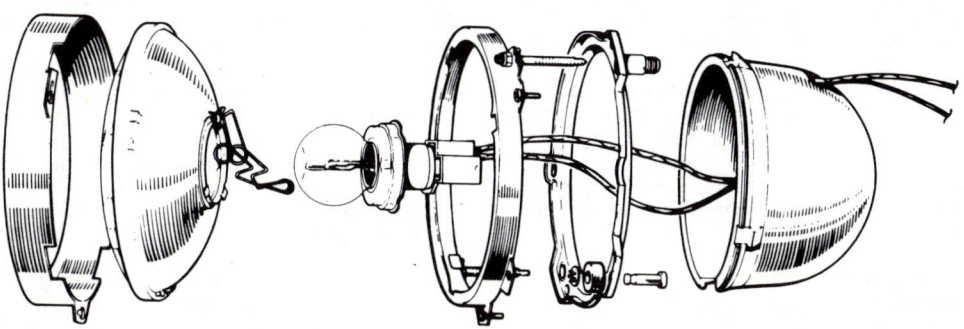

FIG 11:10   Headlamp units of twin system showing (top) Sealed-beam unit, (below) Pre-focus unit

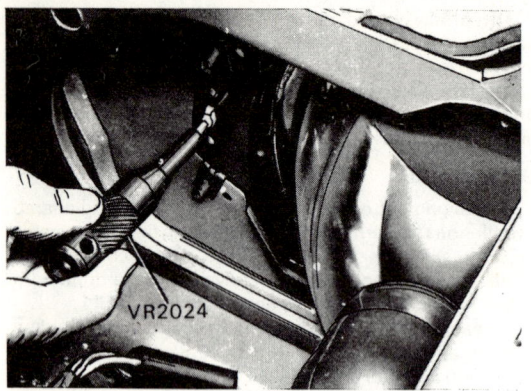

FIG 11:11 Headlamp beam setting

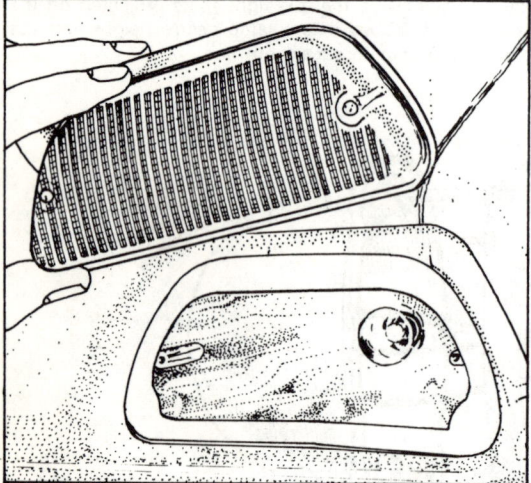

FIG 11:12 Removing front turn indicator lens

Beam adjustment on twin headlamp systems is preferably carried out with an optical type beam setter. The lamps incorporate two beam setting screws which can be rotated with Adjusting Tool VR.2103, access to the screws being from inside the engine compartment.

The correct aiming of the inner lamps is so that the beam is $\frac{1}{2}$ deg. down with no lateral deflection. Aiming the outer lamps is carried out on dipped beam when the setting is 2 deg. down and 2 deg. left or right depending on whether the car is righthand or lefthand drive.

It may be noted that on some cars using the pre-focus units that the inner lamps are fitted with double filament bulbs (15/40 watt). Only one filament (45 watt) is used.

Direction indicators:

The front turn signal lamps are mounted in the front valance panel and secured by three studs and nuts, but access to the bulb is gained by removing two screws and lifting off the lens (see **FIG 11:12**).

On some cars side repeater lamps are wired into the signal lamp circuit which are screwed on to the side of the wings. One screw holds the lens in place.

The vane type turn signal unit is clipped to the vertical section of the drivers parcel shelf close to the steering column where it is readily accessible. The unit is wired through fuse No. 2 which should first be checked in the event of a failure. If the breakdown is traced to the flasher unit it must be renewed as no adjustment is possible.

Hazard warning lights:

This system comprises a switch and flasher unit fed from fuse to No. 1 and connected into the turn signal circuit. The switch is attached to the lower half of the steering column canopy and the unit is clipped adjacent to the turn signal unit.

When the hazard warning switch is pulled out the normal turn signal unit is isolated and the hazard warning unit flashes all four signal lamps simultaneously. Visual confirmation of the system in action is given by a light in the switch as well as the two turn signal warning lamps.

Rear lamps:

The rear lamp assembly contains the combined tail and stop bulb and the turn signal bulb in addition to a red reflector. Being of the wrap-round type. The tail light is also visible from the side of the car.

Access to the bulbs is gained from inside the luggage boot after removing the protecting cover which is held in place by two clamp plates. On estate cars this cover is secured by three screws.

11:9 Windscreen wipers

On early cars the standard fitting is a single speed electric motor for the wipers and a manually-operated windscreen washer. From 1974 all models have a two-speed wiper and an electrically operated pump for the washer. These latter are controlled by a switch mounted in tandem with the direction indicator switch.

The components of the complete assembly are shown in **FIG 11:13** from which it may be seen that there is a girder type mounting bracket with a pivot housing riveted to each end and the motor bolted on in the centre. Access to the wiper unit is gained after detaching the ventilator shroud panel.

Two makes of wiper arms and blades are used, Magnatex and Aeramic, and they are interchangeable only as complete assemblies as they employ different methods of attachment. The Magnatex arm is removed by slackening a screw and tapping it inwards to release the tapered wedge from the spindle. The Aeramic arm can be withdrawn by easing back the spring clip under the arm boss. When refitting the arms they should be located on the spindles so that the centre of the blade is 2 inches from the lower reveal moulding when in the parked position.

To gain access to the unit mounting bolts, the links should be moved clear of the bolts by using the motor or alternatively by detaching the links. Remove the wiper blades, remove the mounting bolts and prise out the rubber retainer. Ease off the unit and detach the harness plug and earth wire.

It is recommended that a faulty motor should be taken to a service station for attention or replacement and not dismantled at home. When assembling the motor to the wiper unit the correct location of the motor and the links will be seen in **FIG 11:14.** It will be noted that the end frame is on the driver's side. Ensure that the crank link is fitted to the crank in the direction shown and that all moving parts are adequately lubricated.

Windscreen wash:

The layout of the washing system is shown in **FIG 11:15.** Two spray jets are housed in a common housing on the bonnet panel and the plastic reservoir is attached to a bracket on the righthand front wheel panel. For identification purposes the tube from the reservoir to the pump inlet is coloured green.

When an electric motor pump is fitted, it is housed in the reservoir cap and is easily removed for servicing by taking out four bolts securing the end cover.

11:10 Instruments

The instrument assembly incorporates a magnetic type speedometer, fuel gauge and on some cars, a water temperature gauge. Both fuel and temperature gauges are of the bi-metal type. Warning lamps for ignition, oil pressure, main beam and turn signal are included and provision is made for backlight demist, brake pressure and water temperature warning lamps.

A printed circuit is attached to the rear of the instrument case and is connected to the wiring harness by a multi-socket plug. Also plugged into the printed circuit is a voltage stabilizer through which the gauges are energized. This prevents fluctuation in the gauge readings resulting from variations in battery voltage.

All instrument and warning lamps have push-in type holders with wedge-base capless type bulbs. Access to the bulb holders is from underneath the assembly, those at the inner end being reached after detaching the filler panel adjacent to the steering column which is held by four screws.

To remove the instrument assembly, first the panel cover must be removed. It is held in place by six nuts 1, two studs 2 and six clips 3 shown in **FIG 11:16.** The instrument assembly is held by three screws and two of the panel cover studs. Remove the screws and detach the multi-socket connector by squeezing the integral catches and withdraw the assembly. On some later cars the instrument assembly can be removed after taking out four retaining screws from the panel.

The printed circuit (see **FIG 11:17**) can be detached after removing all bulb holders, voltage stabilizer and four nuts and washers.

The speedometer is secured in the case by two screws and by plastic supports engaging in channels on the instrument face which is held by two screws.

The fuel and temperature gauges are of the bi-metal type and have a base plate engaging channels on the instrument face and held by spring clips.

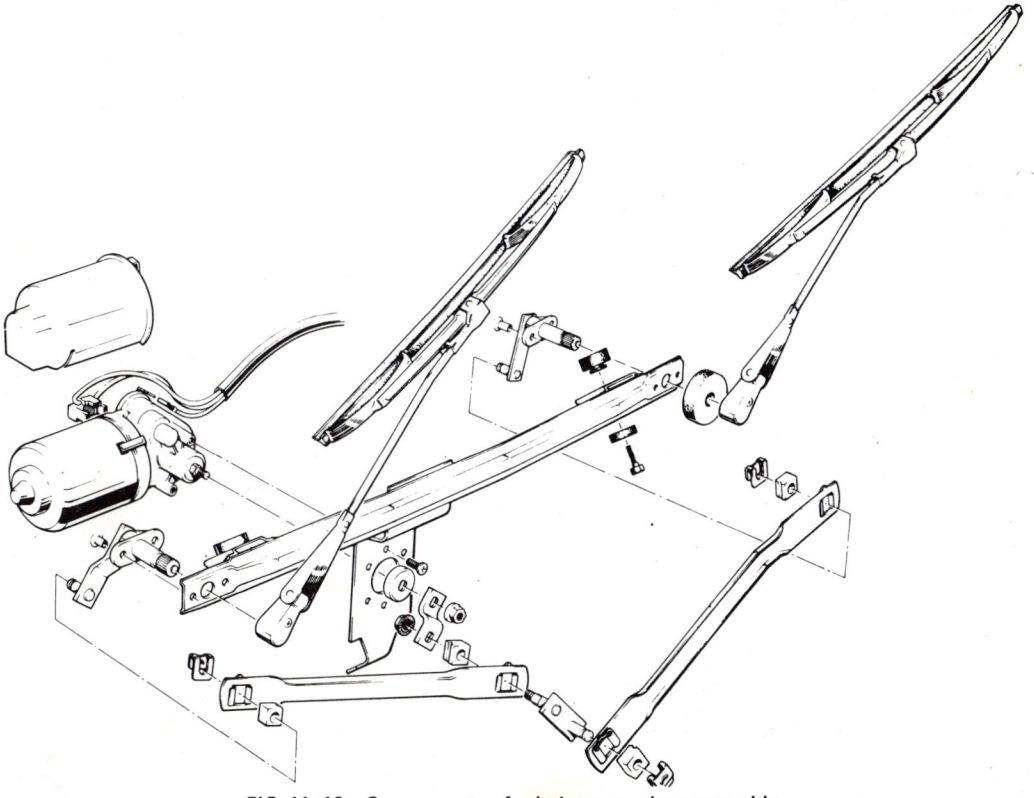

FIG 11:13 Components of windscreen wiper assembly

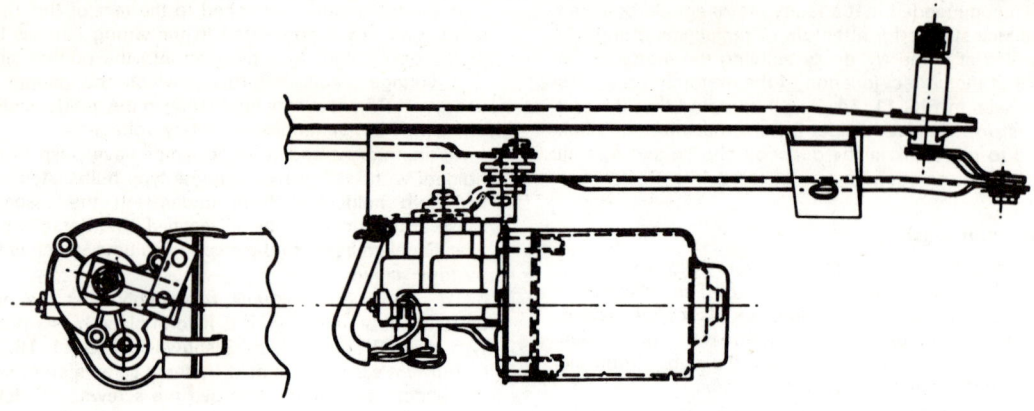

FIG 11:14 Location of wiper motor and links RHD

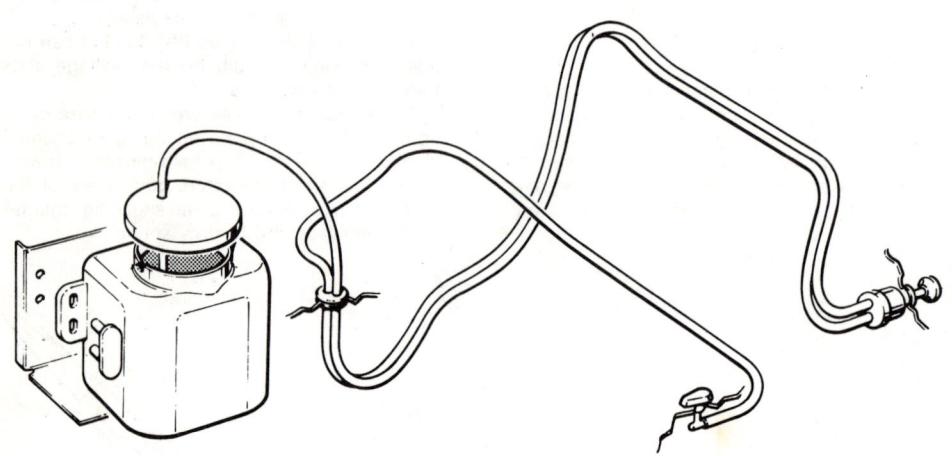

FIG 11:15 Layout of screen washer

The fuel gauge tank unit is a float operated rheostat mounted in the top of the tank and it may be checked when removed from the tank by connecting an ohmmeter between the terminal and the body. When the float is moved through its complete arc the readings should range from 17 to 260 ohms. When refitting see that the terminal points towards the righthand side of the car.

Voltage stabilizer:

This is a sealed unit, plugged in underneath the instrument panel, which ensures a steady supply to the instruments in spite of fluctuation in battery voltage.

It may be tested after removal by wiring up the circuit shown in **FIG 11:18.** There should be regular pulsation on the meter and the reading midway between minimum and maximum should be 10 volts.

If no voltage is recorded or alternatively a steady reading without pulses, the stabilizer is faulty.

Fuel and water temperature gauge tests:

If the operation of the voltage stabilizer has been confirmed these may be checked as follows:

Disconnect the wire from the sender unit and with the ignition switched on short the wire to earth. The needle on the gauge should move slowly to 'F' (full) or 'H' (hot) as appropriate. This will indicate that the sender unit is faulty.

The gauge and wiring are tested by joining the sender terminal on the gauge to earth and switching on the ignition. If the gauge does not move as before it is faulty and should be renewed.

The sender terminal is the outer one on each gauge.

11:11 Combined switch and horn push

The combined turn signal headlamp dip and flasher switch and horn push assembly is clamped to the steering shaft top bearing housing and located by a tongue on the clamp which engages a slot in the column.

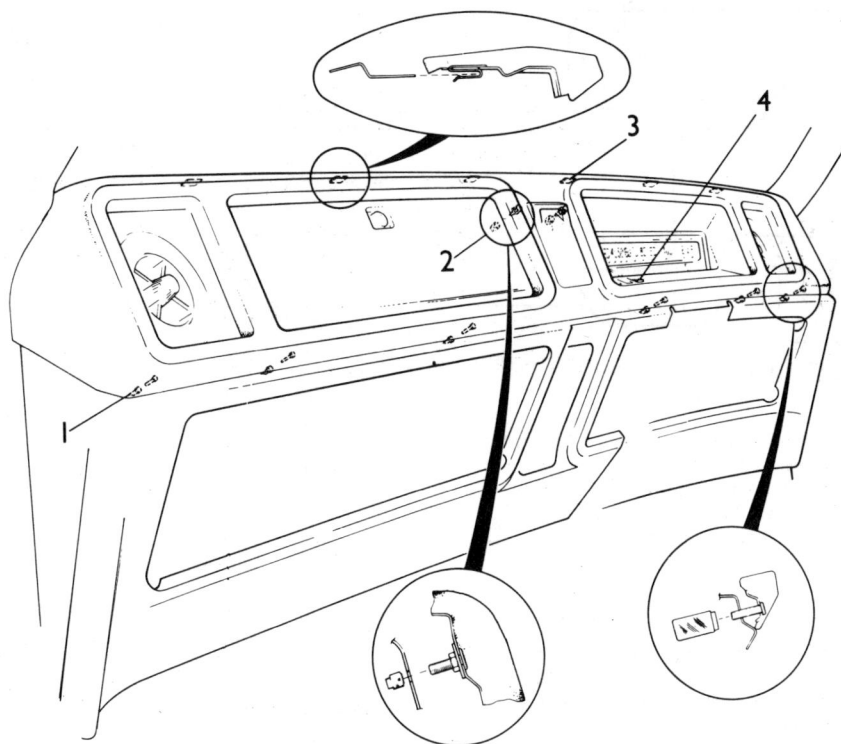

FIG 11:16   Removing instrument panel cover

Key to Fig **11:16**   1 Nuts   2 Studs   3 Clips   4 Switches

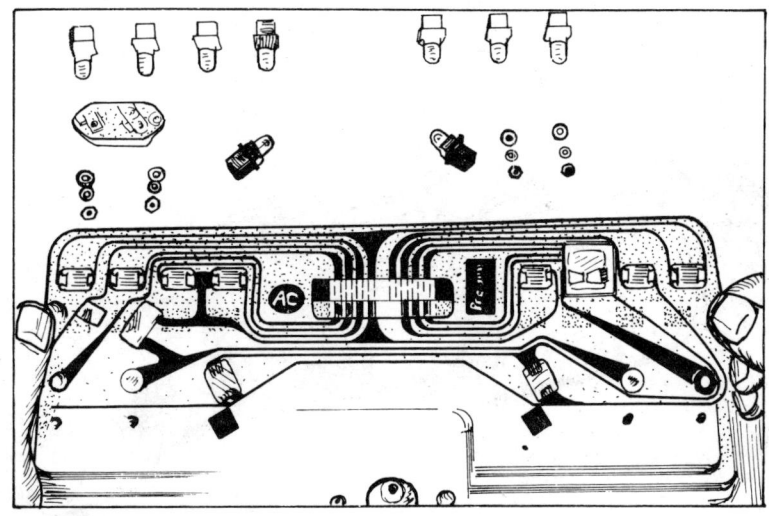

FIG 11:17   Removing printed circuit

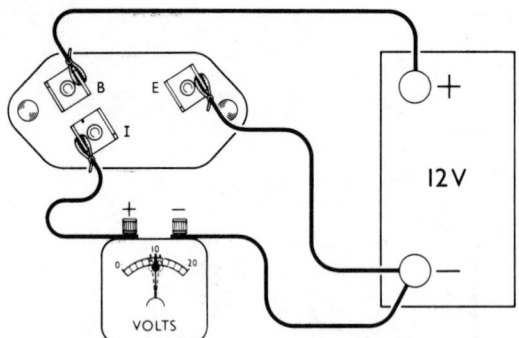

FIG 11:18 Testing voltage stabilizer

The horn contacts are reached by unscrewing the end cap, but to gain access to the remainder of the switch it is necessary to remove the canopy which is held together by four screws. The lower half is secured to the steering column brace by two screws and to the lock housing by one screw.

11:12 Pre-engaged type starter motors

This type of starter, which is fitted as standard to some later cars or as a heavy duty option, differs from the inertia type described earlier in that the actuating solenoid is built-in and positively engages the driving pinion before the motor is energised. Three different types may be used: M35J/PE, M35K/PE or 3M100/PE. They are all basically similar and the components of a typical example are shown in FIG 11:19. Operation is briefly as follows:

When the starter switch is operated, the solenoid pulls in the fork-shaped engagement lever which moves the starter drive pinion into engagement with the flywheel ring gear. When this movement is complete the current for rotating the motor is applied.

When the starter switch is released, the current is switched off and the pinion is retracted under spring pressure. To prevent over speeding the motor if the starter is not released when the engine has started, the pinion drive is taken through a one-way clutch which free wheels under these conditions.

Removal and refitting the starter is quite straight-forward, although in some cases the front engine mounting and the crankcase support bracket may have to be removed.

Testing:

Three simple tests are described in cases where the starter fails to operate. Refer to FIG 11:20.

A Check the electrical supply to the solenoid by disconnecting the white/red wire from the solenoid and connecting a 0–20 voltmeter as shown. Operate the switch and battery voltage should be recorded. No reading indicates a fault in the switch or wiring or, on automatic transmissions, a faulty inhibitor switch.

B To prevent the engine firing, disconnect the LT wire from the coil negative terminal and connect the voltmeter across the main terminals on the solenoid. Battery voltage should be recorded.
Operate the switch and the voltmeter reading should drop to zero. Failure to do so indicates a faulty solenoid which must be renewed.

C Still with the LT wire disconnected, disconnect the white wires from the solenoid IGN terminal and connect the voltmeter between the terminal and a good earth.
Operate the starter switch and turn the engine, at least 8 volts should be shown. If there is no reading, renew the solenoid.

11:13 Fault diagnosis

(a) Battery discharged

1 Terminals or earth connection loose or dirty
2 Lighting circuit shorted
3 Generator not charging
4 Battery internally defective

(b) Insufficient charging current

1 Loose or corroded battery terminals
2 Generator drive belt slipping

(c) Battery will not hold charge

1 Low electrolyte level
2 Battery plates sulphated
3 Electrolyte leaking from casing or top sealing compound
4 Separators ineffective

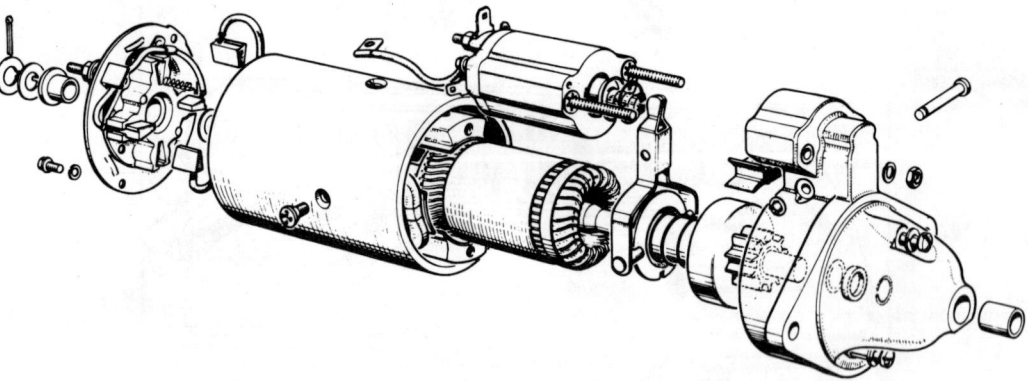

FIG 11:19   Exploded view of a typical pre-engaged starter

(d) Generator output low or nil

1 Belt broken or slipping
2 Worn bearings, loose polepieces
3 Slip rings worn, burnt or shorted
4 Armature shaft bent or worn
5 Rectifier defective
6 Brushes sticking, springs weak or broken

(e) Starter lacks power or will not operate

1 Battery discharged. Loose connections on battery or
  starter. Faulty earth connection.
2 Starter pinion jammed in mesh.
3 Ignition switch faulty. Solenoid switch faulty
4 Brushes or brush leads faulty
5 Commutator dirty or worn
6 Armature or field coils faulty
7 Starter shaft bent
8 Engine abnormally stiff

(f) Starter revolves but does not turn engine

1 Pinion teeth sticking on screwed sleeve
2 Broken teeth on pinion or ring gear

(g) Starter pinion noisy when engine running

1 Anti-drift or control spring weak or broken

(h) Starter motor rough or noisy

1 Mounting bolts loose
2 Damaged pinion or ring gear
3 Main pinion spring broken

(j) Lamps inoperative or erratic

1 Battery low, bulbs burned out, blown fuse
2 Faulty earthing of lamps or battery
3 Faulty switches or wiring

(k) Wiper motor sluggish, taking high current

1 Faulty armature
2 Bearings out of alignment
3 Commutator dirty or shortcircuited

(l) Fuel gauge does not register

1 No battery supply to gauge
2 Gauge not earthed to printed circuit
3 Cable between gauge and tank unit broken
4 Tank unit faulty

(m) Fuel gauge registers FULL

1 Wire between gauge and tank unit earthed

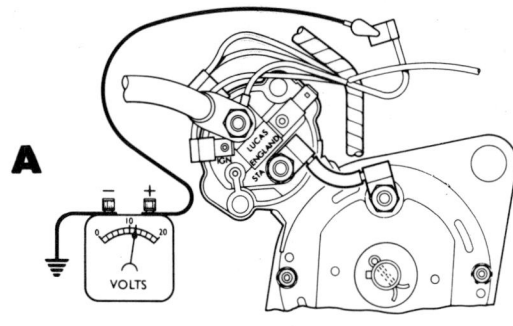

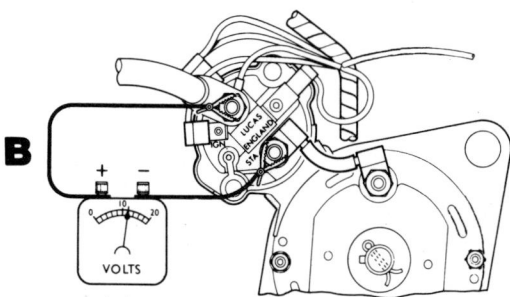

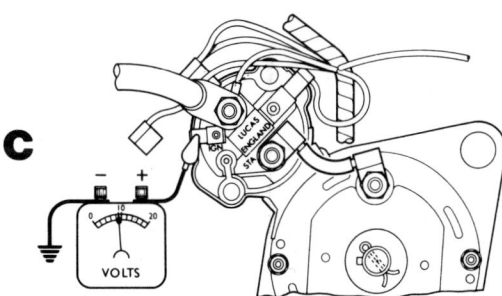

FIG 11:20 Showing the connections for three tests
when the starter fails to operate

NOTES

CHAPTER 12

THE BODYWORK

12:1 Removing door trim
12:2 Servicing door locks
12:3 Servicing window regulators
12:4 Windscreen and back light glass

12:5 Instrument panel cover
12:6 Radiator grille
12:7 Heating and ventilation system

12:1 Removing door trim

On Standard and De-Luxe models the door trim pads are secured round the edge by clips to the inner door panel. The armrest is secured by two screws. On the SL models the trim pad is hung over the top edge of the door panel and secured along the bottom and side with clips. Before the pad can be removed it is first necessary to take off the interior handles.

The escutcheon on the remote control is retained by spring action and is simply prised away from the trim pad.

The handle on the window regulator is secured by a screw in the handle boss, which is accessible after prising out the insert 1 in **FIG 12:1.** On SL models which have thicker trim pads an extension piece 2 is fitted as shown.

There is a polythene sheet stuck on to the inner panel to act as a water deflector and care must be taken not to tear it or water may enter and saturate the trim pad. When replacing the sheet, do not omit to smooth out any wrinkles.

12:2 Servicing door locks

The outside handle of each door incorporates a push button which, in the case of the front doors, is provided with a lock barrel. The locks are of the fork-bolt type in which the fork engages a striker screwed into the door pillar.

The front door lock and catch mechanism is illustrated in **FIG 12:2** and is operated by a series of rods. The remote control rod 3 releases the catch from inside the car and the catch is locked by the rods 1 and 2.

The rod 4 also operates the locking mechanism when actuated by the key in the outside handle. Anti-rattle clips are fitted to the end of each rod except the lower end of rod 4.

The mechanism on rear doors is similar but a little simpler due to the absence of a key operated lock.

To remove the lock, close the window and remove the glass run channel attaching screws. Remove the lock securing screws and detach the control rods, when the lock can be withdrawn.

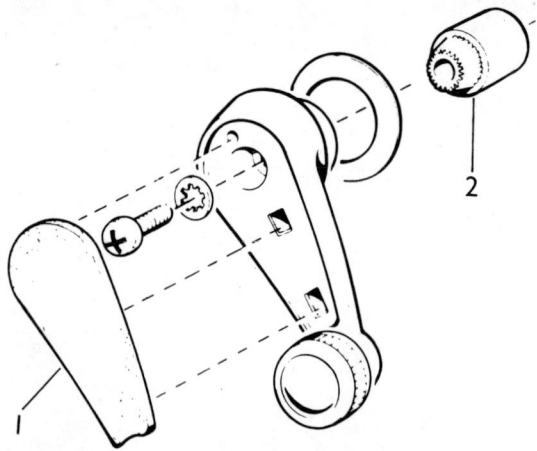

FIG 12:1 Window regulator handle showing 1 spring insert and 2 distance piece (SL only)

When refitting, apply some H.M.P. grease to the friction surfaces of the lock and rods, and do not omit to check the lock to striker engagement.

Forward and rearward adjustment of the striker 1 in **FIG 12:3** is obtained by packing washers 3. Take care to ensure that the fork of the door lock engages the striker over section 2, which incorporates a rubber silencing bush.

Sideways and vertical adjustment is obtained by moving the threaded striker retaining plate.

12:3 Servicing window regulators

Refer to **FIG 12:4**. The front door window regulators incorporate two balance arms riveted to the main arm and they pivot about the rivet to ensure an equal lift at each end of the glass. The lower arm engages a support channel 1 which is bolted to the door inner panel, while the glass support channel incorporates a fixed roller 2 which engages a guide channel attached to the door

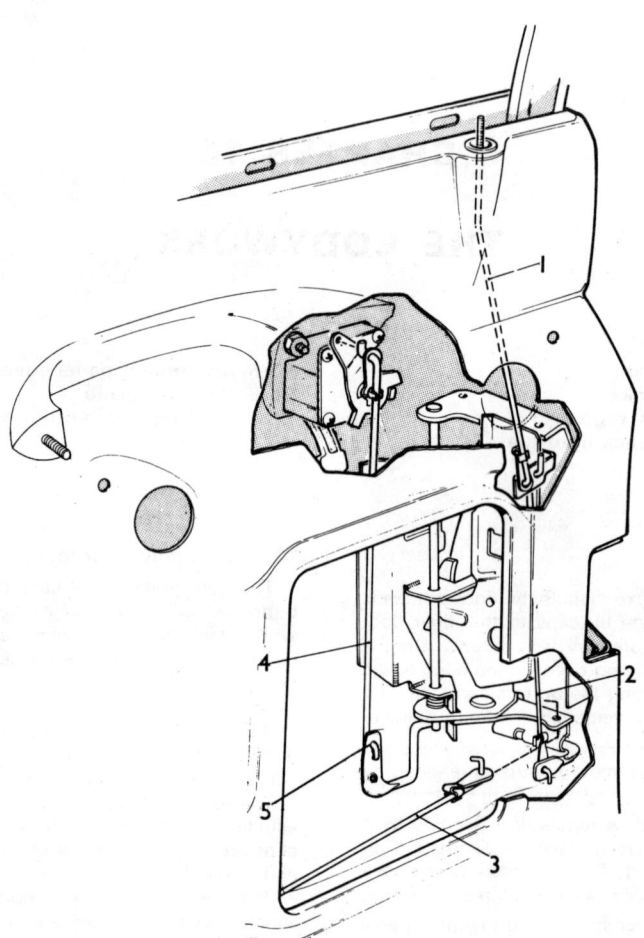

FIG 12:2 Front door locking mechanism

Key to Fig 12:2 1 Rod to lock button   2 Rod   3 Remote control rod   4 Key operated rod (on four-door cars this is fitted in the lower hole in the lock lever)   5 Top hole (two-door cars only)

inner panel to control the sideways movement of the glass. Item 3 is a window stop buffer and bracket.

Access to the guide channel upper bolts is through holes in the door shut which are covered by plastic plugs.

The rear door regulator is similar to the front, but the stop buffer is incorporated in the fixed roller vertical guide.

FIG 12:5 shows the dimensions for fitting a window glass and channel assembly. The inside faces of the channel should be smeared with engine oil and assembled so that the open sides of the channel guides are towards the inside face of the glass.

After installing a regulator, adjust the lower balance arm support channel studs up or down until the upper edge of the glass is parallel with the door frame (see **FIG 12:6**), noting that on four-door models the longer, straight section of the channel must always be towards the front of the car.

The window stop bracket is fitted on two-door cars to the centre of the three holes provided. On four-door models it is fitted to the lower of the two holes.

Do not omit to apply an adequate supply of grease to all friction surfaces when reassembling window glasses and regulators.

12:4 Windscreen and back light glasses

Windscreens are either of wide zone toughened or of laminated safety glass, identified by the maker's mark etched at top or bottom centre of the screen. Windscreens, back light glasses and rear fixed quarter light glasses are mounted in the body apertures in rubber glazing channels. On de-Luxe and SL models the channels incorporate moulding inserts (see **FIG 12:7**).

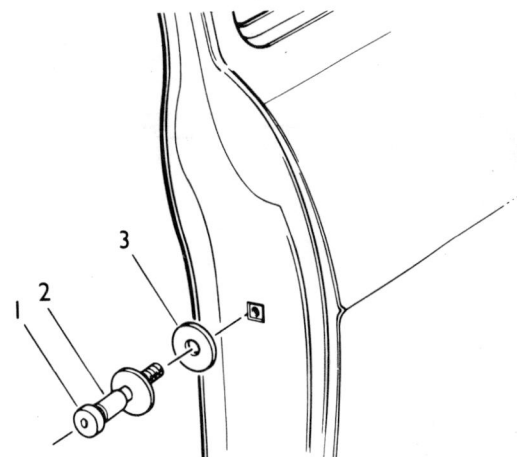

FIG 12:3   Door striker adjustment

Key to Fig 12:3   1 Striker   2 Bush   3 Washers

Toughened glasses are removed by bumping out from the inside of the car with the palm of the hand, **using leather or thick cloth gloves.** An assistant will be needed to prevent the glass from falling. Laminated glass must not be bumped out. To remove, remove moulding insert (where fitted) and cut away glazing channel lip on outer side of glass. Then carefully push glass outwards away from the channel. Protect paintwork, ventilator grille and defrost outlets before removing damaged

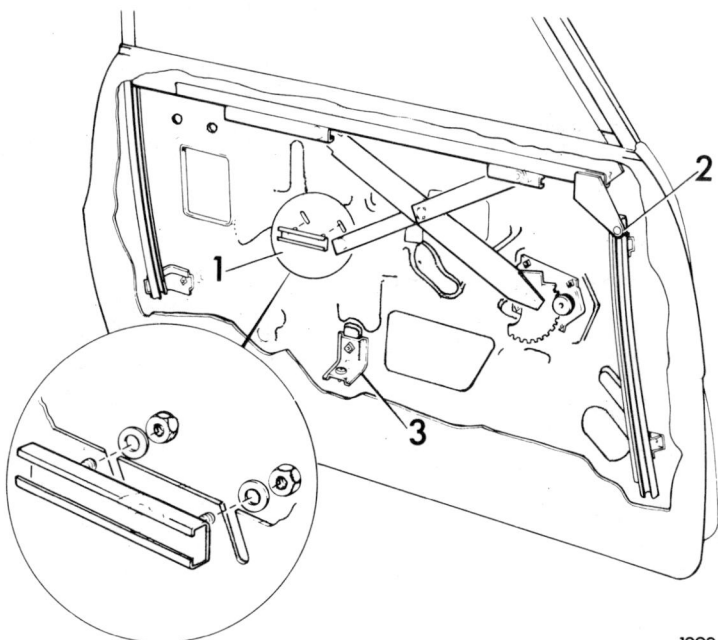

1893

FIG 12:4   Window regulating mechanism (front door)

Key to Fig 12:4   1 Support channel   2 Roller   3 Stop

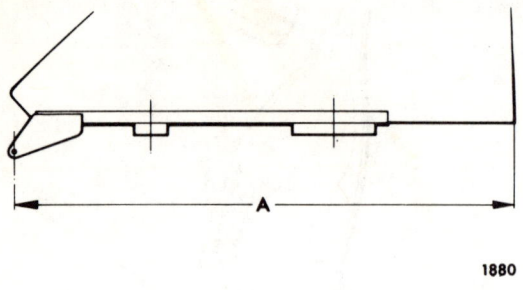

1880

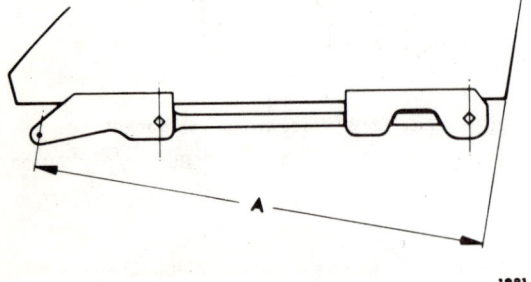

1881

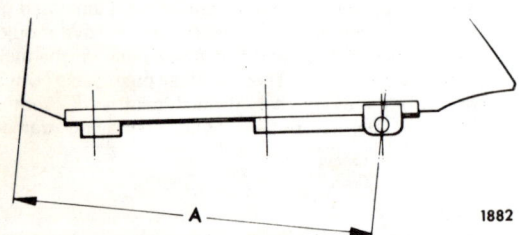

1882

FIG 12:5   Fitting window glass to support channel

Top: Two door cars   ..   ..   **A**=37.80 inches
Centre: Front doors   ..   ..   **A**=26.80 inches
Bottom: Rear doors   ..   ..   **A**=23.20 inches

FIG 12:6   Adjusting level of window

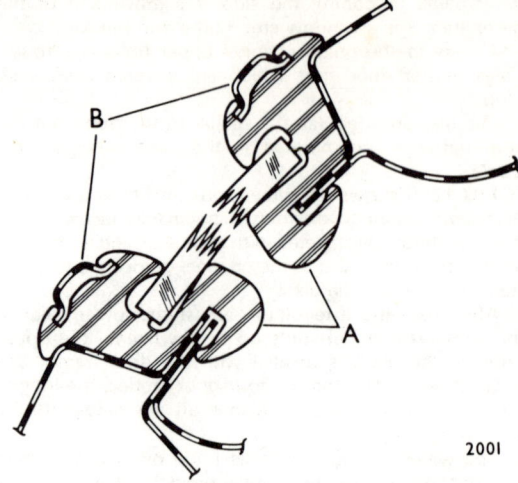

2001

FIG 12:7   Windscreen rubber channel. B shows moulding insert on SL models

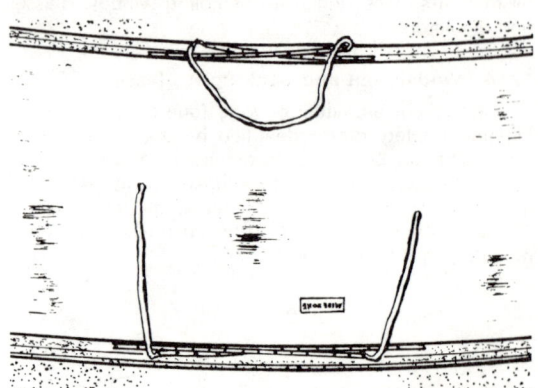

FIG 12:8   Using cord to install windscreen

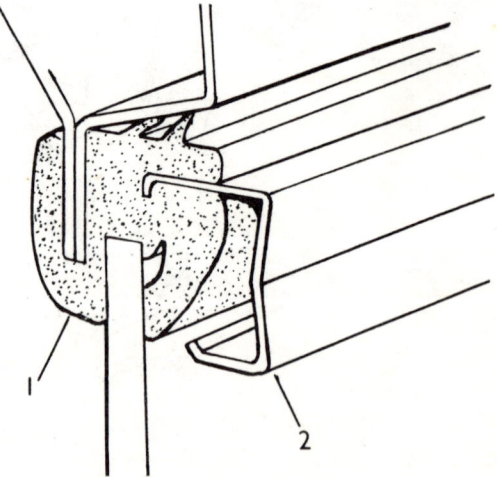

FIG 12:9   Rubber channel 1 for fixed quarter glasses and 2 reveal moulding

windscreens. The mouldings on quarter lights of de-Luxe and SL models are removed from and refitted to the glazing channel with the window out of the car.

To install windscreen, back light or fixed quarter light glasses, fit the glazing channel to the glass and insert strong thin cord around the securing lip groove of the channel. Leave a loop at the top of the glass, crossing the cord here and where the ends emerge at the bottom of the glass (see **FIG 12:8**). Before installing the glass, apply sealing compound all round the root of the body aperture flange. An assistant will also be needed for the next operation. With the glass central in the body aperture and light pressure applied to the outside of the glass, the cord is pulled from the inside to lift the lip of the channel over the aperture flange. Start at the bottom and work to within six inches of the corners. After installing glass, inject sealing compound between the the outside of the glass and the glazing channel. To install the moulding in the channels of windscreen and back light glasses on de-Luxe and SL models a special tool No. D.1163 is needed, the operation being carried out after installation of the glass.

Rear quarter fixed windows:

These are mounted in the body in rubber glazing channels which incorporate reveal mouldings having L-shaped flanges to retain them in the channel as shown in **FIG 12:9**. Before one of these windows can be removed, the three pop rivets later models have screws, which attach the reveal moulding to the door pillar must be drilled out, the window can then be bumped out from the inside. The reveal moulding is detached from the glazing channel after the window is removed.

Before assembling the reveal moulding to the glazing channel, sealing compound must be injected between the glass and the channel. Then attach the reveal moulding, and when applicable, the waist moulding to the glazing channel before assembling the glass to the aperture.

The operation is completed in a similar manner to that described for the windscreen.

12:5 Instrument panel cover

In order to obtain access to a number of components in the course of servicing the car it is necessary to remove the one piece instrument panel and the parcel shelves.

Refer to **FIG 11:16**. The instrument panel cover is secured to the instrument panel by six nuts 1 and six clips 3, on some early cars there may also be two press-on studs 2. The cover can be detached together with the ash tray, air outlets and glove box lid after removing the switches 4 and the six nuts. To gain access to the nuts only the instrument panel aperture filler needs to be removed.

On later cars with rectangular instruments the instrument assembly is left in position when the cover is removed. On Firenza models with twin dials the instruments must be removed to gain access to one cover nut, they are secured by four screws.

Parcel shelves:

The parcel shelf on the passenger side is retained by six screws at the bottom and sides, and one screw through the rear of the shelf to a bracket on the dash panel.

The small parcel shelf on the driver's side is retained by four screws.

Instrument panel aperture filler:

This small panel is situated adjacent to the steering column and carries the windscreen wash pump (manual) or switch (electrical) and the cigarette lighter. It is retained by five screws whose removal will allow the filler to be pulled away and give access to connections at the rear (see **FIG 12:10**).

12:6 Radiator grille

Three types of radiator grille are used on the cars under review as illustrated in **FIG 12:11**. On Standard and de-Luxe models it is a one-piece pressing as shown at **A**, while on SL and Firenza models it consists of a frame and two inserts as shown at **B** and **C**.

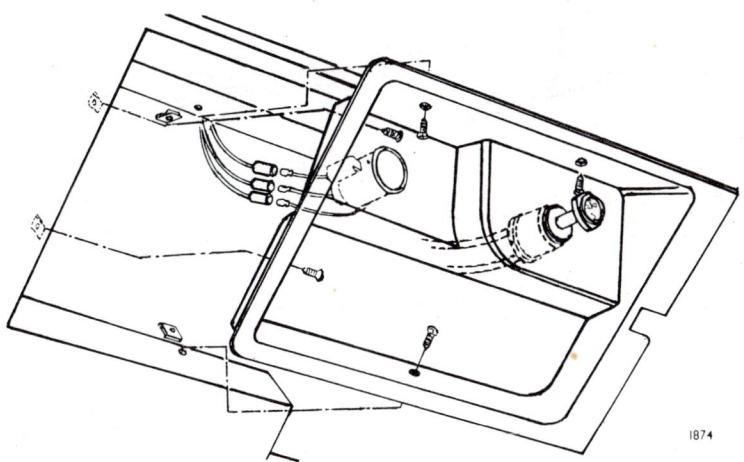

FIG 12:10 Removing instrument panel aperture filler

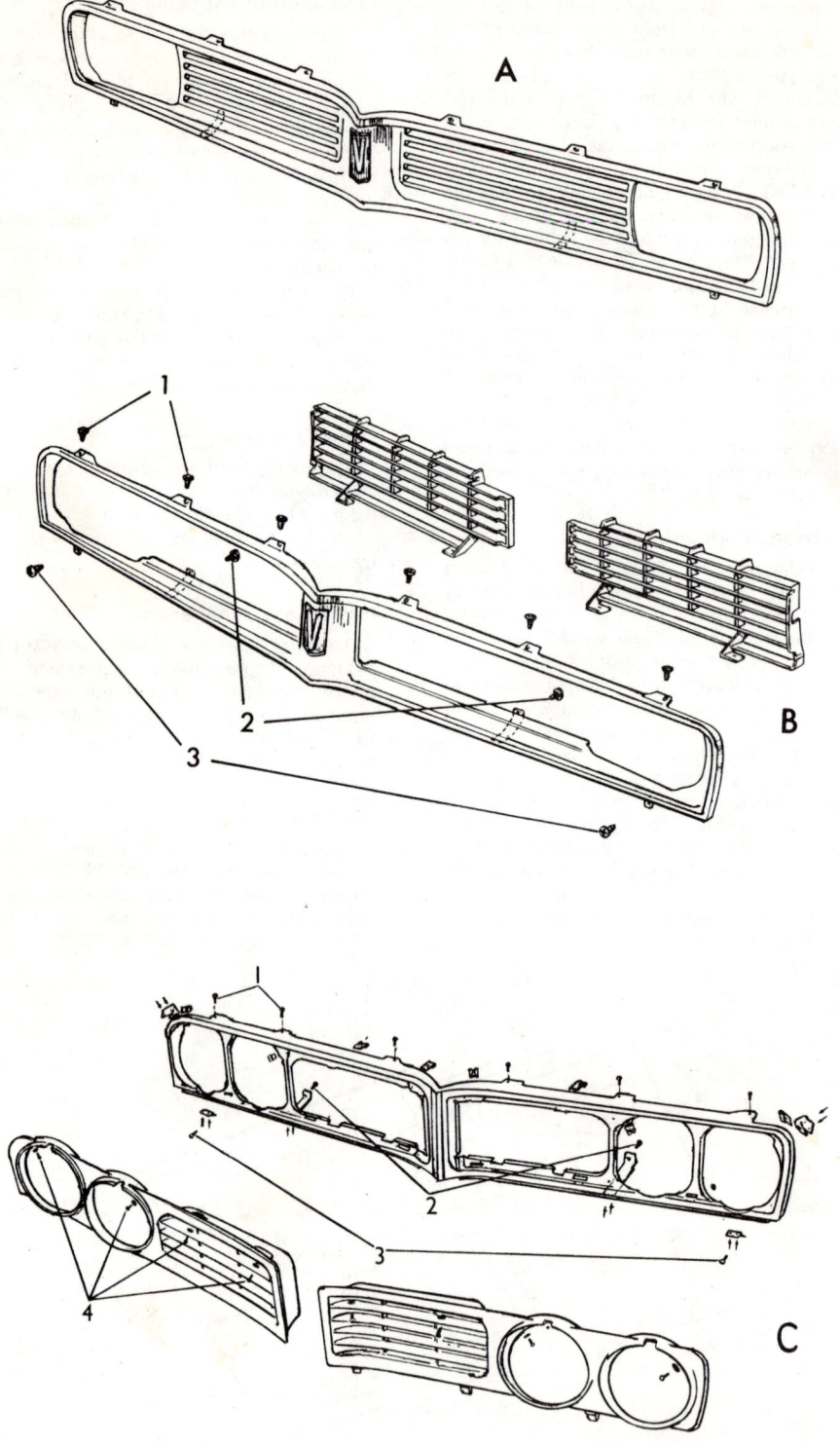

FIG 12:11   Radiator grille. **A** Standard. **B** SL models. **C** Firenza SL

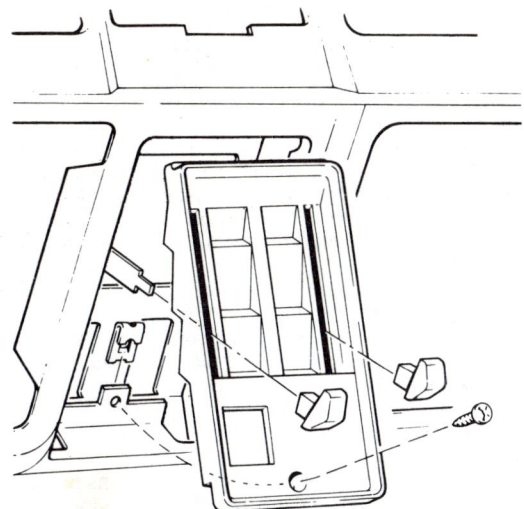

FIG 12:12 Ventilator fan switch

In each case the grille is secured to the front end panel by six screws 1 along the top, two screws 2, which are reached from inside the engine compartment, and two screws 3 to the headlamp mounting panel.

12:7 Heating and ventilating system

Description:

Ventilation of the car interior is by a ball and socket type outlet at each end of the instrument panel, supplied with cool air from two intakes in the bonnet, with the air being extracted through slots below the back light on saloons or above the back door on estate cars.

Additional ventilation is provided by an assembly mounted in the scuttle. When car heating is included, the heater radiator is incorporated in this assembly.

The ventilator and heater controls (see **FIG 12:12**) are mounted in the centre of the instrument panel and may be withdrawn after removing two securing screws.

A two-speed fan motor is used, attached to a cover assembly behind the control aperture.

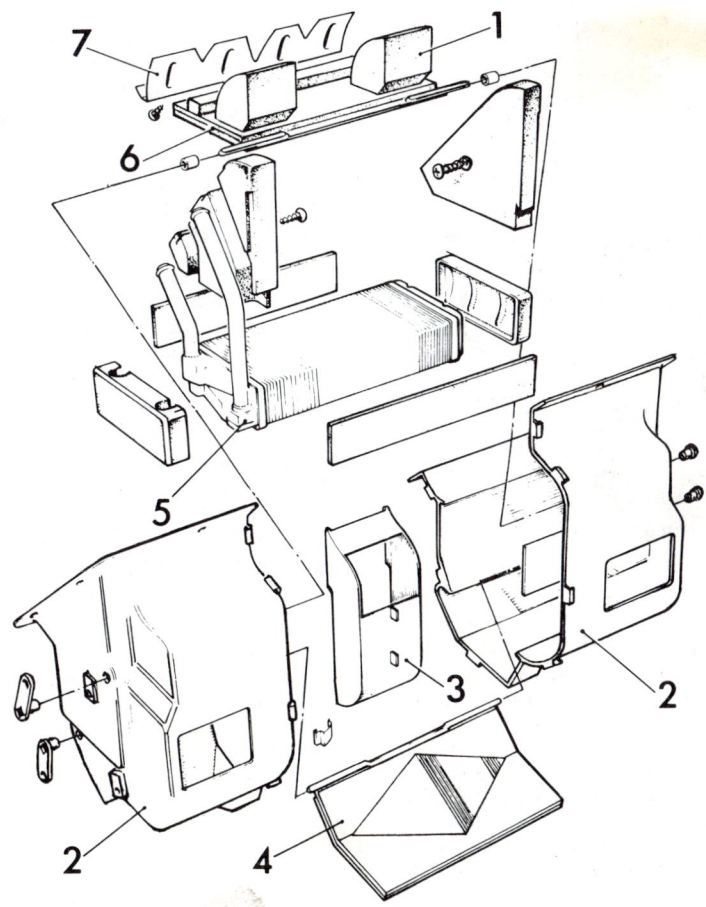

FIG 12:13 Ventilator and heater assembly

Key to Fig 12:13 1 Deflectors   2 Casing   3 Bypass shute   4 Lower flap   5 Radiator   6 Upper flap   7 Graduation plate

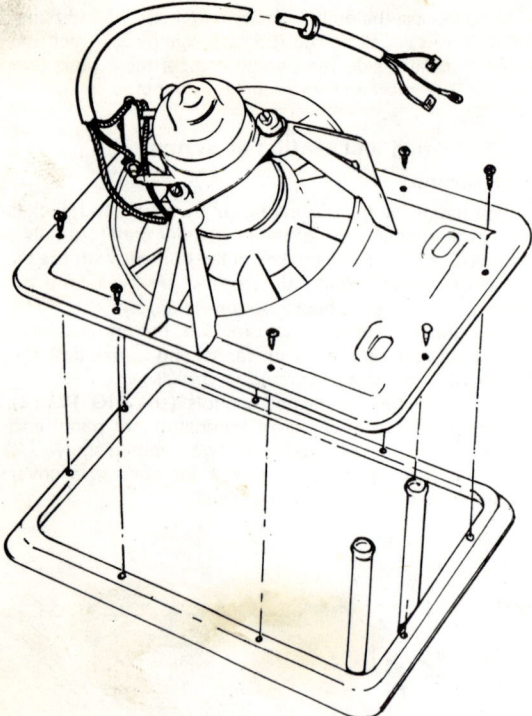

FIG 12:14   Removing fan motor

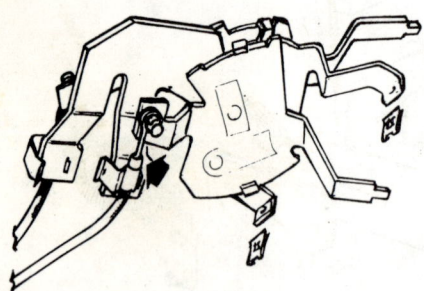

FIG 12:15   Adjusting flap control cables

Ventilator and heater assembly:

This is illustrated in the exploded view of **FIG 12:13** and consists of a heater radiator 5, fed by water from the car's cooling system, mounted in an assembly of ducts and chambers formed inside the two halves 2 of the main casing.

If it is required to take out the ventilator and heater assembly it is first necessary to detach the control cable retaining screws and clips before prising the operating levers from the air flap spindles which will be seen on the side of the casing. It is also necessary to prise out the demist ducts from the casing, but take care not to dislodge them from the outlet slot flanges. To replace the ducts correctly requires the removal of the instrument panel cover, instrument assembly, parcel shelf and glove box.

Ventilator fan:

In order to remove the fan motor and cover assembly it is necessary first to remove the heater control escutcheon and motor switch to disconnect the wires. This latter can be withdrawn from the control aperture by removing the two retaining screws.

Remove the aperture filler adjacent to the steering column to reach the earth connection bolt behind the ash tray. The motor and cover assembly can now be withdrawn after removing eight screws as shown in **FIG 12:14.**

Dismantling the fan will present no difficulty, but when reassembling note that the fan is fitted up to the shoulder on the shaft with the thicker side of the blades towards the motor casing. The toothed washer is fitted with its concave side against the fan hub.

When replacing the motor cover, putty should be applied round the radiator pipes and the eight securing screws to prevent water leaks.

The wires to the switch are connected in the following order: Top (No. 1) terminal blue/black. Centre (No. 2) terminal green. Bottom (No. 3) terminal green/yellow.

Controls:

A diagram showing the heater control panel is given in **FIG 12:12** from which it will be seen that removal is effected by prising off the control knobs, removing the retaining screw and lifting the escutcheon outwards and away from the instrument panel. The control assembly is then withdrawn after removing the two retaining screws.

When refitting the cables to the control, make sure that the outer cable does not protrude more than .10 inch through its retaining clip (see **FIG 12:15**).

To adjust the heater and ventilator cables, slacken the outer cable retaining clips on the ventilator casing, then with both control levers in the OFF position set the upper flap lever in its forward position and the lower flap lever in the rearward position before retightening the clips.

Operation of controls:

The two levers on the control panel shown in **FIG 12:12** operate two flaps in the ventilator assembly. The upper flap, operated by the right hand control lever, covers or exposes the heater radiator to the incoming fresh air, while the lefthand lever operates the lower flap which directs the air flow as required.

When the righthand lever is up, in the C position, the upper flap covers the radiator and any air admitted into the car or on to the screen will be cold and moving it downwards progressively uncovers the radiator with a corresponding increase in air flow temperature until in its lowest or H position all air entering the car will have passed through the radiator. On later cars the HOT position of this lever is UP.

The lefthand lever, when fully down or OFF prevents air from entering the car, although ambient air can still be obtained through the face level vents on the instrument panel.

In the intermediate, or DEF position, it causes all air to be directed to the windscreen at whatever temperature may be determined by the position of the heat lever.

When fully up or in CAR position, both routes are open and the air flow passes to both screen and car interior but with only a small proportion directed into the screen vents.

In any of these positions the air flow selected can be augmented by the use of the two-speed fan.

Thus it will be seen that by selecting a suitable combination of control lever positions an almost unlimited range of air flow direction and temperatures may be obtained.

Bleeding the heater:

When refilling the cooling system it is possible for air pockets to form in the heater system and so reduce its efficiency. The following procedure should be effective in these cars, both on early cars and later cars incorporating a heater water valve.

Fill the radiator and fit the filler cap.

Disconnect the heater hose from the adaptor on the cylinder head and plug he adaptor orifice to prevent coolant loss from the engine. Set the heater water valve control to HOT.

Raise the free end of the hose fully and add coolant in the open end until heater and hose are completely filled. Reconnect the hose to the adaptor, start the engine and check the heater operation.

Stop the engine and top up the radiator as necessary.

NOTES

APPENDIX

TECHNICAL DATA

Engine   Fuel system   Cooling system
Ignition system   Clutch   Synchromesh transmission
Automatic transmission   Rear axle
Suspension and steering   Brakes   Electrical equipment
Capacities   Tightening torques

WIRING DIAGRAMS

HINTS ON MAINTENANCE AND OVERHAUL

GLOSSARY OF TERMS

INDEX

Inches	Decimals	Milli-metres	Inches to Millimetres — Inches	mm	Millimetres to Inches — mm	Inches
1/64	.015625	.3969	.001	.0254	.01	.00039
1/32	.03125	.7937	.002	.0508	.02	.00079
3/64	.046875	1.1906	.003	.0762	.03	.00118
1/16	.0625	1.5875	.004	.1016	.04	.00157
5/64	.078125	1.9844	.005	.1270	.05	.00197
3/32	.09375	2.3812	.006	.1524	.06	.00236
7/64	.109375	2.7781	.007	.1778	.07	.00276
1/8	.125	3.1750	.008	.2032	.08	.00315
9/64	.140625	3.5719	.009	.2286	.09	.00354
5/32	.15625	3.9687	.01	.254	.1	.00394
11/64	.171875	4.3656	.02	.508	.2	.00787
3/16	.1875	4.7625	.03	.762	.3	.01181
13/64	.203125	5·1594	.04	1.016	.4	.01575
7/32	.21875	5.5562	.05	1.270	.5	.01969
15/64	.234375	5.9531	.06	1.524	.6	.02362
1/4	.25	6.3500	.07	1.778	.7	.02756
17/64	.265625	6.7469	.08	2.032	.8	.03150
9/32	.28125	7.1437	.09	2.286	.9	.03543
19/64	.296875	7.5406	.1	2.54	1	.03937
5/16	.3125	7.9375	.2	5.08	2	.07874
21/64	.328125	8.3344	.3	7.62	3	.11811
11/32	.34375	8.7312	.4	10.16	4	.15748
23/64	.359375	9.1281	.5	12.70	5	.19685
3/8	.375	9.5250	.6	15.24	6	.23622
25/64	.390625	9.9219	.7	17.78	7	.27559
13/32	.40625	10.3187	.8	20.32	8	.31496
27/64	.421875	10.7156	.9	22.86	9	.35433
7/16	.4375	11.1125	1	25.4	10	.39370
29/64	.453125	11.5094	2	50.8	11	.43307
15/32	.46875	11.9062	3	76.2	12	.47244
31/64	.484375	12.3031	4	101.6	13	.51181
1/2	.5	12.7000	5	127.0	14	.55118
33/64	.515625	13.0969	6	152.4	15	.59055
17/32	.53125	13.4937	7	177.8	16	.62992
35/64	.546875	13.8906	8	203.2	17	.66929
9/16	.5625	14.2875	9	228.6	18	.70866
37/64	.578125	14.6844	10	254.0	19	.74803
19/32	.59375	15.0812	11	279.4	20	.78740
39/64	.609375	15.4781	12	304.8	21	.82677
5/8	.625	15.8750	13	330.2	22	.86614
41/64	.640625	16.2719	14	355.6	23	.90551
21/32	.65625	16.6687	15	381.0	24	.94488
43/64	.671875	17.0656	16	406.4	25	.98425
11/16	.6875	17.4625	17	431.8	26	1.02362
45/64	.703125	17.8594	18	457.2	27	1.06299
23/32	.71875	18.2562	19	482.6	28	1.10236
47/64	.734375	18.6531	20	508.0	29	1.14173
3/4	.75	19.0500	21	533.4	30	1.18110
49/64	.765625	19.4469	22	558.8	31	1.22047
25/32	.78125	19.8437	23	584.2	32	1.25984
51/64	.796875	20.2406	24	609.6	33	1.29921
13/16	.8125	20.6375	25	635.0	34	1.33858
53/64	.828125	21.0344	26	660.4	35	1.37795
27/32	.84375	21.4312	27	685.8	36	1.41732
55/64	.859375	21.8281	28	711.2	37	1.4567
7/8	.875	22.2250	29	736.6	38	1.4961
57/64	.890625	22.6219	30	762.0	39	1.5354
29/32	.90625	23.0187	31	787.4	40	1.5748
59/64	.921875	23.4156	32	812.8	41	1.6142
15/16	.9375	23.8125	33	838.2	42	1.6535
61/64	.953125	24.2094	34	863.6	43	1.6929
31/32	.96875	24.6062	35	889.0	44	1.7323
63/64	.984375	25.0031	36	914.4	45	1.7717

UNITS	Pints to Litres	Gallons to Litres	Litres to Pints	Litres to Gallons	Miles to Kilometres	Kilometres to Miles	Lbs. per sq. In. to Kg. per sq. Cm.	Kg. per sq. Cm. to Lbs. per sq. In.
1	.57	4.55	1.76	.22	1.61	.62	.07	14.22
2	1.14	9.09	3.52	.44	3.22	1.24	.14	28.50
3	1.70	13.64	5.28	.66	4.83	1.86	.21	42.67
4	2.27	18.18	7.04	.88	6.44	2.49	.28	56.89
5	2.84	22.73	8.80	1.10	8.05	3.11	.35	71.12
6	3.41	27.28	10.56	1.32	9.66	3.73	.42	85.34
7	3.98	31.82	12.32	1.54	11.27	4.35	.49	99.56
8	4.55	36.37	14.08	1.76	12.88	4.97	.56	113.79
9		40.91	15.84	1.98	14.48	5.59	.63	128.00
10		45.46	17.60	2.20	16.09	6.21	.70	142.23
20				4.40	32.19	12.43	1.41	284.47
30				6.60	48.28	18.64	2.11	426.70
40				8.80	64.37	24.85		
50					80.47	31.07		
60					96.56	37.28		
70					112.65	43.50		
80					128.75	49.71		
90					144.84	55.92		
100					160.93	62.14		

UNITS	Lb ft to kgm	Kgm to lb ft	UNITS	Lb ft to kgm	Kgm to lb ft
1	.138	7.233	7	.967	50.631
2	.276	14.466	8	1.106	57.864
3	.414	21.699	9	1.244	65.097
4	.553	28.932	10	1.382	72.330
5	.691	36.165	20	2.765	144.660
6	.829	43.398	30	4.147	216.990

TECHNICAL DATA

Dimensions are in inches unless otherwise stated

ENGINE

Dimensions:	
Bore...	3.062 (77.7 mm)
Stroke	2.400 (61.0 mm)
Capacity	70.7 cu in (1159 cc)
Bore	3.180 (80.97 mm)
Capacity	76.6 cu in (1256 cc)
Firing order	1—3—4—2
No. 1 cylinder ...	At front
Compression ratio:	
Standard engine—Low	7.3:1
High	8.5:1 or 9.2:1
Extra performance engine	9.0:1
Crankshaft:	
Crankpin diameter ...	1.7705 to 1.7712
From engine number 1400011	1.8302 to 1.8310
Crankpin clearance ...	.0010 to .0029
Main journal diameter	2.1255 to 2.1260
Main journal clearance	.0010 to .0025
End float	.002 to .012
Permissible runout ...	.0015
Minimum regrind size—Crankpin ...	Minus .060
Main journal	Minus .040
Main bearing housing bore	2.2835 to 2.2840
Big-end bearing housing bore...	1.8960 to 1.8965
End float	.004 to .010
Pistons:	
Clearance in cylinder bore ...	.0009 to .0014
Piston rings:	*Clearance in groove*
Top ring	.0019 to .0039
Centre ring ...	.0016 to .0036
Scraper ring...	.0015 to .0035
Piston ring gap in cylinder bore, 1159 cc	.009 to .014
1256 cc	.009 to .020 (Not scraper)
Cylinder head, maximum permissible distortion:	
Longitudinally	.005
Transversely...	.003
Manifold faces	.002
Minimum depth after refacing:	
Standard engine, 1159 cc ...	3.185
Extra performance engine, 1159 cc ...	3.157
Standard engine, 1256 cc ...	3.235
From engine number 1400011	3.193

Valves:

Stem diameter—Standard:	
Inlet	.2748 to .2755
Exhaust	.2745 to .2752
Oversizes...	.003, .006, .010, .015
Clearance in guide:	
Inlet	.001 to .0025
Exhaust ...	.0018 to .0033
Seat angle ...	44 deg.

Valve springs:
    Assembled height max. 1.34
    Free length 1.50
    Spring load at 1.32 inch ... ... 44 to 52 lb
Valve clearances—Hot:
    Standard engine:
        Inlet ... ... .006
        Exhaust ... ... .010
    Extra performance and 1256 cc engines:
        Both ... ... .008

Camshaft:
    Journal diameter:
        Front ... ... 1.6127 to 1.6132
        Centre ... ... 1.5930 to 1.5935
        Rear ... ... 1.5733 to 1.5738
    Clearance ... ... .0010 to .0025
    End float ... ... .002 to .009
    Thrust plate thickness ... ... .123 to .126

Oil pump:
    Impeller spindle diameter ... ... .4327 to .4344
    End float ... ... .007 to .010
    Clearance ... ... .0006 to .0017
    Pressure (hot) ... ... 35 to 45 lb/sq in at 3000 rev/min
    Relief valve spring length 1.92
    Spring load at 1.66 inch ... ... 6 lb 10 oz to 6 lb 14 oz
    From engine number 1400011, 1256 cc:
        Pressure, hot ... ... 44 to 55 lb/sq inch at 3000 rev/min
        Relief valve spring length ... ... 1.96 inch
        Spring load at 1.66 inch ... ... 7 lb 15 oz to 8 lb 3 oz

FUEL SYSTEM

Pump:
    Type ... ... AC Mechanical
    Pressure ... ... $2\frac{1}{2}$ to $3\frac{1}{2}$ lb/sq in

Carburetter—Standard:

	Wire gauze	Paper*
Type	Zenith 30 IZ	
Air cleaner element	Wire gauze	Paper*
Identification No.	3345	3346
Main jet	100	107.5
Correction jet	180	175
Economy jet	60	
Econostat outlet		1 mm with .75 mm air bleed
Pilot jet	50	55
Pump injector	50	
Fuel level	23 mm below face of chamber with float removed	
Idle speed	600 to 650 rev/min	

*With positive crankcase ventilation

Carburetter—Extra performance:
    Type ... ... Zenith/Stromberg 150 CDS
    Metering needle ... ... 5 BN
    Air valve spring ... ... Blue
    Fast idle cam—Synchromesh ... ... SA
                Automatic A6
    Cold start needle J6
    Needle valve ... ... 1.75 mm

Needle valve washer	...	...	...	...	1.6 mm		
Float level	...	...	...	...	...	15.5 to 16.5 mm	
Idle speed	...	...	...	...	...	*800 to 850 rev/min	

On automatic with a drive range selected

Carburetter—Extra performance with Code 636:

Type	...	...	...	...	Zenith Stromberg 150 CD-SETV
Identification Number:					
Synchromesh transmission	...	...	...	3393	
Automatic transmission	...	...	...	3356	
Metering needle	...	...	...	...	B5AY
Jet orifice	...	...	...	...	2.29 mm
Jet initial setting	...	...	...	...	2½ turns down from flush with bridge
Air vavle spring identification colour		...	...	Blue	
Fast idle cam	...	...	...	...	A6
Cold start needle	...	...	...	...	F7
Needle valve	...	...	...	...	1.75 mm
Needle valve washer thickness	...	...	...	1.60 mm	
Float position	...	...	...	...	With carburetter inverted and needle valve on seating, highest point of floats should be 15.5/16.5 mm above face of main body, gasket removed
Engine Idling speed	...	...	...	...	*775—825 rev/min

On cars with automatic transmission specified idling speed to be obtained with a drive range selected

Carburetter—1256 cc 1974	...	...	...	...	Zenith Stromberg 150CD-SEV
Identification number, early models	...	...	...	3616 B	
later models	...	...	...	3709 B	
Metering needle, early models	...	...	...	BIDE	
later models	...	...	...	BIDJ	
Jet orifice	...	...	...	...	2.54 mm
Air valve spring identification	...	...	...	Natural	
Fast idle cam	...	...	...	...	M2
Needle valve	...	...	...	...	1.5 mm
Needle valve washer thickness	...	...	...	1.6 mm	
Float position	...	...	...	...	With carburetter inverted and needle valve on seating, highest point of float should be 16 to 17 mm above face of main body, gasket removed
Engine idling speed	...	...	...	...	800 to 850 rev/min

Carburetter—1256 cc Synchromesh:

Make and type Standard engine	...	...	...	Zenith 30 IZ	
Code 636	...	...	...	Zenith 30 IZE	
Main jet	...	...	...	...	105
Correction jet	...	...	...	...	165
Economy jet	...	...	...	...	80
Pilot jet	...	...	...	...	50
Pump injector	...	...	...	...	50

Carburetter—1256 cc:

Synchromesh transmission:

Identification number:					
Standard engine	...	...	...	...	3398
Later standard engine	...	...	...	3632	
Code 636 engine	...	...	...	...	3399
Choke tube	...	...	...	...	24 mm
Main jet	...	...	...	...	105

Correction jet	165	
Economy jet	80	
Pilot jet:		
Code 636 engine and early standard engine ...	50	
Later standard engine	55	
Pump injector	50	
Needle valve	1.6 mm	
Needle valve washer thickness	1 mm	
Fuel level	With float removed, fuel level should be 23 mm below face of float chamber	

Engine idling speed	700-750 rev/min
High altitude jet settings:	
Main jet:	
5000-7000 ft	102
7000-15,000 ft	100
Correction jet:	
10,000-15,000 ft	170

Automatic transmission:

Identification number:	
Standard engine	*3400
Code 636 engine...	3400B
Choke tube	24 mm
Make and type	Zenith 34 IVET
Main jet	80
Compensating jet	105
Idling jet	45
Pump jet	40
Idling speed, drive range selected	700 to 750 rev/min
Part throttle air bleed screw...	Not fitted
Needle valve	1.75 mm
Needle valve washer thickness	2 mm
Float position	With carburetter cover inverted and needle valve on seating, highest points of float should be 30.5/31.5 mm above face of cover gasket

High Altitude jet settings:	
Main jet:	
5000-7000 ft	77
7000-10,000 ft	75
10,000-15,000 ft	70
Compensating jet:	
5000-7000 ft	102
7000-10,000 ft	100

Some early carburetters may have an identification tag stamped 3400X attached to the float chamber cover

COOLING SYSTEM

Filler cap opening pressure	$13\frac{1}{2}$ to $17\frac{1}{2}$ lb/sq in
Thermostat opening temperature:	
Western Thomson	88°C
AC	82°C
Thermostat opening distance	.5
Fan belt tension	.24 inch deflection

IGNITION SYSTEM

Distributor:	
Type	Delco-Remy D202
Rotation	Anticlockwise

Contact breaker gap	...	...	...	...	.020 to .022
Spring tension	...	...	...	...	17 to 21 oz

Timing:

Early engine—low compression	...	...	...	9° BTDC
high compression	...	...	...	4½° BTDC
Extra performance and all late engines	...	...	...	9° BTDC
Coil	...	...	...	Oil filled—ballast type
Sparking plugs	...	...	...	AC 42XLS
Gap—up to 1975	...	...	...	.030
1975	...	...	...	.040

CLUTCH

Type	...	...	...	...	Diaphragm spring
Operation	...	...	...	...	By cable
Fork-free travel	...	...	...	...	.26
Spring colour	...	...	...	...	Pink

SYNCHROMESH GEARBOX

Ratios:

First	...	...	...	...	3.765:1 or 3.460:1
Second	...	...	...	...	2.213:1
Third	...	...	...	...	1.404:1
Top	...	...	...	...	1:1
Reverse	...	...	...	...	3.707:1

AUTOMATIC TRANSMISSION

Type	...	...	...	...	GM
Stall speed—early models	...	...	...	1550 rev/min
later VS models	...	...	...	2200 to 2400 rev/min

REAR AXLE

Ratios:

Standard	...	...	...	...	9/35 (3.89:1)
Extra performance and 1256 cc	...	...	...	8/33 (4.12:1)

SUSPENSION AND STEERING

Front standing height:

Standard	...	...	...	...	9.45 to 10.20
Heavy duty	...	...	...	...	9.95 to 10.70

Rear standing height:

Standard	...	...	...	...	7.96 to 8.76
Heavy duty	...	...	...	...	8.46 to 9.26
Camber angles	...	...	...	...	Nil to 2 deg. negative
Castor angle	...	...	...	...	2° 30' to 4°
Steering pivot inclination	...	...	...	7° 55' to 10° 25' or 6° 50' to 9° 30'
Front wheel alignment	...	...	...	.045 toe-out to .045 toe-in
Toe-out on turns	...	...	...	...	Outside wheel 18° 30' with inside wheel at 20°

BRAKES

Type	...	...	...	...	Girling or Lockheed hydraulic
Rear brakes	...	...	...	...	Drum
Front brakes	...	...	...	...	Drum or disc (with servo)
Drum diameter	...	...	...	...	8
Max. after refacing	...	...	...	...	8.062
Runout—Rear	...	...	...	...	.004
Front	...	...	...	...	.002

Discs:

Thickness	...	...	...	...	.375 to .380
Runout	...	...	...	...	.004

Pads:
Thickness ... ... .295
Minimum ... ... .06

ELECTRICAL EQUIPMENT

Polarity ... ... Negative earth
Voltage 12
Battery... ... ... Exide or Lucas 32 or 55 ah
Alternator ... ... Lucas 15 ACR, 17 ACR or
                                                              Delco-Remy DN 460
Output... ... ... 28 or 36 amps
Regulator ... ... 8 TR
Starter—inertia type ... ... Lucas M35G/I or M35J/I
         pre-engaged type ... ... Lucas M35J/PE, M35K/PE
                                                  or 3M100/PE

CAPACITIES

Engine sump with filter ... ... 5.5 pints
Gearbox ... ... .9 pint
Automatic transmission ... ... 11 pints
Rear axle ... ... 1.8 pints
Cooling system ... ... 9.2 pints
Cooling system with heater ... ... 10.2 pints

TIGHTENING TORQUES

Measurements are in lb ft unless otherwise stated

Connecting rod bolts (oiled threads) 25
Main bearing bolts (oiled threads) 58
Main bearing bolts, $\frac{1}{2}$ inch with 'V' on head 82
Flywheel and flexplate (sealed threads) 25
Cylinder head bolts 49
Oil filter 14
Clutch to flywheel 14
Propeller shaft flange 18
Rear axle flange 75
Axle shaft bearing retainer 13
Rear axle mounting 38
Differential bearing cap 24
Hypoid gear bolts 36
Wheel nuts 51
Upper arm fulcrum bolts 55
Lower arm fulcrum bolts 42
Upper ball joint attaching bolts 22
Steering arm to knuckle bolts 25
Steering knuckle to ball joint 33
Tie rod to steering arm... 25
Damper top mounting 32
Damper lower mounting 57
Control rod to lower arm 32
Control rod rear nuts 47
Steering wheel nut 45
Steering column upper support bracket 17
Steering gear to crossmember 19
Rear springs to lower suspension arms 19
Lockheed caliper bolts... 37
Caliper to steering knuckle 33
Rear brake flange to axle 13
Brake disc to hub (sealed threads) 18

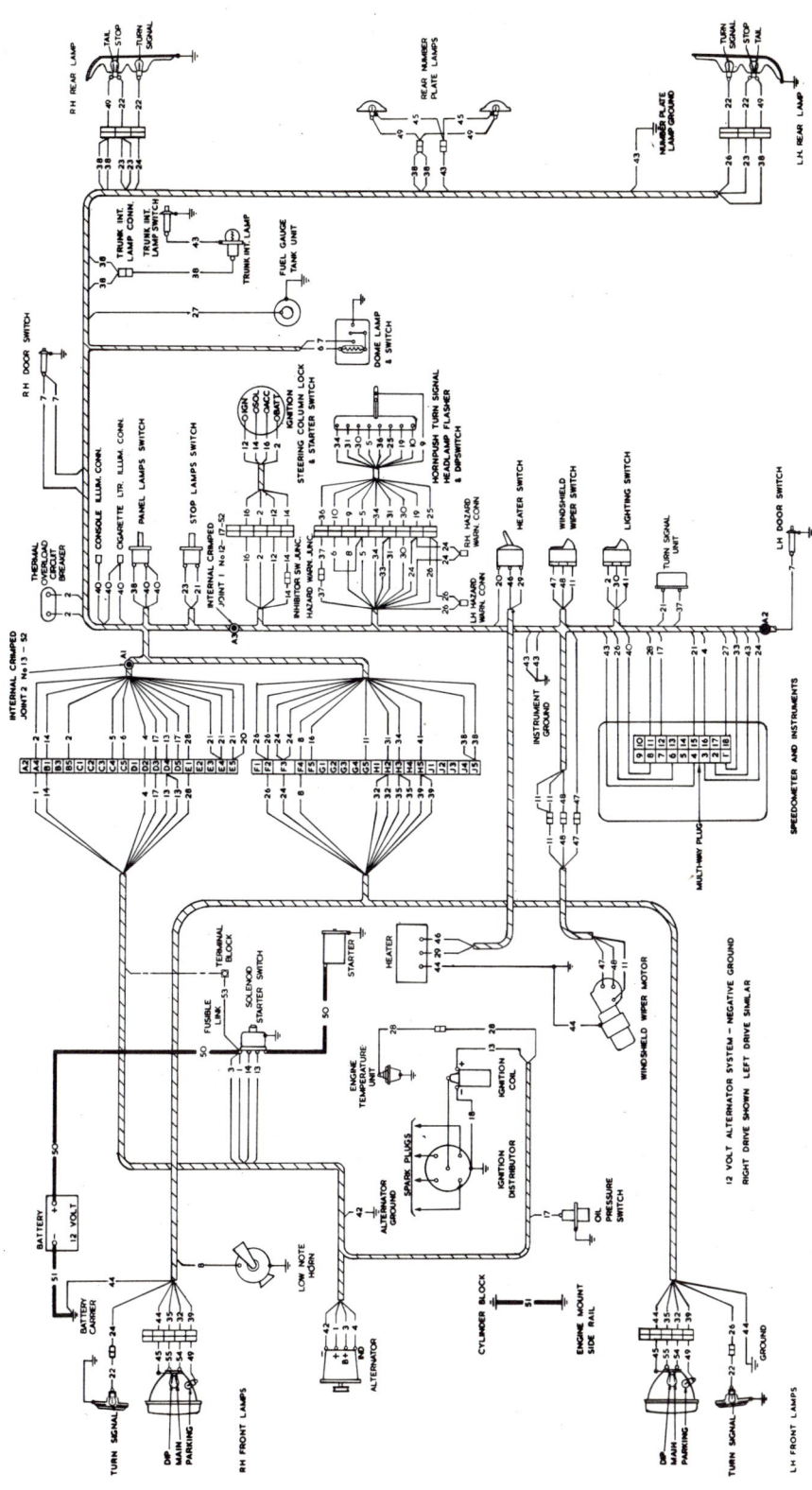

FIG 13:1 Wiring diagram, Viva HC (standard), pre-1974

Key to Fig 13:1

1 Brown (65/012)	2 Brown (35/012)	3 Brown (14/010)	4 Brown/Yellow (9/012)	5 Purple (28/012)	6 Purple (9/012)
7 Purple/White (9/012)	8 Purple/Black (9/012)	9 Purple/Black (14/010)	10 Purple/Brown (14/010)	11 White/Lt. Green (14/012)	12 White (35/012)
13 White (14/012)	14 White/Red (28/012)	15 White/Red (9/012)	16 White/Blue (28/012)	17 White/Brown (9/012)	18 White/Black (7/16/004)
19 Green/White (14/010)	20 Green (14/012)	21 Green (9/012)	22 Green (14/010)	23 Green/Purple (9/012)	24 Green/White (9/012)	25 Green/Red (14/010)
26 Green/Red (9/012)	27 Green/Blue (9/012)	28 Green/Blue (9/012)	29 Green/Yellow (14/012)	30 Blue (28/012)	31 Blue/White (28/012)
32 Blue/White (14/012)	33 Blue/White (9/012)	34 Blue/Red (14/012)	35 Blue/Red (28/012)	36 Lt. Green/Brown (9/012)	37 Lt. Green/Brown (9/012)
38 Red (9/012)	39 Red/Green (9/012)	40 Red/White (9/012)	41 Red/Brown (28/012)	42 Black (65/012)	43 Black (9/012)	44 Black (14/012)
45 Black (14/010)	46 Black/Blue (14/012)	47 Yellow/Lt. Green (14/012)	48 Red/Lt. Green (14/012)	49 Red (14/010)	50 — (37/028)	51 — (16/012)
52 Resistance wire*	53 Brown (35/012)	54 Blue/White (14/010)	55 Blue/White (14/010)		

*Denotes single-strand resistance wire routed between points A1 A2–A3. Resistance wire 1/.028 or 22 SWG. Resistance per inch .0312Ω±5%

*Denotes single-strand resistance wire giving a total of 20Ω routed between points A1 A2–A3 giving a total of 20±20Ω

Figures in brackets denotes size

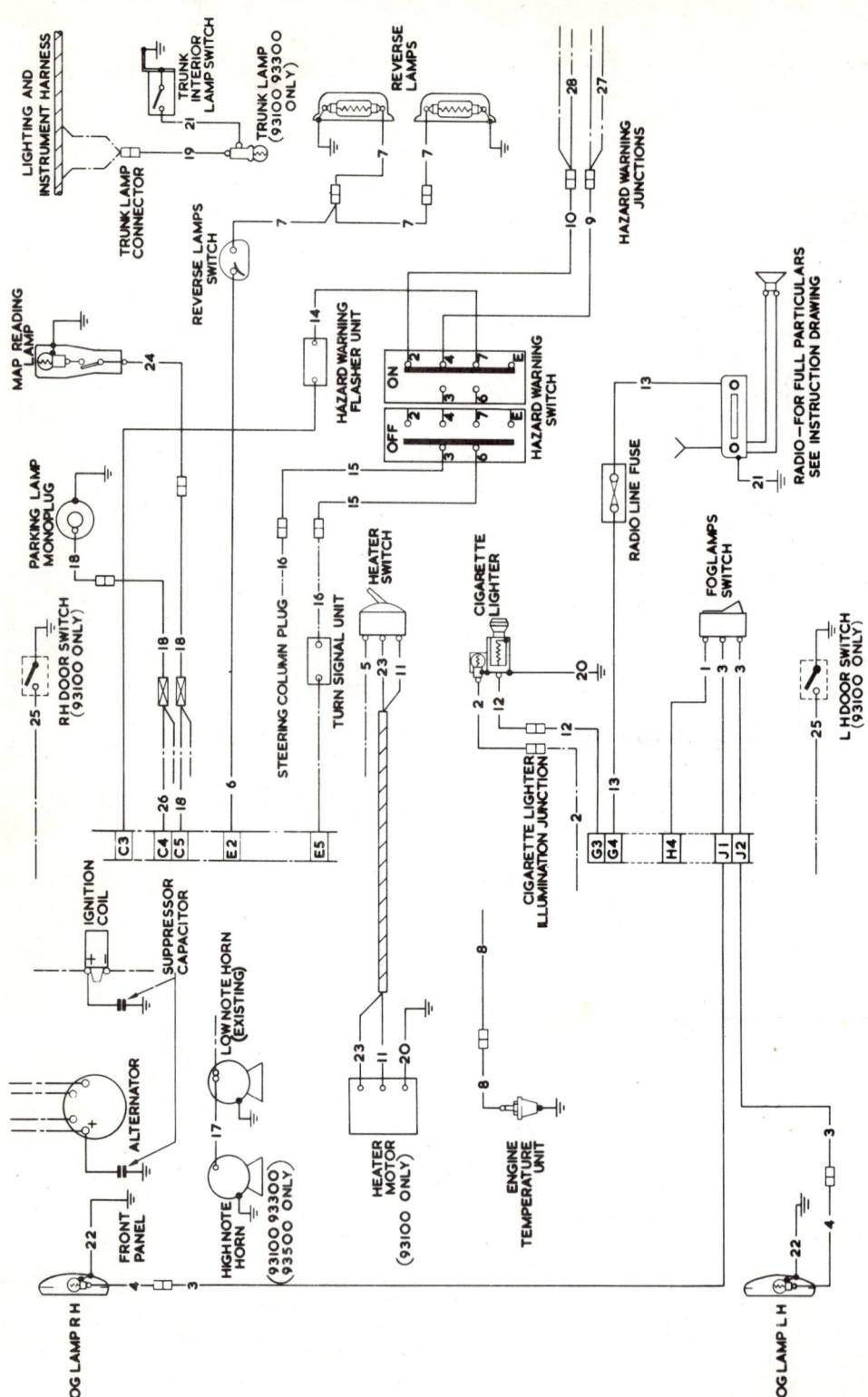

FIG 13:2   Accessory wiring diagram

Key to Fig 13:2   1 Red (28/.012)   2 Red/White (9/.012)   3 Red/Yellow (14/.012)   4 Red/Yellow (14/.012)   5 Green (14/.012)   6 Green (9/.012)
7 Green/Brown (9/.012)   8 Green/Blue (9/.012)   9 Green/Red (14/.012)   10 Green/White (14/.010)   11 Green/Yellow (14/.012)   12 White/Green (14/.012)
13 White/Green (9/.012)   14 Lt.Green/Purple (14/.010)   15 Lt.Green/Brown (9/.012)   16 Lt.Green/Brown (9/.012)   17 Purple (14/.012)   18 Purple (9/.012)
19 Purple/Black (14/.012)   20 Black (14/.012)   21 Black (9/.012)   22 Black (14/.010)   23 Black/Blue (14/.012)   24 Grey (14/.010)   25 Purple/White (9/.012)
26 Purple (28/.012)   27 Green/White (9/.012)   28 Green/Red (9/.012)

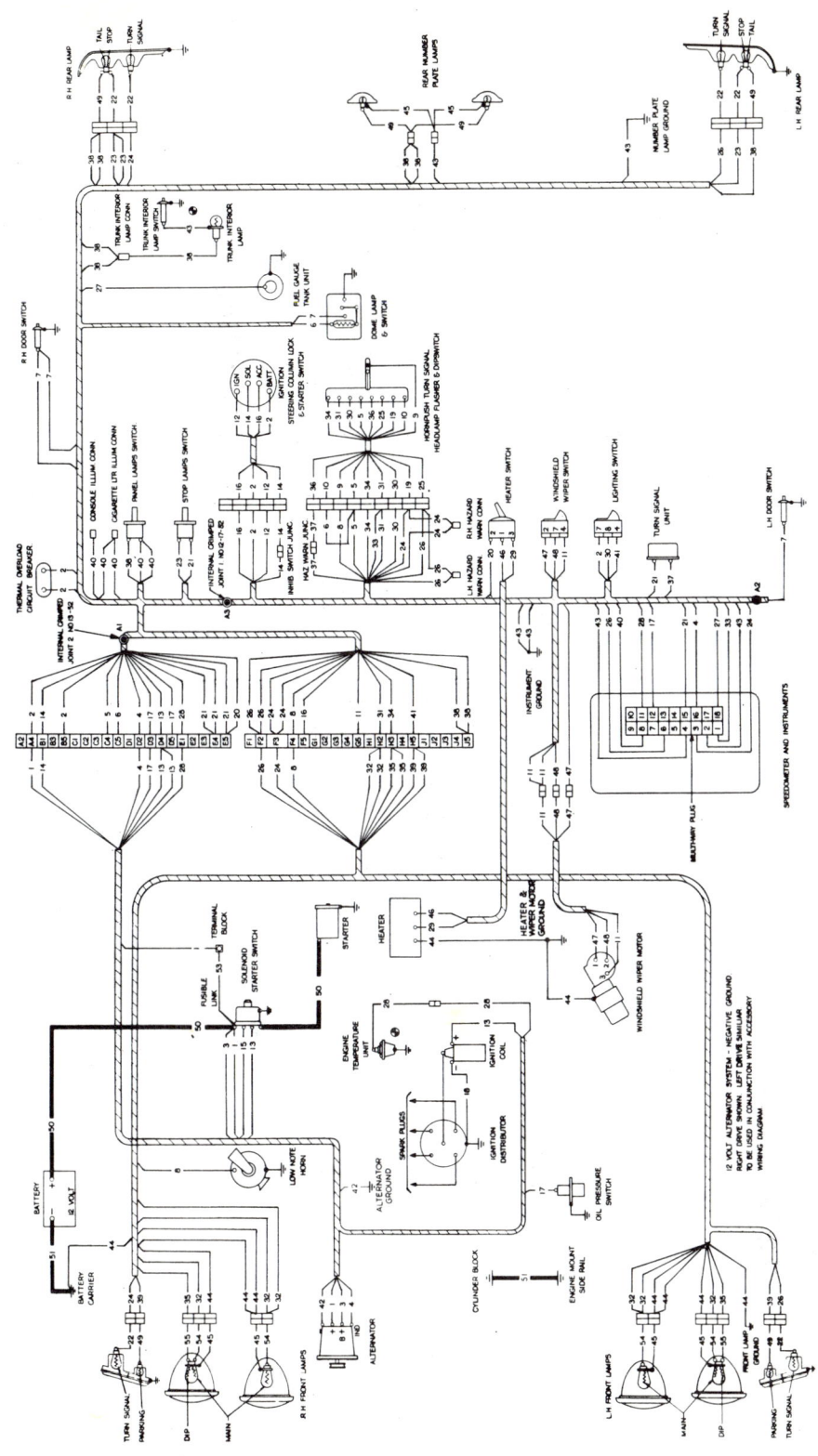

FIG 13:3   Wiring diagram Firenza SL

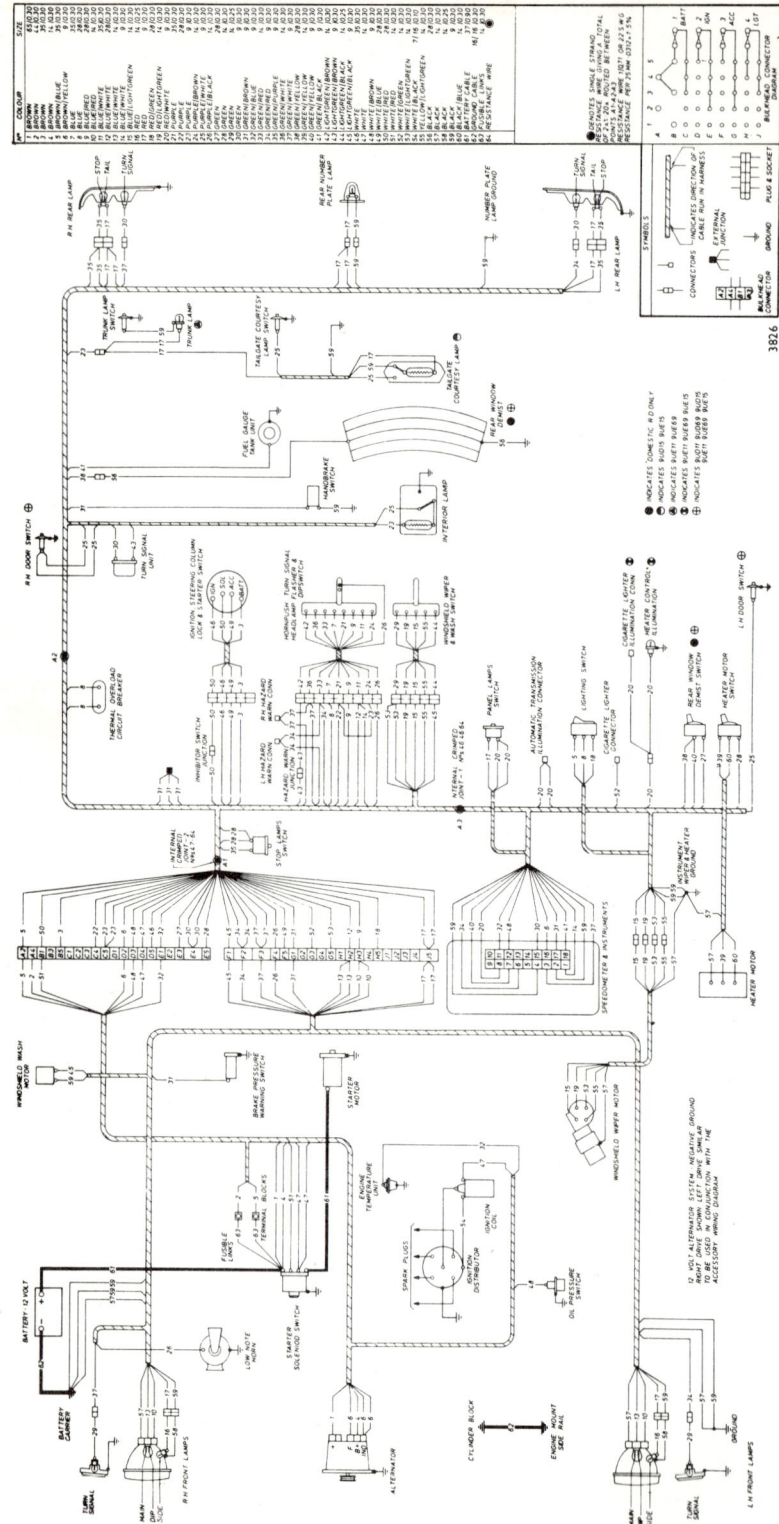

FIG 13:4   Viva with standard instrumentation, 1974 models

144

HINTS ON MAINTENANCE AND OVERHAUL

There are few things more rewarding than the restoration of a vehicle's original peak of efficiency and smooth performance.

The following notes are intended to help the owner to reach that state of perfection. Providing that he possesses the basic manual skills he should have no difficulty in performing most of the operations detailed in this manual. It must be stressed, however, that where recommended in the manual, highly-skilled operations ought to be entrusted to experts, who have the necessary equipment, to carry out the work satisfactorily.

Quality of workmanship:

The hazardous driving conditions on the roads to-day demand that vehicles should be as nearly perfect, mechanically, as possible. It is therefore most important that amateur work be carried out with care, bearing in mind the often inadequate working conditions, and also the inferior tools which may have to be used. It is easy to counsel perfection in all things, and we recognize that it may be setting an impossibly high standard. We do, however, suggest that every care should be taken to ensure that a vehicle is as safe to take on the road as it is humanly possible to make it.

Safe working conditions:

Even though a vehicle may be stationary, it is still potentially dangerous if certain sensible precautions are not taken when working on it while it is supported on jacks or blocks. It is indeed preferable not to use jacks alone, but to supplement them with carefully placed blocks, so that there will be plenty of support if the car rolls off the jacks during a strenuous manoeuvre. Axle stands are an excellent way of providing a rigid base which is not readily disturbed. Piles of bricks are a dangerous substitute. Be careful not to get under heavy loads on lifting tackle, the load could fall. It is preferable not to work alone when lifting an engine, or when working underneath a vehicle which is supported well off the ground. To be trapped, particularly under the vehicle, may have unpleasant results if help is not quickly forthcoming. Make some provision, however humble, to deal with fires. Always disconnect a battery if there is a likelihood of electrical shorts. These may start a fire if there is leaking fuel about. This applies particularly to leads which can carry a heavy current, like those in the starter circuit. While on the subject of electricity, we must also stress the danger of using equipment which is run off the mains and which has no earth or has faulty wiring or connections. So many workshops have damp floors, and electrical shocks are of such a nature that it is sometimes impossible to let go of a live lead or piece of equipment due to the muscular spasms which take place.

Work demanding special care:

This involves the servicing of braking, steering and suspension systems. On the road, failure of the braking system may be disastrous. Make quite sure that there can be no possibility of failure through the bursting of rusty brake pipes or rotten hoses, nor to a sudden loss of pressure due to defective seals or valves.

Problems:

The chief problems which may face an operator are:
1 External dirt.
2 Difficulty in undoing tight fixings.
3 Dismantling unfamiliar mechanisms.
4 Deciding in what respect parts are defective.
5 Confusion about the correct order for reassembly.
6 Adjusting running clearance.
7 Road testing.
8 Final tuning.

Practical suggestions to solve the problems:

1 Preliminary cleaning of large parts—engines, transmissions, steering, suspensions, etc.,—should be carried out before removal from the car. Where road dirt and mud alone are present, wash clean with a high-pressure water jet, brushing to remove stubborn adhesions, and allow to drain and dry. Where oil or grease is also present, wash down with a proprietary compound (Gunk, Teepol etc.,) applying with a stiff brush—an old paint brush is suitable—into all crevices. Cover the distributor and ignition coils with a polythene bag and then apply a strong water jet to clear the loosened deposits. Allow to drain and dry. The assemblies will then be sufficiently clean to remove and transfer to the bench for the next stage.

On the bench, further cleaning can be carried out, first wiping the parts as free as possible from grease with old newspaper. Avoid using rag or cotton waste which can leave clogging fibres behind. Any remaining grease can be removed with a brush dipped in paraffin. If necessary, traces of paraffin can be removed by carbon tetrachloride. Avoid using paraffin or petrol in large quantities for cleaning in enclosed areas, such as garages, on account of the high fire risk.

When all exteriors have been cleaned, and not before, dismantling can be commenced. This ensures that dirt will not enter into interiors and orifices revealed by dismantling. In the next phases, where components have to be cleaned, use carbon tetrachloride in preference to petrol and keep the containers covered except when in use. After the components have been cleaned, plug small holes with tapered hard wood plugs cut to size and blank off larger orifices with grease-proof paper and masking tape. Do not use soft wood plugs or matchsticks as they may break.

2 It is not advisable to hammer on the end of a screw thread, but if it must be done, first screw on a nut to protect the thread, and use a lead hammer. This applies particularly to the removal of tapered cotters. Nuts and bolts seem to 'grow' together, especially in exhaust systems. If penetrating oil does not work, try the judicious application of heat, but be careful of starting a fire. Asbestos sheet or cloth is useful to isolate heat.

Tight bushes or pieces of tail-pipe rusted into a silencer can be removed by splitting them with an open-ended hacksaw. Tight screws can sometimes be started by a tap from a hammer on the end of a suitable screwdriver. Many tight fittings will yield to the judicious use of a hammer, but it must be a soft-faced hammer if damage is to be avoided, use a heavy block on the opposite side to absorb shock. Any parts of the steering system which have been damaged should be renewed, as attempts to repair them may lead to cracking and subsequent failure, and steering ball joints should be disconnected using a recommended tool to prevent damage.

3 It often happens that an owner is baffled when trying to dismantle an unfamiliar piece of equipment. So many modern devices are pressed together or assembled by spinning-over flanges, that they must be sawn apart. The intention is that the whole assembly must be renewed. However, parts which appear to be in one piece to the naked eye, may reveal close-fitting joint lines when inspected with a magnifying glass, and, this may provide the necessary clue to dismantling. Left-handed screw threads are used where rotational forces would tend to unscrew a right-handed screw thread.

Be very careful when dismantling mechanisms which may come apart suddenly. Work in an enclosed space where the parts will be contained, and drape a piece of cloth over the device if springs are likely to fly in all directions. Mark everything which might be reassembled in the wrong position, scratched symbols may be used on unstressed parts, or a sequence of tiny dots from a centre punch can be useful. Stressed parts should never be scratched or centre-popped as this may lead to cracking under working conditions. Store parts which look alike in the correct order for reassembly. Never rely upon memory to assist in the assembly of complicated mechanisms, especially when they will be dismantled for a long time, but make notes, and drawings to supplement the diagrams in the manual, and put labels on detached wires. Rust stains may indicate unlubricated wear. This can sometimes be seen round the outside edge of a bearing cup in a universal joint. Look for bright rubbing marks on parts which normally should not make heavy contact. These might prove that something is bent or running out of truth. For example, there might be bright marks on one side of a piston, at the top near the ring grooves, and others at the bottom of the skirt on the other side. This could well be the clue to a bent connecting rod. Suspected cracks can be proved by heating the component in a light oil to approximately 100°C, removing, drying off, and dusting with french chalk, if a crack is present the oil retained in the crack will stain the french chalk.

4 In determining wear, and the degree, against the permissible limits set in the manual, accurate measurement can only be achieved by the use of a micrometer. In many cases, the wear is given to the fourth place of decimals; that is in ten-thousandths of an inch. This can be read by the vernier scale on the barrel of a good micrometer. Bore diameters are more difficult to determine. If, however, the matching shaft is accurately measured, the degree of play in the bore can be felt as a guide to its suitability. In other cases, the shank of a twist drill of known diameter is a handy check.

Many methods have been devised for determining the clearance between bearing surfaces. To-day the best and simplest is by the use of Plastigage, obtainable from most garages. A thin plastic thread is laid between the two surfaces and the bearing is tightened, flattening the thread. On removal, the width of the thread is compared with a scale supplied with the thread and the clearance is read off directly. Sometimes joint faces leak persistently, even after gasket renewal. The fault will then be traceable to distortion, dirt or burrs. Studs which are screwed into soft metal frequently raise burrs at the point of entry. A quick cure for this is to chamfer the edge of the hole in the part which fits over the stud.

5 **Always check a replacement part with the original one before it is fitted.**

If parts are not marked, and the order for reassembly is not known, a little detective work will help. Look for marks which are due to wear to see if they can be mated. Joint faces may not be identical due to manufacturing errors, and parts which overlap may be stained, giving a clue to the correct position. Most fixings leave identifying marks especially if they were painted over on assembly. It is then easier to decide whether a nut, for instance, has a plain, a spring, or a shakeproof washer under it. All running surfaces become 'bedded' together after long spells of work and tiny imperfections on one part will be found to have left corresponding marks on the other. This is particularly true of shafts and bearings and even a score on a cylinder wall will show on the piston.

6 Checking end float or rocker clearances by feeler gauge may not always give accurate results because of wear. For instance, the rocker tip which bears on a valve stem may be deeply pitted, in which case the feeler will simply be bridging a depression. Thrust washers may also wear depressions in opposing faces to make accurate measurement difficult. End float is then easier to check by using a dial gauge. It is common practice to adjust end play in bearing assemblies, like front hubs with taper rollers, by doing up the axle nut until the hub becomes stiff to turn and then backing it off a little. Do not use this method with ballbearing hubs as the assembly is often preloaded by tightening the axle nut to its fullest extent. If the splitpin hole will not line up, file the base of the nut a little.

Steering assemblies often wear in the straight-ahead position. If any part is adjusted, make sure that it remains free when moved from lock to lock. Do not be surprised if an assembly like a steering gearbox, which is known to be carefully adjusted outside the car, becomes stiff when it is bolted in place. This will be due to distortion of the case by the pull of the mounting bolts, particularly if the mounting points are not all touching together. This problem may be met in other equipment and is cured by careful attention to the alignment of mounting points.

When a spanner is stamped with a size and A/F it means that the dimension is the width between the jaws and has no connection with ANF, which is the designation for the American National Fine thread. Coarse threads like Whitworth are rarely used on cars to-day except for studs which screw into soft aluminium or cast iron. For this reason it might be found that the top end of a cylinder head stud has a fine thread and the lower end a coarse thread to screw into the cylinder block. If the car has mainly UNF threads then it is likely that any coarse threads will be UNC, which are not the same as Whitworth. Small sizes have the same number of threads in Whitworth and UNC, but in the $\frac{1}{2}$ inch size for example, there are twelve threads to the inch in the former and thirteen in the latter.

7 After a major overhaul, particularly if a great deal of work has been done on the braking, steering and suspension systems, it is advisable to approach the problem of testing with care. If the braking system has been overhauled, apply heavy pressure to the brake pedal and get a second operator to check every possible source of leakage. The brakes may work extremely well, but a leak could cause complete failure after a few miles.

Do not fit the hub caps until every wheel nut has been checked for tightness, and make sure the tyre pressures are correct. Check the levels of coolant, lubricants and hydraulic fluids. Being satisfied that all is well, take the car on the road and test the brakes at once. Check the steering and the action of the handbrake. Do all this at moderate speeds on quiet roads, and make sure there is no other vehicle behind you when you try a rapid stop.

Finally, remember that many parts settle down after a time, so check for tightness of all fixings after the car has been on the road for a hundred miles or so.

8 It is useless to tune an engine which has not reached its normal running temperature. In the same way, the tune of an engine which is stiff after a rebore will be different when the engine is again running free. Remember too, that rocker clearances on pushrod operated valve gear will change when the cylinder head nuts are tightened after an initial period of running with a new head gasket.

Trouble may not always be due to what seems the obvious cause. Ignition, carburation and mechanical condition are interdependent and spitting back through the carburetter, which might be attributed to a weak mixture, can be caused by a sticking inlet valve.

For one final hint on tuning, never adjust more than one thing at a time or it will be impossible to tell which adjustment produced the desired result.

NOTES

GLOSSARY OF TERMS

Allen key — Cranked wrench of hexagonal section for use with socket head screws.

Alternator — Electrical generator producing alternating current. Rectified to direct current for battery charging.

Ambient temperature — Surrounding atmospheric temperature.

Annulus — Used in engineering to indicate the outer ring gear of an epicyclic gear train.

Armature — The shaft carrying the windings, which rotates in the magnetic field of a generator or starter motor. That part of a solenoid or relay which is activated by the magnetic field.

Axial — In line with, or pertaining to, an axis.

Backlash — Play in meshing gears.

Balance lever — A bar where force applied at the centre is equally divided between connections at the ends.

Banjo axle — Axle casing with large diameter housing for the crownwheel and differential.

Bendix pinion — A self-engaging and self-disengaging drive on a starter motor shaft.

Bevel pinion — A conical shaped gearwheel, designed to mesh with a similar gear with an axis usually at 90 deg. to its own.

bhp — Brake horse power, measured on a dynamometer.

bmep — Brake mean effective pressure. Average pressure on a piston during the working stroke.

Brake cylinder — Cylinder with hydraulically operated piston(s) acting on brake shoes or pad(s).

Brake regulator — Control valve fitted in hydraulic braking system which limits brake pressure to rear brakes during heavy braking to prevent rear wheel locking.

Camber — Angle at which a wheel is tilted from the vertical.

Capacitor — Modern term for an electrical condenser. Part of distributor assembly, connected across contact breaker points, acts as an interference suppressor.

Castellated — Top face of a nut, slotted across the flats, to take a locking splitpin.

Castor — Angle at which the kingpin or swivel pin is tilted when viewed from the side.

cc — Cubic centimetres. Engine capacity is arrived at by multiplying the area of the bore in sq cm by the stroke in cm by the number of cylinders.

Clevis — U-shaped forked connector used with a clevis pin, usually at handbrake connections.

Collet — A type of collar, usually split and located in a groove in a shaft, and held in place by a retainer. The arrangement used to retain the spring(s) on a valve stem in most cases.

Commutator — Rotating segmented current distributor between armature windings and brushes in generator or motor.

Compression ratio — The ratio, or quantitative relation, of the total volume (piston at bottom of stroke) to the unswept volume (piston at top of stroke) in an engine cylinder.

Condenser — See capacitor.

Core plug — Plug for blanking off a manufacturing hole in a casting.

Crownwheel — Large bevel gear in rear axle, driven by a bevel pinion attached to the propeller shaft. Sometimes called a 'ring gear'.

'C'-spanner — Like a 'C' with a handle. For use on screwed collars without flats, but with slots or holes.

Damper — Modern term for shock-absorber, used in vehicle suspension systems to damp out spring oscillations.

Depression — The lowering of atmospheric pressure as in the inlet manifold and carburetter.

Dowel — Close tolerance pin, peg, tube, or bolt, which accurately locates mating parts.

Drag link — Rod connecting steering box drop arm (pitman arm) to nearest front wheel steering arm in certain types of steering systems.

Dry liner — Thinwall tube pressed into cylinder bore

Dry sump — Lubrication system where all oil is scavenged from the sump, and returned to a separate tank.

Dynamo — See Generator.

Electrode — Terminal, part of an electrical component, such as the points or 'Electrodes' of a sparking plug.

Electrolyte — In lead-acid car batteries a solution of sulphuric acid and distilled water.

End float — The axial movement between associated parts, end play.

EP — Extreme pressure. In lubricants, special grades for heavily loaded bearing surfaces, such as gear teeth in a gearbox, or crownwheel and pinion in a rear axle.

Fade	Of brakes. Reduced efficiency due to overheating.	**Journals**	Those parts of a shaft that are in contact with the bearings.
Field coils	Windings on the polepieces of motors and generators.	**Kingpin**	The main vertical pin which carries the front wheel spindle, and permits steering movement. May be called 'steering pin' or 'swivel pin'.
Fillets	Narrow finishing strips usually applied to interior bodywork.	**Layshaft**	The shaft which carries the laygear in the gearbox. The laygear is driven by the first motion shaft and drives the third motion shaft according to the gear selected. Sometimes called the 'countershaft' or 'second motion shaft.'
First motion shaft	Input shaft from clutch to gearbox.		
Fullflow filter	Filters in which all the oil is pumped to the engine. If the element becomes clogged, a bypass valve operates to pass unfiltered oil to the engine.		
FWD	Front wheel drive.	**lb ft**	A measure of twist or torque. A pull of 10 lb at a radius of 1 ft is a torque of 10 lb ft.
Gear pump	Two meshing gears in a close fitting casing. Oil is carried from the inlet round the outside of both gears in the spaces between the gear teeth and casing to the outlet, the meshing gear teeth prevent oil passing back to the inlet, and the oil is forced through the outlet port.	**lb/sq in**	Pounds per square inch.
		Little-end	The small, or piston end of a connecting rod. Sometimes called the 'small-end'.
		LT	Low Tension. The current output from the battery.
Generator	Modern term for 'Dynamo'. When rotated produces electrical current.	**Mandrel**	Accurately manufactured bar or rod used for test or centring purposes.
Grommet	A ring of protective or sealing material. Can be used to protect pipes or leads passing through bulkheads.	**Manifold**	A pipe, duct, or chamber, with several branches.
		Needle rollers	Bearing rollers with a length many times their diameter.
Grubscrew	Fully threaded headless screw with screwdriver slot. Used for locking, or alignment purposes.		
Gudgeon pin	Shaft which connects a piston to its connecting rod. Sometimes called 'wrist pin', or 'piston pin'.	**Oil bath**	Reservoir which lubricates parts by immersion. In air filters, a separate oil supply for wetting a wire mesh element to hold the dust.
Halfshaft	One of a pair transmitting drive from the differential.	**Oil wetted**	In air filters, a wire mesh element lightly oiled to trap and hold airborne dust.
Helical	In spiral form. The teeth of helical gears are cut at a spiral angle to the side faces of the gearwheel.	**Overlap**	Period during which inlet and exhaust valves are open together.
Hot spot	Hot area that assists vapourisation of fuel on its way to cylinders. Often provided by close contact between inlet and exhaust manifolds.	**Panhard rod**	Bar connected between fixed point on chassis and another on axle to control sideways movement.
		Pawl	Pivoted catch which engages in the teeth of a ratchet to permit movement in one direction only.
HT	High Tension. Applied to electrical current produced by the ignition coil for the sparking plugs.	**Peg spanner**	Tool with pegs, or pins, to engage in holes or slots in the part to be turned.
Hydrometer	A device for checking specific gravity of liquids. Used to check specific gravity of electrolyte.	**Pendant pedals**	Pedals with levers that are pivoted at the top end.
Hypoid bevel gears	A form of bevel gear used in the rear axle drive gears. The bevel pinion meshes below the centre line of the crownwheel, giving a lower propeller shaft line.	**Phillips screwdriver**	A cross-point screwdriver for use with the cross-slotted heads of Phillips screws.
		Pinion	A small gear, usually in relation to another gear.
Idler	A device for passing on movement. A free running gear between driving and driven gears. A lever transmitting track rod movement to a side rod in steering gear.	**Piston-type damper**	Shock absorber in which damping is controlled by a piston working in a closed oil-filled cylinder.
		Preloading	Preset static pressure on ball or roller bearings not due to working loads.
Impeller	A centrifugal pumping element. Used in water pumps to stimulate flow.	**Radial**	Radiating from a centre, like the spokes of a wheel.

Radius rod	Pivoted arm confining movement of a part to an arc of fixed radius.
Ratchet	Toothed wheel or rack which can move in one direction only, movement in the other being prevented by a pawl.
Ring gear	A gear tooth ring attached to outer periphery of flywheel. Starter pinion engages with it during starting.
Runout	Amount by which rotating part is out of true.
Semi-floating axle	Outer end of rear axle halfshaft is carried on bearing inside axle casing. Wheel hub is secured to end of shaft.
Servo	A hydraulic or pneumatic system for assisting, or, augmenting a physical effort. See 'Vacuum Servo'.
Setscrew	One which is threaded for the full length of the shank.
Shackle	A coupling link, used in the form of two parallel pins connected by side plates to secure the end of the master suspension spring and absorb the effects of deflection.
Shell bearing	Thinwalled steel shell lined with anti-friction metal. Usually semi-circular and used in pairs for main and big-end bearings.
Shock absorber	See 'Damper'.
Silentbloc	Rubber bush bonded to inner and outer metal sleeves.
Socket-head screw	Screw with hexagonal socket for an Allen key.
Solenoid	A coil of wire creating a magnetic field when electric current passes through it. Used with a soft iron core to operate contacts or a mechanical device.
Spur gear	A gear with teeth cut axially across the periphery.
Stub axle	Short axle fixed at one end only.
Tachometer	An instrument for accurate measurement of rotating speed. Usually indicates in revolutions per minute.
TDC	Top Dead Centre. The highest point reached by a piston in a cylinder, with the crank and connecting rod in line.
Thermostat	Automatic device for regulating temperature. Used in vehicle coolant systems to open a valve which restricts circulation at low temperature.
Third motion shaft	Output shaft of gearbox.
Threequarter floating axle	Outer end of rear axle halfshaft flanged and bolted to wheel hub, which runs on bearing mounted on outside of axle casing. Vehicle weight is not carried by the axle shaft.
Thrust bearing or washer	Used to reduce friction in rotating parts subject to axial loads.
Torque	Turning or twisting effort. See 'lb ft'.
Track rod	The bar(s) across the vehicle which connect the steering arms and maintain the front wheels in their correct alignment.
UJ	Universal joint. A coupling between shafts which permits angular movement.
UNF	Unified National Fine screw thread.
Vacuum servo	Device used in brake system, using difference between atmospheric pressure and inlet manifold depression to operate a piston which acts to augment brake pressure as required. See 'Servo'.
Venturi	A restriction or 'choke' in a tube, as in a carburetter, used to increase velocity to obtain a reduction in pressure.
Vernier	A sliding scale for obtaining fractional readings of the graduations of an adjacent scale.
Welch plug	A domed thin metal disc which is partially flattened to lock in a recess. Used to plug core holes in castings.
Wet liner	Removable cylinder barrel, sealed against coolant leakage, where the coolant is in direct contact with the outer surface.
Wet sump	A reservoir attached to the crankcase to hold the lubricating oil.

NOTES

INDEX

A

Air cleaner	30, 35
Alternator	110
Armature starter motor	113
Automatic ignition controls	39
Automatic transmission GM	61
Axle shafts	68
Axle shaft bearings	69

B

Ball joints, front suspension	80
Ball joints, tie rod	88
Battery maintenance	107
Belt tension	46
Big-end removal	18
Big-end refitting	21
Bleeding brake system, drum brakes	100
Bleeding brake system, disc brakes	105
Brake adjustment	95
Brake cylinders	98
Brake discs	101
Brake dismantling	97, 102
Brake hoses	97
Brake linings	99
Brake pads, disc brakes	102
Brake shoes	96, 99
Breather, crankcase	20
Brushes, starter motor	112
Bulb replacement	114

C

Calipers, disc brake	102
Camber angle	85
Camshaft bearing renewal	15
Camshaft removal and refitting	14
Capacitor	40
Carburetter, Zenith 30.IZ	27
Carburetters, Zenith Stromberg	31, 33, 36
Castor angle	85
Centrifugal ignition advance	39
Circuit breaker, thermal	114
Clutch adjustment	49
Clutch construction	49
Clutch disc alignment	51
Clutch friction linings	50
Clutch pedal	51
Clutch release mechanism	49
Clutch removal	18
Clutch refitting	18
Clutch spigot bearing	51
Coil, ignition	43
Coil springs, front	79
Coil springs, rear	71
Commutator, starter motor	113
Condenser (capacitor)	40
Connecting rod removal	18
Connecting rod refitting	21
Contact breaker	40

Control rod, front suspension

Control rod, front suspension	83
Crankshaft removal and refitting	19, 21
Crankshaft regrinding	20
Cylinder head removal	10
Cylinder head refitting	14
Cylinder head servicing	12
Cylinder rebore sizes	19

D

Dampers, front	84
Dampers, rear	74
Differential	68
Diodes, alternator	111
Direction indicators	116
Disc brakes	100
Distributor	39
Doors	123
Door windows	124
Downshift and throttle control, auto transmission	63
Draining precautions, auto transmission	62
Draining cooling system	45

E

Electrical system polarity	39
Electrolyte, battery	108
Engine mounting	23
Engine reassembly	21
Engine removal	9
Engine refitting	23
Engine type	9

F

Fan belt	46
Field windings, alternator	111
Flywheel removal	18
Flywheel refitting	22
Flywheel ring gear	18
Front hubs	77
Front spring removal and refitting	79
Front standing height check	79
Front suspension, description	77
Fuel gauge	118
Fuel pump	25
Fulcrum bolts and bushes, front suspension	82
Fuses	114

G

Gasket, cylinder head	14
Gaskets, engine	21
Gear control	54
Gear ratios	139
Gearbox, description	53
Gearbox oil seal	56
Gearbox overhaul	57
Gearbox removal	56
Gearbox refitting	59
Gearbox selectors	54
Gudgeon pins	19

H

Handbrake adjustment	96
Handbrake shoe lever	101
Hazard warning system	116
Headlamps	114
Heater	129
Heating and ventilating system	129
Horns	118
High-tension cables	43
Hubs, front	77
Hydraulic brake operation	95
Hydraulic components servicing	97
Hydraulic system bleeding 99,	104
Hydrometer	108

I

Idling adjustment, Zenith 30.IZ	27
Idling adjustment, Zenith Stromberg ..	33
Ignition automatic controls	39
Ignition timing	42
Impeller, automatic transmission	61
Impeller, water pump	47
Inlet manifold removal	11
Instrument assembly	117

J

Jet centralisation, Zenith Stromberg ..	31

L

Locks, door	123

M

Main bearings	19
Manifold, inlet	11
Master cylinder	96

O

Oil control rings	19
Oil filter	20
Oil pump	16
Oil relief valve	18
Oil seal, crankshaft	21
Oil seals, front hub	77
Oil seal, gearbox	56
Oil seals, rear axle	69
Oilways	20

P

Pedal, clutch	51
Pedals, removal	52
Piston oversizes	19
Piston removal	18
Piston refitting	21
Piston rings	19
Propeller shaft	67
Pushrod removal	12

R

Rack and pinion steering	87
Radiator	46
Radiator grille	127
Rear axle removal and refitting	70
Rear spring removal and refitting	71
Rear standing height check	71
Rear suspension arms	73
Reboring	19
Remote control, door lock	123
Rocker removal and refitting 12,	14
Rotor, alternator	111

S

Screen wash	117
Selector mechanism, gearbox	54
Selectors, automatic transmission	63
Servo, disc brake systems	101
Shock absorbers (dampers) 74,	84
Slow-running adjustments, Zenith 30.IZ ..	27
Slow-running adjustments, Zenith Stromberg	33
Solenoid switch, starter	112
Sparking plugs	43
Specific gravity, battery electrolyte	108
Springs, front	79
Springs, rear	71
Starter	112
Starter inhibitor switch, automatic transmission	63
Stator, alternator	111
Stator, automatic transmission ..	61
Steering column removal and refitting ..	90
Steering gear removal and refitting	87
Steering geometry	89
Steering wheel	90
Sump removal	15
Sump refitting	22
Suspension, front	77
Suspension, geometry	84
Suspension, rear	71
Switches	118

T

Tappets 14,	15
Thermal circuit breaker	114
Thermostat	48
Throttle valve cable, automatic transmission .. 35,	63
Tie rod ball joints	88
Timing case oil seal	15
Timing chain	15
Timing chain tensioner	15
Timing gear	14
Timing ignition	42
Timing valve	15
Toe-in	90
Torque converter, automatic transmission ..	61
Transmission, automatic	61
Trim removal, doors	123
Turbine, automatic transmission	61

U

Universal joints   67

V

Vacuum ignition advance   39
Vacuum servo, disc brakes   101
Valves, engine   12
Valve timing   14
Ventilating and heating system   129
Ventilator, crankcase 20, 24

W

Water circulation   45
Waterways, engine   21
Water pump..   47
Window glasses   125
Window winders   124
Windscreen renewal   125
Windscreen wash   117
Windscreen wipers   116
Wiring   107
Wiring diagrams   141

NOTES

Alfa Romeo Giulia 1600,
  1750, 2000 1962 on
Aston Martin 1921-58
Auto Union Audi 70, 80,
  Super 90, 1966-72
Audi 100 1969 on
Austin, Morris etc.
  1100 Mk. 1 1962-67
Austin, Morris etc. 1100
  Mk. 2, 3, 1300 Mk. 1, 2, 3
  America 1968 on
Austin A30, A35, A40
  Farina 1951-67
Austin A55 Mk. 2, A60
  1958-69
Austin A99, A110 1959-68
Austin J4 1960
Austin Allegro 1973 on
Austin Maxi 1969 on
Austin, Morris 1800
  1964 on
Austin, Morris 2200 1972 on
Austin Kimberley, Tasman
  1970 on
Austin, Morris 1300, 1500
  Nomad 1969 on
BMC 3 (Austin A50, A55
  Mk. 1, Morris Oxford
  2, 3 1954-59)
Austin Healey 100/6,
  3000 1956-68
Austin Healey, MG
  Sprite, Midget 1958 on
Bedford CA Mk. 2 1964-69
Bedford CF Vans 1969 on
Bedford Beagle HA Vans
  1964 on
BMW 1600 1966 on
BMW 1800 1964-71
BMW 2000, 2002 1966 on
Chevrolet Corvair 1960-69
Chevrolet Corvette V8
  1957-65
Chevrolet Corvette V8
  1965 on
Chevrolet Vega 2300
  1970 on
Chrysler Valiant V8
  1965 on
Chrysler Valiant Straight
  Six 1963 on
Citroen DS 19, ID 19
  1955-66
Citroen ID 19, DS 19, 20,
  21 1966 on
Citroen Dyane Ami 1964 on
Daf 31, 32, 33, 44, 55
  1961 on
Datsun Bluebird 610 series
  1972 on
Datsun Cherry 100A, 120A
  1971 on
Datsun 1000, 1200 1968 on
Datsun 1300, 1400, 1600
  1968 on
Datsun 240C 1971 on

Datsun 240Z Sport 1970 on
Fiat 124 1966 on
Fiat 124 Sport 1966 on
Fiat 125 1967-72
Fiat 127 1971 on
Fiat 128 1969 on
Fiat 500 1957 on
Fiat 600, 600D 1955-69
Fiat 850 1964 on
Fiat 1100 1957-69
Fiat 1300, 1500 1961-67
Ford Anglia Prefect 100E
  1953-62
Ford Anglia 105E, Prefect
  107E 1959-67
Ford Capri 1300, 1600 OHV
  1968 on
Ford Capri 1300, 1600,
  2000 OHC 1972 on
Ford Capri 2000 V4, 3000 V6
  1969 on
Ford Classic, Capri
  1961-64
Ford Consul, Zephyr,
  Zodiac, 1, 2 1950-62
Ford Corsair Straight
  Four 1963-65
Ford Corsair V4 1965-68
Ford Corsair V4 2000
  1969-70
Ford Cortina 1962-66
Ford Cortina 1967-68
Ford Cortina 1969-70
Ford Cortina Mk. 3
  1970 on
Ford Escort 1967 on
Ford Falcon 6 1964-70
Ford Falcon XK, XL
  1960-63
Ford Falcon 6 XR/XA
  1966 on
Ford Falcon V8 (U.S.A.)
  1965-71
Ford Falcon V8 (Aust.)
  1966 on
Ford Pinto 1970 on
Ford Maverick 6 1969 on
Ford Maverick V8 1970 on
Ford Mustang 6 1965 on
Ford Mustang V8 1965 on
Ford Thames 10, 12,
  15 cwt 1957-65
Ford Transit V4 1965 on
Ford Zephyr Zodiac Mk. 3
  1962-66
Ford Zephyr Zodiac V4,
  V6, Mk. 4 1966-72
Ford Consul, Granada
  1972 on
Hillman Avenger 1970 on
Hillman Hunter 1966 on
Hillman Imp 1963-68
Hillman Imp 1969 on
Hillman Minx 1 to 5
  1956-65
Hillman Minx 1965-67

Hillman Minx 1966-70
Hillman Super Minx
  1961-65
Jaguar XK120, 140, 150,
  Mk. 7, 8, 9 1948-61
Jaguar 2.4, 3.4, 3.8 Mk.
  1, 2 1955-69
Jaguar 'E' Type 1961-72
Jaguar 'S' Type 420
  1963-68
Jaguar XJ6 1968 on
Jowett Javelin Jupiter
  1947-53
Landrover 1, 2 1948-61
Landrover 2, 2a, 3 1959 on
Mazda 616 1970 on
Mazda 808, 818 1972 on
Mazda 1200, 1300 1969 on
Mazda 1500, 1800 1967 on
Mazda RX-2 1971 on
Mazda R100, RX-3 1970 on
Mercedes-Benz 190b,
  190c, 200 1959-68
Mercedes-Benz 220
  1959-65
Mercedes-Benz 220/8
  1968 on
Mercedes-Benz 230
  1963-68
Mercedes-Benz 250
  1965-67
Mercedes-Benz 250
  1968 on
Mercedes-Benz 280
  1968 on
MG TA to TF 1936-55
MGA MGB 1955-68
MGB 1969 on
Mini 1959 on
Mini Cooper 1961-72
Morgan Four 1936-72
Morris Marina 1971 on
Morris (Aust) Marina
  1972 on
Morris Minor 2, 1000
  1952-71
Morris Oxford 5, 6 1959-71
NSU 1000 1963-72
NSU Prinz 1 to 4 1957-72
Opel Ascona, Manta
  1970 on
Opel GT 1900 1968 on
Opel Kadett, Olympia 993 cc
  1078 cc 1962 on
Opel Kadett, Olympia 1492,
  1698, 1897 cc 1967 on
Opel Rekord C 1966-72
Peugeot 204 1965 on
Peugeot 304 1970 on
Peugeot 404 1960 on
Peugeot 504 1968 on
Porsche 356A, B, C 1957-65
Porsche 911 1964 on
Porsche 912 1965-69
Porsche 914 S 1969 on
Reliant Regal 1952-73

Renault R4, R4L, 4 1961 on
Renault 5 1972 on
Renault 6 1968 on
Renault 8, 10, 1100 1962-71
Renault 12, 1969 on
Renault 15, 17 1971 on
Renault R16 1965 on
Renault Dauphine
  Floride 1957-67
Renault Caravelle 1962-68
Rover 60 to 110 1953-64
Rover 2000 1963-73
Rover 3 Litre 1958-67
Rover 3500, 3500S 1968 on
Saab 95, 96, Sport
  1960-68
Saab 99 1969 on
Saab V4 1966 on
Simca 1000 1961 on
Simca 1100 1967 on
Simca 1300, 1301, 1500,
  1501 1963 on
Skoda One (440, 445, 450)
  1955-70
Sunbeam Rapier Alpine
  1955-65
Toyota Carina, Celica
  1971 on
Toyota Corolla 1100,
  1200 1967 on
Toyota Corona 1500 Mk. 1
  1965-70
Toyota Corona Mk. 2
  1969 on
Triumph TR2, TR3, TR3A
  1952-62
Triumph TR4, TR4A
  1961-67
Triumph TR5, TR250,
  TR6 1967 on
Triumph 1300, 1500
  1965-73
Triumph 2000 Mk. 1, 2.5 PI
  Mk. 1 1963-69
Triumph 2000 Mk. 2, 2.5 PI
  Mk. 2 1969 on
Triumph Dolomite 1972 on
Triumph Herald 1959-68
Triumph Herald 1969-71
Triumph Spitfire, Vitesse
  1962-68
Triumph Spitfire Mk. 3, 4
  1969 on
Triumph GT6, Vitesse
  2 Litre 1969 on
Triumph Stag 1970 on
Triumph Toledo 1970 on
Vauxhall Velox, Cresta
  1957-72
Vauxhall Victor 1, 2, FB
  1957-64
Vauxhall Victor 101
  1964-67
Vauxhall Victor FD 1600,
  2000 1967-72

Continued on following page

VIVA HC

THE AUTOBOOK SERIES OF WORKSHOP MANUALS

Vauxhall Victor 3300,
    Ventora 1968-72
Vauxhall Victor FE
    Ventora 1972 on
Vauxhall Viva HA 1963-66
Vauxhall Viva HB 1966-70

Vauxhall Viva, HC Firenza
    1971 on
Volkswagen Beetle 1954-67
Volkswagen Beetle 1968 on
Volkswagen 1500 1961-66

Volkswagen 1600 Fastback
    1965-73
Volkswagen Transporter
    1954-67
Volkswagen Transporter
    1968 on

Volkswagen 411 1968-72
Volvo 120 series 1961-70
Volvo 140 series 1966 on
Volvo 160 series 1968 on
Volvo 1800 1960-73

NOTES

NOTES